ABSOLUTE BEGINNER

MEMOIRS OF THE WORLD'S BEST LEAST-KNOWN GUITARIST

KEVIN ARMSTRONG

JAW BONE

ABSOLUTE BEGINNER

MEMOIRS OF THE

WORLD'S BEST

LEAST-KNOWN

GUITARIST

A Jawbone book
First edition 2023
Published in the UK and the USA by
Jawbone Press
Office G1
141–157 Acre Lane
London SW2 5UA
England
www.jawbonepress.com

ISBN 978-1-911036-17-3

Printed by Short Run Press, Exeter

1 2 3 4 5 27 26 25 24 23

ABOVE I wasn't normally in the habit of sitting like this before a gig. I think I may have been put there for the photo op. *Paul McAlpine.*

Dedicated to Matthew Seligman (July 14, 1955–April 17, 2020)

INTRODUCTION

ON THE MORNING OF SATURDAY, JULY 18, 1985, SOUTH LONDON WAS EERILY QUIET. Usually, the hum of traffic where I lived on New Park Road between Brixton and Streatham was constant, but there was good reason for the silence in the streets on that day. It was the day of Live Aid.

Part of the South Circular Road, which funnels traffic from Kent through to Battersea Bridge and across the river to Chelsea and Kensington, flows right past Angus House, where I lived at the time. My building was a nineteenth-century Peabody-style block, typical of many in the area: a solid redbrick structure with balconies and walkways connecting hundreds of small apartments, designed by philanthropic Victorians to provide social housing for the poor.

Like a lot of struggling youngsters in London, I moved around a great deal in the late 70s and early 80s. I had lived in everything from cheap bedsits to rooms in run-down houses and illegal squats. After a tipoff from a friend a few months earlier that there might be empty units in the estate, I had discovered and broken into an abandoned two-bedroom flat on the third floor of Angus House. I changed the locks and moved in—or 'squatted'—there with my girlfriend.

Actually, it turned out to be a bit better than just squatting. After forcing the door, I opened some old mail that was on the mat, addressed to the previous occupant. It was clear from the number of official reminders present that he had fled abruptly, leaving some outstanding rent. I went to the local council housing department and pretended to be he.

'I am Hubert Barwell, and I've come to pay the rent arrears on 62 Angus House, if that's okay,' I said to the housing officer.

'Ah, Mr Barwell,' he began. 'We've been wondering how long it would take you to contact us. When did you get out of prison, and is your wife quite recovered from her injuries?'

After mumbling some apologies and saying I had paid my debt to society, I left with a new rent book and a plan to pay back the debts at £5 a week, on top of the (very cheap) council rent. A squat had thereby become an official residence, and even though it was on one of the roughest estates in South London, it would provide me with a relatively safe home for the next couple of years. I sincerely hoped that the real Mr Barwell would never return, and, happily for me, he never did.

One morning at Angus House, I woke to the sound of sirens. The place was soon crawling with police looking for a guy with a gun. Happily, it wasn't Hubert. Another time, one of the relatively scarce fathers who lived there *en famille* was taken away for sexually abusing some of his ten kids. Directly beneath my flat, the pervasive odour of sewage kept bubbling up in the warm weather. The sounds of smashing furniture and high-pitched screaming could be heard for a week until the police came and carted away one barking mad tenant, who shouted that he was a monk in training as he was locked into a secure vehicle. It took three days' work by people in hazmat suits to clear the bottles of piss and boxes of faeces from his flat.

It was from this humble, illegally occupied dwelling that I went, on that unusually quiet July morning, to catch a helicopter across the city with David Bowie, to play guitar next to him at the biggest rock concert in the history of the planet, in front of a global audience of a billion souls.

From that day to this, my life would never be the same.

CHAPTER ONE

ABSOLUTE BEGINNINGS

§

BEFORE 1967, MY EXPERIENCE OF MUSIC WAS ALL ABOUT WHAT MY PARENTS LISTENED TO. We'd often have the radio on while we were having a family meal together. Sunday lunch was often accompanied by *Two-Way Family Favourites* on the Home Service of the BBC, with Ed 'Stewpot' Stewart or Pete Murray. It specialised in novelty children's songs like 'Nellie The Elephant', 'The Laughing Policeman', 'Rawhide', 'The Ugly Bug Ball', and 'The Runaway Train'.

My parents had picked up an odd selection of records, too. Apart from such aberrations as The Singing Postman, who may well be due a twenty-first-century reappraisal—'*Molly Wimbley, sche schmowks loik a chimbley, but sche's moy li'ol nicotine gal*'—they did actually like some good stuff. They had a few Deutsche Grammophon LPs of Bach's Brandenburg concertos and piano recitals by Sviatoslav Richter and Artur Rubenstein, and my dad had loads of old jazz 78s by people with crazy-sounding names like Bix Beiderbecke and Jelly Roll Morton.

They also had albums by the American pianist and comedic genius Tom Lehrer, whose songs I particularly liked. Lehrer was a Harvard professor with a brisk piano style and a mind like a steel trap. I have never heard a wittier songwriter or a sharper rhymer and lyricist. Very few people have such a strict, economical, and syllable-perfect way with a lyric or a tune. Nowadays, it's common to find words in songs mangled and twisted out of all proportion to the way they are normally used in conversation. The meaning is often lost or at least blunted by stresses on the wrong syllable of a word, or by clunking mis-rhymes. A few songwriters, however, set a bar that is higher than the rest, and Lehrer is word perfect every time, which is even more impressive when you are delivering comedy.*

One of the first records that my brother and I loved was a version of 'Tom Hark' by a group called Elias & His Zig-Zag Jive Flutes. It's an insanely catchy and joyous three-chord South African jam with duelling recorders, and we responded to it as only little kids can—by playing it over and over and over again until our elders and betters wanted to jump screaming out of the windows. Those familiar with *Stewart Lee's Comedy Vehicle* will know it as the theme tune.

Pop radio simply didn't exist in the UK until I was nine, so I was only exposed to it through other people who had records. I did have a couple of friends who collected the early Beatles stuff in the mid-60s. I remember games with them where we would wear moulded plastic Beatle wigs and play toy guitars with the Fabs' pictures on and red and green plastic strings. We would bounce along with the tunes and pretend that we were they. I imagined myself standing next to Paul McCartney, waving my guitar and going *Wooooo!* like in 'She Loves You'. My leg would start pumping vigorously up and down as I took the guitar solos.

I am part of the generation that literally hid under the bedcovers with a transistor radio tuned in to the static-filled pioneers of pirate radio broadcasting illegally from stations based on old forts and leaky ships in the North Sea. I remember hearing 'Flowers In The Rain' by The Move—the very first record ever played on BBC Radio 1 by Tony Blackburn, on September 30, 1967. My young life was struck by lightning then, and I've never grown up.

---

* George Brassens does this in French, and tragicomic English troubadour Jake Thackray is worthy of an honourable mention in the 'flawless use of language' stakes too, as is The Divine Comedy's Neil Hannon.

Apart from these childish fantasies of being a Beatle—strangely prescient, as you will see later—the first time in my life that music felt as if it might have something to do with me was in the very early 1970s. My friends and I would talk about what we had seen on *Top Of The Pops* that week. When Marc Bolan, Slade, or Rod Stewart was on, there was always something to talk about.

But when David Bowie and the Spiders From Mars appeared doing 'Starman', it seemed as if the world had shifted on its axis. Bowie and Mick Ronson ramped (and camped) it up in a way that nobody had ever seen before. They redefined how to do rock'n'roll overnight, and even what it was to be male. We had seen the future and left Elvis, The Beatles, and Motown firmly in aspic. Who were these men from another planet? Bowie had changed the whole game, and nothing about pop music could ever be the same. Our ancient walnut radiogram that shook to the sounds of *Motown Chartbusters Volume Three* and 'Hello Goodbye' by The Beatles made way for far headier stuff.

The name Iggy Pop first appeared to me as that of a somewhat mythical protégé of Bowie's when I was about thirteen and really starting to take a keen interest in rock music. Before I had heard a note he sang, I had seen those startling images of him onstage with The Stooges at his first London gig: silver hair, mouth agape, his lithe, half-naked body held aloft on outstretched hands, seemingly levitating on the adoring crowd. As soon as I heard his wild screams and yelps on 'Down On The Street', from The Stooges' *Fun House* LP, he got me. Here was someone who represented my adolescent yearning for something *other*. A new way of living that transcended my suburban upbringing. Here was the embodiment of danger and madness that seemed to challenge the humdrum certainties of our safe little English lives. He did what? Burned and cut himself onstage? Took out his massive great schlong? He made singers like Rod Stewart and Marc Bolan seem tame. Like people acting out a part. Here was a guy who was cooler than the rest. No wonder Bowie was envious of him.

In 1971, the only people who seemed like authentic stars to me were Bowie, Iggy, Jimi Hendrix, and Jim Morrison. They were impossibly committed to life on the edge—to an exploration of how far out rock music and excess could go. I was fascinated and scared by them in equal measure. I had no possible way to imagine what it might be like to meet any of these people, let alone stand on a stage and play guitar with them. They were as remote as aliens and as unreachable as angels. Finding myself in later life working alongside a few of these iconic artists, as I have, has given me a little glimpse behind the curtain, an insight into what goes on beyond the public façade. I couldn't have possibly imagined such a life as a star-struck teenager.

Even after all these years, part of me still can't quite accept that I've been allowed to be up there, standing next to these demigods, much less playing guitar with them and getting paid for it, but there it is and here we are.

* * *

In 1964, I was six years old. My family were living in one of those 1920s solid semi-detached Arts and Crafts houses that can be seen the length and breadth of Britain. We lived in Orpington in Kent. I suppose if you had to rank us in the way that the British did in those days, we would have been firmly in the category of lower-middle class. We weren't poor, but mine certainly wasn't a privileged upbringing. Though neither of my parents went to university, there were proper books around in our house, and my dad even attempted to speak a little French (with limited success). They had the aspiration to better themselves and transcend their working-class origins.

My grandparents had been domestic servants, had served in the forces, and had worked in retail. The big idea of post-war British society was 'upward mobility', and it was this convenient fiction that drove their efforts. A noble and hopeful undertaking, no doubt, even though we lived through the era when class division was subtly revealed every time you opened your mouth by whether you said 'sitting room' or 'lounge', the kind of books you read, what school you went to, and whether or not you had an outside toilet. Back then, the war seemed to have cleared the way for people to dream of better things. Everything seemed up for grabs.

An abiding childhood memory is of the house being overrun at election time with 'Young Liberals'—bearded students wreathed in cigarette smoke with black and orange rosettes and piles of leaflets. My dad was politically active with the Liberal Party, and I have definitely clung to his tolerant and humanistic values. In his capacity as chairman of the Young Liberals, Dad even developed something of a friendship with Eric Lubbock (the late Lord Avebury), who rather sensationally was elected Liberal MP for Orpington in 1962 and had a distinguished career as a human rights campaigner. I went to school with one of his sons, and for a while we referred to the MP as 'Uncle Eric'. We visited the family house at Downe in Kent a few times, but Eric, Victoria, and the lads never popped round to ours for tea, and I suspect the relationship was rather one-sided, given the stark difference in status.

Most of the time, my mum was what was then referred to as a housewife. Dad had a white-collar job. He worked as a humble accountancy clerk in a bank (not the kind of banker that gets bonuses or share packages). Mum sometimes worked from home assembling costume jewellery or did occasional part-time shifts in a factory.

There was a twelve-acre pasture at the bottom of the back garden of our house in Chelsfield Lane. An old brown horse called Fred who lived there would sometimes wander in and be found munching the apples off our tree. My dad would patiently persuade him to back off by waving a broom in his general direction. Fred would turn lazily and walk out of the gate, letting off a giant fart in his wake and loping back to his field again.

One day, bulldozers came and started to flatten the whole area beyond our back gate. Other heavy machinery joined them in digging up the entire twelve acres and levelling it in preparation for a new housing development. Poor old Fred most probably ended up in the glue factory. My parents were offered the brand-new house that emerged at the end of our garden (at a knockdown price) in exchange for part of the land on which our present house stood.

My brother Ross and I and our bunch of scruffy mates enjoyed playing on the emerging site. There were enormous concrete sewer pipes waiting to be installed in deep trenches that were being dug—perfect for war games or hide-and-seek. Half-built shells of houses with scaffolding were a big lure. One time, we were fooling around in the un-tarmacked streets of new builds. I was sitting on a window ledge on the upper storey of a house under construction when I fell. I tumbled inward, dropped between the exposed ceiling joists, and landed on a pile of rubble on the ground floor that was going to be somebody's living room one day. A split lip and a dozen stitches in my head were the inevitable results of being an unsupervised child in such a dangerous place.

We moved into the still-incomplete estate in 1963, just before the snowiest winter anyone could remember. I was five and Ross was four. All the new houses looked very similar to each other in that anodyne 1960s style. The maze of wide streets that made up the estate was named after Battle of Britain pilots. We lived on Mungo Park Way, so named after World War II Spitfire ace John Mungo-Park. The houses were reasonably well made but utilitarian and boxy and without much architectural merit. The broad, newly surfaced streets, with their neat gardens sporting not-yet-grown shrubs and trees, along with the generally spacious layout of it all, made us feel part of a hopeful, shiny suburban future. I never thought of it while growing up, but it was less than twenty years after the end of the war, so the experiences of rationing and bombing were still echoes that rang in our parents' and grandparents' heads and peppered their conversation.

My mother had always played the piano very well. We had an old black upright Rönisch from Germany that had been with her since her teenage years. She had done the thing expected of women in the 50s when she got married: given up any ambition to be a professional concert pianist (or a professional anything) to have kids, cook meals, and clean the house for my father. When I was six years old, my mother offered me the opportunity to learn the piano. I don't know why I jumped at it. Ross hadn't. But it just felt like something I should do and might like. I wanted to please her.

It also may have been a way to help me adjust to a world where I had become bespectacled at age five. The curse of being 'four-eyes' took a while to get used to. The expectation of having your goggles smashed by a bigger kid was an ever-present anxiety once you had been labelled 'short-sighted' and you had to accept that you'd be looking at the world through glass for the rest of your days. Maybe music could help me return to the world.

One of the first memories I have of that new house is when the piano teacher sat me down on the piano stool and showed me the names of the notes. Dr Biurski was a musty-smelling man dressed in blacks and greys with a thick Polish accent. After the third or fourth lesson, I heard the good doctor speaking in hushed tones to my mother in the hallway before collecting his twelve shillings:

'Ze boy has a touch of chenius.'

I didn't know what this meant, but I knew it was probably good.

* * *

As it turned out, my aptitude for the piano was a real thing, but my reluctance to learn to sight-read ultimately steered me toward a life as a musical autodidact. I loved to learn the pieces and I loved to play, but all that theory was a real turn-off.

I soon learned to play Grade Five and then Grade Seven piano pieces fluidly, but I never actually sat an ABRSM exam. My natural ear and physical ability way outstripped my patience or respect for study. That's why I would never become a jazz musician or have the capacity to read a score at anything other than at a snail's pace. And I would never (thank the angels) end up working in a theatre's orchestra pit. I would learn music mostly by myself, through trial and error. My 'good ear' was going to save me, or so I naively believed.

While I was growing up, my mother joined a group of folksingers, and four or five of them would appear at our house on a regular basis to sing through 'Puff The Magic Dragon', 'Michael Row The Boat Ashore', 'Over The Sea To Skye', and other such whimsy. One of them was a bushy-bearded guy in his late twenties called Roger Ferris. Roger was the proud wielder of a Levin Jumbo acoustic guitar, and everything about it fascinated me: the shiny varnish, the white ivory pins holding the strings in place behind the bridge, the huge twangy vibrations of the thing when he strummed a chord. I wanted one.*

Before long, and after much pestering from me, my mum had enlisted Roger's help in choosing a cheap, second-hand guitar for me to learn on. My first instrument was an unbranded acoustic guitar with a trapezoid tailpiece, a floating, unglued bridge that kept moving about, and a roughly painted finish. In short, it was nothing at all like Roger's beautiful, handmade Levin. He showed me three or four chords and I practised them until my fingers bled.

That guitar was little more than a barely playable toy. Nevertheless, I wrote my first song on it—something about being 'a drinking, gambling man and living in disgrace', as I recall—and performed it, aged eleven, at a school fête, to indifference from the crowd but astonished praise from my mother. After my early efforts to teach myself how to play, I soon realized that, in order to join the pantheon of rock gods like the ones on posters that adorned my bedroom walls, I would have to 'go electric'.

---

* Fun factoid: Roger Ferris was at that time the lead singer of David Bowie's first band, The Konrads, in which the young David Jones played sax. I only learned this decades later; I wish I'd known this sooner and could have talked to David about those early days in Bromley, where we might even have crossed paths.

At that time, there was a magazine you could get through the post called *The Bell's Guitar Catalogue*. It was my earliest encounter with what has since become known as guitar porn. I drooled over the black-and-white photos of the weird and wonderful creations in there: the Hofner Verithin, the Watkins Rapier 44, the Vox Teardrop, the Guyatone; the ugly, over-engineered Burns Black Bison, with its rows of plastic buttons and giant horns; and, of course, the pages of genuine, American Fenders and Gibsons at dizzying prices.*

It's hard to put into words the aspirational effect these pictures of shiny things had on a young wannabe like me. I dreamed of just seeing them in real life, let alone handling and playing them. I still get a thrill from the actual sight and feeling of a nice guitar, despite decades of interaction with quality instruments. I prop them up against the couch in my studio sometimes and just admire them as beautiful pieces of art and engineering. I guess it's something like the feeling car collectors get. It's definitely a fetish. Anyway, as a boy, these things cast a spell over me that was to bewitch me for a lifetime.

* * *

Thanks to my above-average literacy and rat-like cunning, by the time of my last year at St Mary Cray primary school I was asked to help other classmates with their reading skills. I sailed through my eleven-plus exam and into the rarefied air of candidates for the higher bracket of what in the 1970s was called selective schooling. I have my parents to thank for this. As kids we were read to from toddlerhood and always encouraged to discover books for ourselves, and we did love them; from Richmal Crompton's *Just William* to Sir Walter Scott's *Ivanhoe*, we lapped it up. My successful application to the single-sex St Olave's Grammar School must have made my parents proud, and it promised much. As it turned out, however, they and the school were to be seriously disappointed.

* In 1969, a Gibson Les Paul would cost an eye-watering £239; kept in good condition until today, it might fetch £25,000 or more.

In the summer before I started at St Olave's, I knocked around with my best friend Raymond Friend (yes, really), listening to Deep Purple's *Fireball* and walking the streets dressed in brightly coloured nylon shirts with huge pointy collars and matching cravats, trying to get noticed. Once, we even accessorised these with some horse-brasses borrowed from Raymond's mum's wall. What absolute pillocks we must have looked.

In September of 1970, it was time for St Olave's Grammar School. Previously located in the heart of London at Southwark, on the South Bank of the Thames, it was one of the better high schools I could have aspired to attend. It had a lot of leftover Tom Brown-ish characteristics from its three-hundred-year history; teachers were masters and mistresses, and, even after the institution's relocation to very well-appointed, brand-new buildings in my hometown of Orpington, they still wore mortarboards and gowns. We addressed them as 'Sir' and 'Ma'am'.

The headmaster while I was there was the eminent Dr R. C. Carrington, known colloquially as The Oaf—a severe and terrifying begowned figure whose very arrival in the dinner hall would cause it to fall silent. Only a few days after I started at the school, I was half striding, half bouncing across a quadrangle while exuberantly practising ejecting saliva through my front teeth when I collided with Dr Carrington's enormous stomach, mid-bounce, as he loomed from behind a pillar. I stood almost paralysed with fear while he fixed me with a hawk-like expression and boomed down at me, 'Walk, boy, and don't spit!'*

In a throwback to the old public-school system, senior boys of supposedly exemplary character at St Olave's were given the power to punish their juniors for misdemeanours and get them to run errands.

---

* Dr Carrington succumbed to dementia during my time at the school, and he was sometimes to be seen prowling the corridors carrying a small stepladder and stopping only to micro-adjust the angle of every picture hanging on the walls.

These 'monitors' were feared and respected in equal measure. Some of them seemed impossibly olde-worlde to me, with their putative facial hair (or bum fluff, as we called it), grey waistcoats, and zip-up Chelsea boots.

Even during the few years I was there, a number of teachers were quietly and unceremoniously escorted off the premises by the police for so-called 'inappropriate conduct'. They were the ones who would tuck your shirt in for you and take a little too long over it. One of them was a priest, you may be somewhat unsurprised to learn.

The school sport was rugby-football, a violent contact sport involving charging about pulling people to the ground to take a weird-shaped ball off them, then throwing it backwards to a teammate so they could plunge headlong into a thicket of legs. If two teams with different-coloured 'house' shirts could not be made up into an even number, one team would be made to play in 'shirts' and the other in 'skins'—i.e., with no shirts on. Games took place in all weather, so you could easily find yourself ploughing face down onto the thick, wet mud of the sports field, half-naked and nursing a broken collarbone, or at the very least a black eye.

Another peculiar form of character-building sport (or acute physical torture) that St Olave's had a fondness for was compulsory, twice-weekly, cross-country running. This was undertaken over a six-mile course across rough farmland and through woods, often in freezing fog. I succumbed, the first time out, to such a serious chest infection and subsequent asthma attacks that I was forced to miss thirteen weeks of school in my first year.

It was this bout of illness, more than anything, that sounded the death knell for my high-school education. I simply couldn't catch up with my classmates in the new subjects of Latin, Biology, or Italian. I floundered and ended that year at the bottom of the class, and there I doggedly remained throughout the next four. I soon gravitated toward other boys for whom disruptive behaviour was a plausible substitute for unattainable academic success. The only fond memories I have of my school days are ones connected with mischief. My reports were invariably of the 'much room for improvement', 'lets himself down', and 'could do better' variety.

My old piano teacher Dr Biurski's ministrations soon gave way to my musical development being entrusted to the music master at St Olave's, Mr Swinburn. Des Swinburn was a man whose sarcastic and scathing manner made him seem seriously tired of life, although he went on into his nineties playing the organ at Peterborough Cathedral. Everything about him was brown by default—his wavy brown hair, his scuffed brogues, his jacket with obligatory leather elbow patches— and his outlook on music was as exhausted as his wardrobe. His own efforts at creativity extended to the most bizarre and turgid improvised meanderings from the seat of the school's impressive pipe organ at morning assembly. He was such an uninspiring presence that I wonder now why it didn't kill off my desire to make music entirely. I tried but I couldn't maintain an interest in his tedious classes. Any boy even mentioning any music that wasn't entirely classical in nature was scornfully humiliated. He did his best to put me off progressing much further as a pianist, too.

My musical life at school limped on, and I did once audition to be a 'treble' singer in the Savoy Chapel Choir, mostly because its few privileged members were paid to skip lessons and ride up to London on the train to sing at the queen's private chapel. The Savoy had choristers exclusively provided by St Olave's. My voice had started to break, though, and was deemed too unstable, so I never made the cut.

Mr Swinburn was assigned to give me one-on-one piano lessons after school on Wednesdays. I made a real effort, but I always struggled to read through the pieces he set me. I would learn a piece of Chopin by painfully working through the score at home. Once I had learned it fluently, I just pretended to follow the music at my piano lesson but really played it from memory. This was quite effective, as long as I didn't make a mistake. When, inevitably, I did, it would elicit a heavy sigh from Des and a sardonic comment like, 'Well, I *love* what you've done with bar seventeen, but it's not what the composer actually *wrote*, is it, laddie?'

Clearly, I didn't possess the studiousness necessary for serious attainment at the piano, and I wasn't going to be a very well-behaved or respectful scholar, either. It wasn't long before I turned against the whole deal of education, lock, stock, and smoking lunchbox.

Toward the premature end of my school career, a friend who would later become a roadie for Motörhead and I stole a couple of life-sized model llamas that had been made from papier mâché and painted gold, out from under the stage in the school hall. They were props for a sixth-form production of *The Epic Of Gilgamesh* or some such pretension. We mounted them, in a copulating position, on top of the cricket pavilion, which rendered them visible to four classrooms full of delighted boys. Setting the llamas on fire with lighter fluid added to the final *fuck-you* effect.

One highly successful and subversive phenomenon was the so-called 3D Dirge Choir. My form started a trend at morning assembly of singing the hymns in a deep and tuneless monotone, thereby causing consternation among the masters, who didn't know how to react but just kept staring around the hall on tiptoes, trying in vain to identify the devilish din. We would start singing confidently and tunefully until it was our prearranged moment to 'dirge', when we'd unleash a disturbing discordant rumble up to the rafters of the school hall while maintaining our angelic expressions. It sounded like the soundtrack from a sacrifice scene in a Hammer Horror movie.

The summer holidays were spent strolling or cycling around the streets all day. Sometimes my brother Ross and I would end up miles from home on our bicycles, just exploring the countryside and getting chased by farmers when we strayed across somebody's barley field or into the wrong orchard. To paraphrase Spinal Tap's description of the

Druids, 'No one knew, where we were . . . or what we were doing.'

From dawn 'til dusk we were exploring our corner of northwest Kent and getting into trouble. We'd often be pursued by a flock of angry geese, or we'd cause mayhem in a pigsty by throwing pignuts in by the handful and enjoying the ensuing porcine riot. Once, we were with a bunch of mates on our bikes and came across a huge, abandoned greenhouse about fifty yards long. Though it was derelict and overgrown, it still had enough acreage of intact glass to attract us. After an hour or so there wasn't a pane that we hadn't trashed. It would be unthinkable now for most kids to have an unsupervised 'range' of forty square miles, but back then it was totally normal.

One summer (possibly 1972) was spent with an older teenage friend called Gaz who had a Reliant Robin three-wheeled van. Four or five of us would pile in the back of that death trap and tool around the town. Once, we ended up outside the gates of Haddon Hall in Beckenham, hoping to catch a glimpse of David Bowie, but we waited in vain. We had to make do with listening to *Hunky Dory* and *Space Oddity* on the eight-track in the car.

At that time, record shops like Ajax in Orpington High Street were the place to get music. They sold washing machines and vacuum cleaners in the front of the shop but had a large room at the back equipped with listening booths made out of thick soundproof material, each with a set of headphones on a hook. You could ask to hear any record you wanted, and the guy would send you to a booth and put it on for you. I spent so much time in there, sorting through the racks of vinyl albums. Savoy Brown, Ten Years After, Yes, Kevin Ayers, King Crimson, Tractor, Budgie, Hawkwind, Led Zeppelin, Badfinger, Grand Funk Railroad, Captain Beefheart, Moondog. I would gaze at the weird cover art and avidly read the credits on the sleeves.

During my early teenage years, I had three life-changing experiences of live music. The first was at the Empire Pool Wembley (now Wembley Arena). My classmate Jim had offered me a spare ticket to see Alice

Cooper play just after the release of the *Killer* album, so I jumped at the chance.* Alice's preoccupation with the macabre, his first-person songs about the experience of being locked up in mental hospitals for killing babies, and his habit of appearing to be decapitated on a large scaffold, made me very curious to go to the gig. Us kids knew it was all just a bit of theatrical fun, but it didn't stop a prominent Tory MP from having a pink fit in parliament over Alice's 'sick antics corrupting our youth', which made me want to go and see him even more. The band was amazing. It was thrilling to hear the fearsome duelling guitars of Glen Buxton and Michael Bruce and Alice's sneering, but engagingly melodic vocal delivery. The opening act was an unknown Roxy Music in all their glam glory. I think Brian Eno caused me some partial hearing loss that day with his screaming synth sounds.

Life-changer number two was at the Oval cricket ground in September 1972. I arrived early for the all-dayer and lay on the grass with my schoolmates, who had also come to worship at the altar of Frank Zappa beneath the grey skies and the gasworks of South London. They had assembled the biggest PA system that had ever visited the UK—it may have been part of the famous rig made by Stanley Owsley for the Grateful Dead, but I can't be sure about that. Smoking a joint and listening to 'Close To The Edge' by Yes blasting across the field was mind-blowing enough, but to see Zappa play guitar and conduct his big band *Grand Wazoo* was incredible. Hawkwind closed out the day, and I dragged myself home with Lemmy screaming 'I've Got A Silver Machiiiine' ringing in my ears.

For number three, in December of that same year, I queued all day outside the BBC's old Alexandra Palace HQ to see the mighty Led Zeppelin play.† When the doors were opened I ran to the front of the stage and staked out a place from where I could look up Jimmy

---

* I still listen to the album before *Killer*, *Love It To Death*—a truly epic rock record.
† This enormous gothic structure overlooking North London now has an ice rink in the giant concert hall.

Page's trouser leg. That must have been one of the best gigs they'd ever delivered. Zeppelin, at that time, were absolutely in their pomp and at a shining peak. To a wide-eyed lad like me, it felt like I had seen the top of Mount Olympus.

That gig made such an impression on me that I can still smell it—a mixture of hash smoke, patchouli oil, and a kind of burning electrical miasma coming from the stage gear and the lights.

CHAPTER TWO

AXE NO. 1

AS SOON AS I COULD, I SAVED UP £14 FROM THE MONEY I'D EARNED WORKING A PAPER ROUND AND WASHING CARS. I cycled over ten miles on major A roads to something called the Swop Shop in Lewisham, on the edge of South London. It was a sort of pawnshop and junk shop rolled into one. I returned triumphantly carrying a real electric guitar in a bag on my back.

Audition is not a brand of instrument that will go down in the annals of rock history, even though there are still a few die-hard collectors (or mugs) buying them on eBay. It was mass-produced down to a cost by the Teisco Corporation in Japan for the budget chain store Woolworths. Despite this, to me it represented my ticket to Mars. It was a passport to another world.

My dad helped me make a connector with a bare jack socket and a pair of matchsticks, then jam the two wires from it into the back of an old Pilot valve radio. This bodged-up modification enabled me to turn the radio into a rudimentary amplifier. It probably had an output of half a watt pushed through its cheap, oval speaker, but it made quite a warm, full sound and was enough to practise with until such time as I could obtain a real amp. I was up and running, learning to play Wishbone Ash and Led Zeppelin songs and listening slavishly to the radio to pick out anything I could copy.

Fairly soon in 1972, when I was becoming a seriously maladjusted grammar-school boy, my early efforts at the guitar came to the attention of a classmate who was also a gifted singer and rhythm guitarist. Martin Osborn was a tall, thickset, mop-topped Beatles obsessive. He was an imposing specimen. An alpha male. Not like me with my asthma and my tortoiseshell, standard-issue NHS specs. With the help of his equally alpha (and slightly gangster-ish), cigar-chomping father and manager, George Osborn, Martin had carved out a nice little niche for himself playing on weekends in what were known as working men's clubs across South London and Kent. I soon joined the band, with another classmate, Mark Foster, on bass, and a precocious twelve-year-old drummer called John Jacobs.

Martin's dad styled us in frilly, pale mauve dress shirts and purple bow ties, and as The Young Ones we trotted out limp and inept versions of Slade, Mud, and Beatles songs, as well as horrific numbers like 'Tie A Yellow Ribbon Round The Ole Oak Tree', which I absolutely hated. Once, we got to accompany a somewhat faded one-hit-wonder called Crispian St Peters (probably not his real name) doing his song 'You Were On My Mind' in a smelly old club in Eltham. It was a small glimpse of my far-off future, even though Crispian was clearly a washed-up alcoholic with delusions of grandeur.

* * *

We would sometimes rehearse in the Osborns' back garden, which overlooked the enormous cornfields I had to cross between my house and his. One day, on the way to a band practice, I was carrying my Japanese guitar—possibly the cheapest electric guitar money could buy—in a duffle bag over my shoulder. It was a hot summer afternoon under a clear blue sky that rang with the high, twittering peal of skylarks as they hovered over the waving corn. Halfway across the field, in a wide-open space, quite alone, I stopped and sat down. I had a sort of moment of clarity that I have never really had before or since. In that instant, I experienced the absolute certainty that the guitar would carry me around the world and be my companion throughout my life. Not necessarily *that* guitar, of course, but the guitar as a thing. It was going to be me, and I was going to be it. Nothing was going to stop me.

I got up and continued over the field to Martin's house. Setting up in the garden, we attempted to play 'Stairway To Heaven' and some Alice Cooper songs. We were rubbish but we were keen. I knew that there was so much to learn but I felt blissfully happy. My epiphany among the corn that day had revealed to me that I was certain to learn it. It was my version of a 'Robert Johnson at the crossroads' moment.

Martin's mum, Kath Osborn, watched us practising. She had long, jet-black hair and wore black velvet zip-up trouser suits. She was always smoking a Benson & Hedges and cradling a glass of white wine. She had a husky voice, high cheekbones, heavy makeup, and a slim but very shapely figure. I suppose she must have been in her mid-thirties. She was the fuel for my teenage fantasies for a while.

I enjoyed being in Martin's group, but I wanted to do more than just play pop songs to old men playing dominoes and drinking brown ale. I became closer friends with Mark Foster, the bass player in The Young Ones, who also harboured a wish to progress to a wider world of music than just trotting out the popular hits of the day for old geezers in clubs.

The Fosters were quite a dysfunctional family who kind of adopted me. They were the first Irish Catholics I'd met. I started spending hours after school hanging out at Mark's, listening to records. The Rolling Stones, The Allman Brothers, Fleetwood Mac, and Mountain were our favourites.

Also, there was Mark's sister Jane. Jane was only twelve when I started hanging out at the house, but I fell hopelessly in love with her. Her freckles, her dark curls. Her cute lisp and coquettish laughter at my jokes. Her soulful brown eyes. The way they lit up when she smiled. My fourteen-year-old heart was sick with longing whenever I saw her. It was my shameful secret to be besotted with Jane. I spent many of my visits just trying to impress her by learning the songs I knew she liked and playing them on the guitar.

The reason for my acceptance at the Fosters' was twofold. Number one, they were kind. They were always very nice to me and allowed me refuge there anytime my own family got too much. My parents argued often, and my brother and sister fought a lot too, so I needed a place to go that felt more open and relaxed. There were dark secrets at play in my parents' lives, of which I was only dimly aware. The true extent of their dysfunctional marriage has only really been revealed to me decades later, but I sensed that something wasn't right back then, even if I didn't know what it was. But Ann Foster was like a second mum to me. Her easy laughter and *laissez-faire* attitude were what my anxious young soul needed—a refuge from the tension at home.

Reason number two that I was accepted by the Fosters was because, as I was starting to realise, I had some talent. I could help Ann's lover, Andrew, with his guitar classes. I could teach Jane to play—which meant I actually got to touch her fingers. The whole vibe of the Fosters' lapsed-catholic, smoke-filled, alcohol-fuelled, music-centred, slightly chaotic household felt like a nurturing environment to me. More so than my own home, it spoke of a future, of freedom, of love.

All the time I had been playing in The Young Ones, I had been developing a keen interest in the alternative side of music. I knew that it was not going to be my destiny to play pop covers in clubs to disinterested bingo players and drinkers. I developed a close friendship with another boy in my year, Philip Butcher. He had long ginger hair and thick glasses and was clearly a bit of an outsider. I liked his original, arty way of thinking and bizarre sense of humour. Time hanging out at his house was a real learning curve. We stole *Penthouse* magazines from his older brother's room (or 'one-handed literature', as we called it) and raided his rather esoteric record collection. This is how I got to hear and learn to love Frank Zappa & The Mothers' early work. I heard Captain Beefheart and Soft Machine, too.

Phil's brother, John, was to become a leading experimental saxophonist in the free-jazz world, and Phil and I would eventually tour with Iggy Pop together. As teenagers, we were already starting to carve out a niche as mavericks and 'the weird kids' among our peers, who were mostly more conventional in their tastes. We shunned the hits of the day and what we saw as a slavish devotion to so-called hard-rock groups like Black Sabbath and Deep Purple. We convinced ourselves— in the way only pretentious teenagers can—that our blind devotion to the music of Zappa, Soft Machine, and The Mahavishnu Orchestra made us intellectually superior to those who followed the herd.

Phil and I made it our business to hang out with a few of the coolest older kids at school and find out what they were listening to (and what they were smoking). Once, when my parents were out for the day, I offered the sixth-form freaks our house for a jam session. I invited all the long-haired, Afghan-wearing, diffident hippies, with their proper Fender guitars and real Vox and Watkins amplifiers. They duly arrived, smelling heavily of patchouli, smoked a lot of dope, and ate everything in the fridge. Then they turned up the volume and jammed for hours. I had no idea what they were doing but it felt as if I had staged a free festival in our living room. By the time my mother came home, all but the stragglers had left, and I was drunk on cheap whisky mac and rock'n'roll and immune to her scolding.

To give them their due, my mum and dad soon realised that I wasn't going to quit my obsession with music. They became entirely supportive of my ambition to become an actual guitar player. They drove me to and from early gigs and rehearsals. They let me spend hours in my room, absorbing all the records I could. By the time I was fifteen, I had lost all interest in anything except guitars and girls. I had become quite good at the guitar but was fairly rubbish at girls.

I had an older friend, a very talented drummer named Rob Todd, who lived about half a mile away. He was seventeen and lived with his mum, who kept herself closeted upstairs and just seemed to leave Rob to fend for himself. His dad had died and left them an inheritance, but a palpable sense of loss pervaded their home. His mum's grief seemed to leave her unable or unwilling to intervene much in Rob's development, so he did pretty much what he wanted. He had quite a good car (a white Triumph 2000), a sparkly silver Pearl drumkit, a fantastic stereo, endless bags of Thai grass, and hundreds of great records.

I used to wait until all was quiet at night and leave the house via my bedroom window. I could jump out onto the porch and climb down, putting my feet into the holes in the ornamental bricks by the front door. I'd skip off down the road and be at Rob's house in ten minutes. We would sit on his sofa in between a set of very expensive hi-fi speakers, smoke weed, and totally immerse ourselves in some of the trippiest music I had ever heard. Pink Floyd, Todd Rundgren, Can, Genesis, Yes, and King Crimson all swirled around us in a cloud of dope smoke and teenage wonder.

I'm so glad that I have—at one or two brief periods in my life— enjoyed the habit of just sitting in front of a really good record player, often while indulging in mild hallucinogens, and just drowning in sound. Full immersion in music like that was a powerful thing at my impressionable age. Though I don't do it much now, outside of my work, it taught me how to really hear music in fine detail. My life as a studio musician has been, I'm sure, immeasurably affected by having listened to records in that way.

I liked the things I heard on the radio a few years before. 'The Days Of Pearly Spencer', 'I Heard It Through The Grapevine', 'Nathan Jones', the early Bowie hits, 'Maggie May' by Rod Stewart. I liked the music I had explored with Mark Foster—The Rolling Stones and Fleetwood Mac—and the freaky shit I heard at Phil's house. But it was the nocturnal exploration of so-called progressive rock at Rob's that opened my mind to the possibilities of how far the imagination could wander in the recording studio.

This feverish world of dreams conjured from guitars, drums, pianos, and organs, fronted by exotic mysterious characters singing about things I only dimly understood, called me away from the crushingly dull environment of family life and school. The album artwork was great to look at, too, when you were stoned. The visions I saw and heard on that Orpington sofa made me want to follow these phoney prophets, somehow to take my place there among the lost and found sages of rock'n'roll. I had no idea how I was going to get near their world, but I had to try, and to do that I had to up my game.

I borrowed the deposit for a real American Fender Stratocaster from my dad and struggled to keep up on the payments with various Saturday jobs in local shops, more cleaning of cars, delivering leaflets, and so on.* By now, my school life had become a total joke, something I had turned against in a serious way. But I was making some real progress with the guitar. I spent hours every day in my room with it, obsessing over Led Zeppelin, Hendrix, and Wishbone Ash guitar parts and learning how to play T. Rex and David Bowie songs. That gave me focus, and people were starting to notice.

---

* I wish I still had that guitar now—it would be worth thousands!

CHAPTER THREE

ESCAPE FROM SUBURBIA

§

MY O-LEVEL EXAMS WERE A PREDICTABLE NON-EVENT. I passed English but either failed or didn't even turn up for the others. I had spent the last year of school, from the age of fifteen, not even showing up except to register in the morning. I would then sneak off and do shifts in a coffee bar in town. The café had one album, which they played on a continuous loop. To this day, I still can't listen to David Gates and Bread without becoming nauseous.

My father was working at his London office job, and neither he nor my mother seemed to notice that I wasn't attending school. They had their own problems, so I just kept getting away with it until they received a bill for entrance fees for exams that I hadn't turned up for. I can't remember them even being mad with me over my total rejection of secondary education. My younger brother was a model student, and that seemed to make up somewhat for my wayward behaviour. Plus I think they had some faith in my obvious doggedness with regard to music, and maybe they hoped it might present a way forward for me.

As an early teenager, I cast around looking for other bands to play with. I joined a rock group called Pigpen, made up of cool kids from school. On Sundays, I would walk a mile to the bus stop in Orpington with my guitar over my shoulder, wait sometimes an hour for a 61 bus that would take another hour to get to Bromley, where I'd finally join a rehearsal at Al Brown's house. Al's mum, Mona, would be drinking gin in bed in the room next door to the rehearsal space while we made an unholy racket. I don't even think we ever did a gig.

The back pages of the *Melody Maker* were full of wanted ads for young players. Many well-known bands had started out looking there for members so, at fifteen, I started going to auditions. I once got a call back after turning up to try out for Chris Spedding's band. I also went to Southend and got a five-minute chance to play with The Kursaal Flyers. They were very kind to a kid who clearly wasn't ready and encouraged me to keep going anyway.

There was an annual sale in those days at the legendary Orange Music shop at 3 New Compton Street in London. I camped out on the pavement for two nights to be one of the first in the queue. It was rumoured that you could pick up a Gibson guitar for some ridiculous giveaway price.

On the first day, I caught a glimpse of Free's guitarist, Paul Kossoff, going into the shop. I came away with some dodgy speaker cabinets and a couple of microphones, which must have involved one of my parents driving up to get me. It was a little taste of independence and adventure that made me want to live in London.

Eventually, after travelling on the train to another *Melody Maker* audition, I got offered a gig with a band of self-described 'nice Jewish boys' from Northwest London who said they had a record deal. I told my dad that I wanted to go, and he gave me the one piece of golden, fatherly wisdom he ever dispensed.

'Son,' he said, 'if you don't do this now, you'll always regret it.'

So it was that in 1974 I left my hometown in Kent to join a band in London. I was sixteen years old, as fresh as a daisy and as green as grass. The band I had auditioned for and joined turned out to be a bit of a dead loss, though. Fiver (as they were terribly named) did have a real record deal with EMI, but, alas, it was an early experiment in the creation of a manufactured 'boyband', and they weren't allowed to write their own songs. We weren't required to be anywhere near a studio when 'our' records were being made, either. The whole thing was a sort of proxy project cooked up by a couple of old Tin Pan Alley queens, Ken Howard and Alan Blaikley, who had written hits for Dave Dee, Dozy, Beaky, Mick, And Titch and other 70s horrors. ('Xanadu', anyone?) We were only there to have our pictures taken and, possibly, to mime, if the band ever had a hit. (We didn't.)

The lead singer, Michael, had been a child movie actor with a bit of a profile, so all the focus was on him. Our only role was to be props while he sang over the session men's dreary backing. I went along for the ride in the mistaken belief that all this Tin Pan Alley crap was a necessary way to break into the music business, but I mostly spent my time soaking up every musical influence other than pop.

For my first couple of years in London, '74–'75, I lived in a series of squats and boarding houses filled with a cast of diverse characters the like of which I'd only read about in Henry Miller and Jack Kerouac novels. For a brief while I even found myself sharing a tiny room in a house with a guy and his dog, and, having no money for tube fare, I walked the entire length of Edgware Road from Dollis Hill to the West End (two and a half hours) to my day job in a small warehouse, packing clothing in boxes.

Pretty soon, 70s London being what it was, I developed other, shadier interests. My head turned toward getting as much sex as I could and buying the best weed my budget would allow. I hung around with lots of what my mother would have called 'quite unsavoury types' during this time, and I would spend a number of years in denial as to how destructive a habit marijuana became for me. It seemed that drugs were everywhere I turned. My dope smoking was possibly a cause for arrested development and a lack of focus. What it did do, though, was furnish me with that indefinable sense of immersion in the sensual that can be such a direct connection to how music is heard. I still think that there are some definite benefits to listening to things while stoned out of your mind. Though I don't do it anymore (and haven't since the age of thirty-odd), I did the trip with an open mind.

Meanwhile, my first 'professional' band, Fiver, had finally realised that there was no future in just being sock puppets and left EMI. We actually tried to be a proper band. We met and hired a new manager, Terry Collins, who turned out to be one of the dodgiest spivs I have ever encountered, in or outside the music business.

In 1977, Terry somehow obtained the lease on an old cinema in Harlesden, Northwest London, and rechristened it the Roxy Theatre. His idea was to showcase the band there. He soon realised, though, that the place would have to make money on its own, so he started renting it out for gigs. At first, his group of decrepit golfing buddies persuaded him to book rotten, washed-up 60s acts like Clodagh Rodgers and Bobby Crush and horrible, racist throwback 'comedians' like Jim Davidson. But after a much-needed change of direction, some authentic Jamaican reggae stars were booked to play there, like The Gladiators and Gregory Isaacs. The locals in Harlesden loved that (and so did I). Terry also hired out the cinema as a rehearsal space, and the classic line-up of Thin Lizzy rehearsed there—the one with the duelling Les Pauls of Scott Gorham and Brian Robertson. And I remember sitting in the dark at the back of the stalls, watching Johnny Guitar Watson routine his band before a tour.

One day, an oddball called Malcolm turned up to meet Terry with a wad of cash. A 'national scandal' that revolved around him and the group he managed was about to become big news. This was Chelsea boutique owner and anarchist entrepreneur Malcolm McLaren, and the scene that had sprung up around him, known as punk rock, was about to go global. Malcolm's protégés, the Sex Pistols, were already known to the cognoscenti who read *NME* and *Sounds*. They were about to become household names to a far wider demographic—and inflict a seismic shock on the pop world to boot.

Punk was just starting to attract headlines and disapproving noises from various stuffed-shirt politicians and church leaders. Another youth movement was being characterised as undermining the very foundations of society. It was about to give the haters something to really hate. The Pistols and various acolytes had been invited to appear on a live, early evening TV news show, primarily in order to be ridiculed. The cynical editors must have thought it would be good telly to parade these stupid ne'er-do-wells in front of a jeering public. The Pistols turned the tables, though, to great howls of tabloid hysteria and faux tabloid outrage. What has become known as 'The Bill Grundy Incident' established them as the biggest threat to civilisation since the *OZ* trials in the 60s. One day they were an unknown band, but after the *Today* show, even my granny knew who they were.

On the day they arrived to rehearse at the Harlesden Roxy, Johnny Rotten was already Public Enemy Number One with his disdainful sneer splashed over every front page in the country as a result of the TV farce the evening before. I accompanied him across the street during a break from rehearsals to buy some beers for the band. We went into a corner shop in Harlesden High Road, and people stood there with their mouths open just at the sight of him. The whole punk circus of the Sex Pistols, The Damned, The Clash, and Johnny Thunders' Heartbreakers rehearsed for a week at the Roxy for the doomed Anarchy Tour, which was quickly hounded out of existence by shocked and morally outraged local councils up and down the country. I sat in the back of the darkened theatre and listened as they played what have become the foundation songs of punk: 'Anarchy In The UK', 'White Riot', 'New Rose', all fresh out of the box.

As a matter of personal taste, I didn't quite 'get' punk on a musical level when it first appeared in 1976. Being raised on classic rock, I was too enamoured with the amazing technique and sensuality of what those artists made to be particularly tolerant of the cheap, dustbin-lid noises made by many of the early punks. Despite this, I looked on with excited interest at these young iconoclasts who seemed to be doing something brave and free with their rudimentary and aggressive approach.[*]

Spotting a commercial opportunity, the Roxy Theatre booked Hersham punks Sham 69 to play. I had heard about Sham 69's shows and urged Terry Collins to remove the seating before the gig, but he and his masonic, puce-faced mates knew better and dismissed my concerns. Of course, the Hersham Boys' fans had trashed the place after the riotous gig. It was bloody funny to see that there was nothing left but piles of shredded firewood, horsehair stuffing, and velvet rags where the original seats had been. It must have cost them most of their profit just to get rid of the debris.

Despite my reservations on a purely musical level, I could see that the attitude the punk rockers had toward the creative process was revolutionary, and it definitely breathed fresh air into a music scene that was becoming bloated with self-importance and super-egos (not to mention misogyny, wizards, dragons, and too many psychedelic drugs). I fully understood the need to overthrow the idea that you had to be a musical genius to make a record, even if I didn't much like the results.

In those early years, punk *music* sometimes seemed secondary in importance to the haircut and the artwork. The more ideological bands were wedded to the idea of 'DIY' to the extent that (in public, at least) they dismissed everyone who could actually play as bourgeois and corrupt, even though, inevitably, many of them learned their craft really well. Bands like the Stranglers had reinvented themselves as popular punk acts. I saw them play in a pub in West London in 1975, and the raw sound that made them into a hit band was fully formed even then. Many of the early punks pretended they couldn't play, even though they could, to avoid the suspicions of the 'back to basics' crowd.

---

[*] Years later, I would work with both John Lydon and Steve Jones, with John as a sideman for PiL on *Top Of The Pops*, and alongside Steve onstage and on record for Iggy Pop and toured with Glen Matlock.

Around this time, I was living at a particularly tawdry house full of bedsits in Belsize Park with a somewhat older American girlfriend. It was the kind of place that attracted more than its fair share of misfits and marginal people, and, in fact, it was a hive of addiction, violence, and criminality. An Irish family had been designated as 'managers' on behalf of the (absent) Middle Eastern owners. The father, Billy, was in charge of collecting rent from the hundred or so occupants of the shabby rooms. He and his sidekick—a Charles Manson lookalike—would intimidate the tenants and often physically threaten late payers, and they held the whole place in a carefully curated atmosphere of menace. They were also rumoured to spy on lone women through holes in the walls. One day, Billy and his entourage disappeared, having stolen a month's takings, and were never seen again.

An elderly Swiss man called Franz Ernst and his young male lover introduced us to the joys of LSD. Franz was the chauffeur to Nord Ringling, owner of the famous Ringling Brothers Circus. He had been Nord's driver for years and had the use of a twenty-foot-long Mercedes stretch limo and sort of latched on to me and my girl. One night, Franz and his Italian boyfriend drove us in the limo to see New York band Television's London debut as they opened for Blondie. As the acid took hold of me during the gig, I 'saw' great plumes of orange and purple notes flying out from Tom Verlaine's guitar and arcing over the crowd at the Hammersmith Odeon. The Pistols' 'God Save The Queen' was pumped over the PA too, and it sounded fabulous.*

Tripping on acid was both thrilling and incredibly scary. I never took LSD again, but I can still see those flying streamers. Something about having 'seen' sound in this way stays in the brain forever. Something about living on the edge in that house of horrors was getting to me, too. The potential for unpleasantness was never far from the surface in that squalid labyrinth. Most of the people there were

---

* I think Television's album *Marquee Moon* remains a timeless classic—a masterclass in clean Fender guitar sounds and angular songwriting.

drawing unemployment benefit or social-security money. Some were ex-military with mental health issues, or addicts, or crooks on the run. Many of them spent their Giro cheques on drink and drugs and were skint again two days after payday.

One day, I went to put my key in the lock and found the door had been kicked in. The beautiful Japanese stereo equipment that had been gifted by my girlfriend's parents was now just a bunch of wires dangling from the wall. All my records were gone. It felt like time to move on.

Being in Fiver—always told what to play and how to dress, while not even earning enough to live on—wasn't what I signed up for. It was imperative to do something 'real' with my music. If I was going to be a career musician, I needed to do something for the love of it and work with people I could truly respect as artists. Otherwise, I might as well look for a job in an office or a factory. Though the guys in Fiver were good blokes, the hopelessly outmoded Tin Pan Alley world in which they operated was getting to me. They weren't going to be my true musical brethren.

I left the band, and, for a while at least, quit the life of druggy pennilessness in London. Some of my old schoolmates in Orpington had started punk bands, and I got involved in the local scene by virtue of the little bit of experience I'd had in studios and playing in a 'pro' band. I became the go-to guy whenever any of them wanted help at a recording session or wanted to borrow an amplifier or have someone sit in the room while they rehearsed and suggest how they could improve. Even then, I was being steered into the sort of bandleader/producer role that would become part of my natural skillset later.

One Orpingtonian guy around at that time was an inveterate loony and local wild man who would drink anything, smoke or inject anything, take on anyone twice his size in a fight, and generally cause hilarious mayhem wherever he went. He lived with his mum in a flat over a shop in Orpington High Street. I once saw him throw fresh turds out of his window onto passers-by. Another time he faced down a whole gang of skinheads in the high street (before getting the living shit kicked out of him). Max Splodge, as he had christened himself, had gathered together a loose collection of likeminded loons and miscreants who became known as Splodgenessabounds. The band was made up of various school dropouts and hippies from the neighbourhood. Some of them could play instruments; some of them just supplied the drugs.

One summer, they broke into and squatted in Cromlix, an enormous Edwardian mansion in nearby Chislehurst with a two-acre garden and a derelict swimming pool. Huge wood-panelled rooms would play host to amazing parties, overflowing with drugs, orgiastic behaviour, and all-night jam sessions. The whole band lived there. The fun continued for two years until an eviction notice finally put paid to the shenanigans and the place was repossessed. It was fantastic while it lasted.

I was occasionally on hand to cover various instruments and give support when songs for their album were recorded in Manfred Mann's Warehouse Studio on the Old Kent Road. Splodgeness's 'Two Pints Of Lager And A Packet of Crisps Please' became Orpington's first number-one hit. The glory was somewhat muted, though, as there was a technician's strike at the BBC, which meant their *Top Of The Pops* slot was cancelled, so their record remains probably the most obscure number one in British chart history. When they did get on *Top Of The Pops* with the follow-up single in '81, the band's luck didn't improve much. It was a cover version of Rolf Harris's 'Two Little Boys' introduced by Jimmy Savile, preceded by Jonathan King, and followed on the show by Gary Glitter.*

Despite my ambivalence about punk, I joined in with the general milieu and followed my friends. Weekends would often be spent getting the train with my brother Ross and our mates up to the Roxy in Covent Garden. We'd take cheap sulphate and pogo to Eater or The Damned or Slaughter & The Dogs and chat up depressed-looking girls in heavy

---

* Note for non-British readers: these people all turned out to be predatory paedophiles and rapists. Three were jailed and the worst one is dead.

makeup and fishnets (the girls, not us). We'd either leave just in time to get the last train from Charing Cross or stay out late, haunting the desolate wastelands near Butler's Wharf, speeding off our nuts, and get the milk train at 5am. I knew a few of those who became known as the Bromley Contingent, so punk felt like it had many local connections for us South London suburbanites. Most of us weren't what you'd call hardcore punks, just weekend ones. Nobody had gone as far as having a cock piercing or getting trepanned. We just used to dye our hair and wear a few bits from the shops in Kings Road like Sex (later Seditionaries), which was where Vivien Westwood sold her first clothes designs, and from where Malcolm McLaren had launched those naughty Sex Pistols.

I preferred it when more sophisticated bands like Devo and Talking Heads emerged from America to counter the fashion against any kind of technique or prowess, which had become the crushing orthodoxy for what seemed like too long. Pretty soon, proper grown-up songwriting was 'allowed' again, following the emergence of artists like Blondie and Elvis Costello. New wave, they called it. Looking back, punk was like living through the cultural equivalent of some kind of Stalinist purge or the Pol Pot years in Cambodia. I'm overegging the analogy, obviously, but for a few years you couldn't own up to having liked any record that was made before 1976 unless it was Bowie, T. Rex, or Iggy Pop. People hid their former tastes for fear of ridicule. As a Led Zeppelin fan, I had to treat my past as a shameful dirty secret. I'm sure Joe Strummer was a fan of loads of great pre-punk records, even Elvis, Beatles, and The Rolling Stones (Clash lyrics notwithstanding). For a long while, though, it was still Year Zero, and former classic-rock fans like me had to stay well in the closet.

* * *

Growing up in a suburban town, I often heard my school friends tell racist jokes. Their parents did it too. I joined in as well because that's what you did. We had no real understanding of what we were doing.

We had one Asian kid in school, but we never met any black people. Blackness was an alien concept. It was common to hear friends or their parents refer to black people in offensive terms that you rarely hear today. Thankfully, my parents never did this, but plenty of attitudes from my peers' families affected me. It wasn't until I first moved to London that I realised what kind of poison I had been drinking. After going to a few 'blues parties' in Harlesden and Brixton, hanging out with reggae bands, and developing a serious love for that music, I would never again laugh at a racist joke, or hear one without calling it out. The rise of right-wing cults like the National Front and the BNP (British National Party), and the nasty way the police behaved to locals, was enough to turn me into a rabid anti-racist. Late-70s London was changing. This was when white punks found something more important to say than, 'Look at my funny haircut.'

The Rock Against Racism gig in 1978 was headlined by The Clash and Steel Pulse and took place in Victoria Park, Hackney, in London's East End. Eighty thousand people were there because they hated racism as much as they loved music. It was events like this that helped to destroy the pretend Nazis of the NF and break up the elite police squads and right-wing goons that caused so much friction in some London communities. The youth had found a voice, and its message was 'Fuck you, racists.'

We felt like we were making a difference back in the late 1970s, but over five decades later, despite the gains, there is still so much work to be done. With the continued inequalities based on skin colour alone— Windrush, Grenfell, George Floyd—sometimes it feels remarkably like we've not learned much.

I've been lucky that music is a rarefied world where different cultures are encountered and bonds are made far more easily than in wider society. My children have grown up in a truly mixed world and have many lifelong friends from different backgrounds. This was not available to me growing up and, as ever, I take hope from the young.

CHAPTER FOUR

WHERE'S CAPTAIN KIRK?

§

TO MAKE AN HONEST CRUST, I SIGNED ON WITH A TEMPORARY WORK AGENCY CALLED MANPOWER—a popular way in the late 1970s to make a quick buck with no strings attached.

Sometimes, on certain street corners in some parts of London, you see groups of men hanging around, hoping for a gang master to offer a day's casual work for cash. Back then, before undocumented cheap labour, there was a good living to be made in temporary agency jobs where extra or replacement staff were needed. Agency workers are paid more than regular employees, so it was a good gig.

I would jump on a 6am train, turn up at Manpower's offices in Elephant and Castle at 7am, and find myself doing anything from banging the plastic feet onto garden chairs to moving pool tables to mundane office work, answering the phone or filing. The beauty of it was that none of it lasted for more than a few days, or at most a few weeks, so you didn't get bored. It was like being a job tourist, but quite a well-paid one.

I once spent a few days packing false teeth in boxes, which sounds like sheer hell, but then I started chatting with the guy at the next bench. He turned out to be alternative punk poet Wavis O'Shave, whose album *Anna Ford's Bum* I'd heard bits of on *The John Peel Show*. He later morphed into a character called Foffo Spearjig (aka The Hard) with his own slot on Channel 4's rock show, *The Tube*. His catchphrase, as he rammed his head into a fence post, was, 'I'm that haaard I felt nowt,' delivered in his broad Geordie accent.

I became a temporary theatre porter for a few months at the Nuffield Centre of Guy's Hospital. It was my job to ferry patients and their beds along the warren of underground tunnels between the wards and the operating theatres. The Nuffield was a private wing specialising in cosmetic surgery, but other operations were done there too. I had to move lamps around and fetch and carry surgical instruments to and from the sterilisation centre, deep in the bowels of the building (and I saw deep into the bowels of several people while doing that job, too). I also heard and marvelled at the things that the eminent consultants said about the patients on whom they were operating. They were mostly knights of the realm and professors. I wiped the blood off their white rubber boots as they bantered with each other:

'Why on earth this woman thinks that a nose job will make her look any less like a horse is anyone's guess, Rodney.'

'Good God, Lancelot, it's not like this one's tits aren't big enough already, phwah phwah!'

Another time I did a stint at New Cross Hospital, stoking the incinerator. The giant chimneys at Guy's Hospital, several miles away, had been closed for repairs, and the very much smaller incinerator at New Cross was consequently expected to cope with all of its own waste and the stuff from Guy's too. Vans full of it would arrive twice a day, and the vile, minging pile never seemed to shrink.

Clad head-to-toe in Formica helmets, boilersuits, and thick gloves, an old Jamaican bloke called Winston and I manned the brick shed at the back of the hospital where the incinerator was housed, far away from visitors' eyes. We would crank open the heavy iron doors of the furnace and shove in the plastic sacks full of hospital waste by hand. A lot of it was toxic chemicals, needles, surgical waste like limbs and organs, and dirty, used dressings or nappies. Sometimes it was whole animals, decaying goat and dog carcasses—really disgusting, gory stuff.

These plastic bags of filth would pile up inside and outside the shed and attract swarms of flies and wasps. It was too much for the little place to cope with.

One day, Winston had gone home early but I decided to stay late to try and tackle the heaving mountain of shite on my own. I started loading the furnace for all it was worth, chucking in bag after bag. I was oblivious to my surroundings in my protective clothing and helmet. It wasn't until I heard the sirens that I realised that six fire engines were approaching.

Stepping out of the shed, I was greeted by a lot of firemen waving their arms and looking up. I saw, to my alarm, that the steel chimney above the furnace was glowing orange almost up to its entire height of twenty feet. Thick black toxic smoke poured out the top and blanketed half of Millwall. The stench in the nearby blocks of flats must have been overwhelming.

By far my favourite Manpower assignment was an extended period working for a company that delivered tax-free booze from a bonded warehouse on the South Bank of the Thames to various foreign embassies around London. I was teamed up with a driver called Jos Grain. A natural humourist from Heckmondwicke in Yorkshire, Jos would make extremely off-colour jokes and maintain a constant barrage of pithy, northern wit and wisdom that would keep me entertained all day. He was also a bit of a speed freak. We would munch through a bag of 'blues' that he kept stashed behind the steering wheel of the truck and get buzzed off our faces.

In the morning we would load the boxes of expensive liquor, beer, and wine onto the three-tonner and then spend an enjoyable day driving around the city, stopping to drop off crates of whisky for Saudi diplomats or marvel at the ineptness of the staff at India House. They would all gather on balconies, looking down at us in the lobby, with seemingly no one in charge or able to sign off on our delivery without at least a thirty-minute wait. The Nigerians always had crates and crates of Guinness, I remember, and we would swap friendly banter with Red Army guards at the Russian mission as we replenished their stocks of quality vodka.

That same Jos Grain went on to work in music for decades, for many big names, and he's still Iggy Pop's most trusted roadie. Our working relationship goes back further than any other in my life. It was Jos who, upon learning that I was a budding guitar player, offered me my first professional touring opportunity. He happened to be sharing his flat with a singer and talented graphic artist from Walsall called Kenneth Spiers, who would become known to a legion of fans as Spizz. His song 'Where's Captain Kirk?' became something of a punk classic. He changed the name of his band every year—Spizzoil, Spizzenergi, Athletico Spizz 80, et cetera.

I was drafted in for the iteration called Spizzles. A brief tour of northern cities and rock clubs followed, and I really got a taste for the life of a touring musician. Travelling, playing gigs, getting drunk, and engaging in a certain amount of casual sex seemed like the way forward for a young gunslinger like me.

Spizz himself was a curious mixture of visual artist and self-deprecating comedian who had a good go at singing. His natural exuberance and sense of fun seemed to grab attention very easily, and a sort of friendly gang mentality held sway. We played a lot of punk dives up and down the country. Some small venues were slightly hostile environments for punk bands who occasionally wore eyeliner and women's clothing. Years later, when the internet started to rear its head as the fount of all information, my youngest daughter, Olivia, searched for pictures of her dad's guitar-wielding exploits in order to impress her friends. The first image she came up with was a photo of me and Spizzles bass man Jim Solar changing into fishnet stockings and suspenders in a pub toilet in Barnsley.

* * *

After the Spizzles tour, it seemed like I was getting somewhere, but I still had to earn a living. The last job I had from Manpower was as an internal postboy for the accountancy firm Price Waterhouse, based in a shiny gold tower block next to my old haunt, Guys Hospital. At the Christmas office party in the basement, I downed about nine double scotches in quick succession and then realised that I had one more post round to make before clocking off. So, at about 5pm on Christmas Eve, I took the fast elevator to the twenty-fifth floor. By the time I got there, my head was reeling from the whisky. Somehow, I managed to collect the post from my little office. There was a sort of dumb waiter pulley system in it to drag the letters up from the post room. I wobbled around the empty offices on the top floor, trying to match the names on the envelopes to the names on the desks.

When I had done my round and returned to the cubbyhole I got the mail from, I sat down. *Oh no*, I thought. *I'm going to puke.* I staggered to the nearest toilet, and the next thing I knew it was Christmas morning and I was on my knees, hugging a toilet, on the top floor of a darkened, empty office block near London Bridge, fifteen miles from home.

On another day in that tiny post room in the sky, I read an interview with DJ Charlie Gillett in the *Melody Maker*. He had a label called Oval Records, which he ran from the basement of his house. I looked him up in the phone book, called him, and convinced him to listen to my songs.

Charlie was a music writer and a highly respected DJ on Radio London and Capital Radio with a reputation as a talent spotter. He'd written a great book called *Sounds Of The City* and been instrumental in discovering Ian Dury, Elvis Costello, Dire Straits, Lene Lovich, and many more. I turned up at his place in Clapham one afternoon, plonked an amplifier down in the middle of his basement office, plugged in a guitar, and sang him three of my own songs. My stuff was somewhat Elvis Costello-like and quite catchy. Charlie and his partner, Gordon Nelki, offered me a record contract on the spot.

I experienced a huge sense of elation, assuming that now, at the age of twenty-one, I had made it. I really thought I'd cracked the music business and would now automatically find a path to instant success. I mustered the confidence to form a band with Soft Boys bassist Matthew Seligman and drummer Kim Barti, and so Local Heroes was born.

We rehearsed together and played gigs everywhere we could. In those days, there was a network of pubs and clubs around London that welcomed new bands. We soon found ourselves playing regularly at the 101 in Clapham, the Moonlight in West Hampstead, the Rock Garden in Covent Garden, and the Old Queen's Head in Stockwell, which was virtually opposite Bowie's birthplace in Stansfield Road.

We went into some local eight-track studios and made our first demos. It was the culmination of all my efforts to get noticed up until that point. I'd even phoned John Walters at the BBC—John Peel's producer. Somehow, I got through to him from a phone box. While frantically shovelling ten pence pieces into the slot, I gabbled to him about how good I was and how John Peel ought to have me do a session on his show. He must have thought I was a right nut, but he was very kind and patient, nonetheless. At least he gave me the time of day and listened.

People like Peel and Walters had to keep an ear to the ground at all times. They couldn't dismiss anybody as a no-hoper, especially in this post-punk period. They might just be the next big thing. Either way, I was now an Oval Records artist with a real record contract and—so it seemed to me—one big step closer to my proper place in the world. Local Heroes became the focus of my whole life. We opened for Tom Robinson at the Ritzy in Brixton and Cabaret Voltaire at the ICA. We played all over London and started to get some momentum going and even a bit of a following, until everything changed overnight.

* * *

On December 18, 1979, my brother Ross was killed, through no fault of his own, in a motorbike smash, and my exciting new world fell to pieces.

Ross was riding back from work in Central London in the dark. It was raining, and a broken-down flatbed truck without lights had been left on the busy main road, two miles from home. It was directly in his path. He never saw it—never even braked. I had played a Local Heroes gig in South London that night and got back to my flat in Orpington late, so, in the age before mobile phones, I knew nothing about the accident that had happened eight hours before. At 7am on the 19th, there was a frantic banging on the door and my grandfather, Colin Studart, burst in and told me the terrible news.

Ross and I were very tight brothers. We'd shared a room until we were twelve and thirteen. As kids, being so close in age, we were always together, and we shared everything. We were very different people, but we properly loved each other, as brothers should. I have always been about language and music, whereas he was very clever with his hands and could make things and take them apart and find out how they worked. It was no surprise that he became a Post Office engineer, working on cabling and telecom infrastructure in tunnels under the city. It wasn't until we went to different high schools that our lives diverged much at all. While I went to the grammar school and rebelled, he went to the local technical school and excelled. We had an overlapping circle of friends, and we often used to frequent the local pubs together at weekends (drinking far more than was strictly necessary). We always had a real laugh together on these very hedonistic occasions, and I don't think we upset too many people.

Ross had been a big supporter of my music and came to all the Local Heroes gigs he could, along with his mates. He was clearly proud of me. It was Ross who had introduced me to the David Bowie albums. Bowie was his absolute idol. If only he'd been able to see me play with David a mere six years later.

Ross's sudden death shattered my family into fragments. The grief I felt knocked me sideways. I spiralled off into a desperate search for new and darker experiences. I slept with some of Ross's old girlfriends, who gravitated toward me for 'sympathy sex' the way that some people do around grievers. I wore some of his clothes. I was an emotional mess for months. Suddenly, Local Heroes seemed like an irrelevance.

It's hard to calculate what the loss of a close sibling does to you. Sometimes it seems not to matter so much, but then you meet up in a dream and it's like he's been away somewhere and just come back, as if it's the most normal thing in the world. That still happens to me today. The effects of the loss are lifelong, but you are not always aware of them. I've written songs, even recently, and not noticed for ages that he's in there. It's just bubbled up from inside, from somewhere unbidden. Certainly, my family never really recovered. I tore up all my old songs and started life (and my relationship to music) from scratch.

CHAPTER FIVE

SQUAT ROCK HEROES

§

I MET TOM BAILEY AND HIS BAND, THE THOMPSON TWINS, AT GIGS AROUND LONDON. They invited me to share a house he was squatting at in Lillieshall Road, Clapham, with his manager, John Hade. It was only a couple of streets away from Oval Records, so it made complete sense to me to live there.

The Thompson Twins were a six-piece guitar-based anarcho-syndicalist collective fond of cruising around to CND (Campaign for Nuclear Disarmament) festivals in a huge LDV van stuffed with PA equipment and all their backline amps. My band became sort of camp followers of theirs. We shadowed them in our fairly unreliable Ford Transit minibus to gigs around the country.*

The world knows The Thompson Twins as a pop trio with hits like 'Doctor Doctor' and 'In The Name Of Love', but the original band that I knew was about three hundred times more interesting than the brittle pop phenomenon they turned into. The big hits happened only after John and Tom ditched the guys from the original band and reapplied the name to a pop trio consisting of Tom, his girlfriend Alannah, and the band's roadie, Joe Leeway. It caused quite a stir when they did this, particularly among former band members

---

* I'd only come by the Transit van because of the insurance pay-out on Ross's death. It was a valuable thing for a band to own, and the small consolation was that I knew that that he would have wanted me to have it.

Pete Dodd, John Roog, and Chris Bell, who were each given £500 to fuck off.

Lillieshall Road was made up of abandoned semi-detached Victorian cottages in very run-down condition. London had numerous streets like this in the late 70s and early 80s. Enterprising young things like us would just break in and somehow get the power and water hooked up, then declare that we were living there and asserting our 'squatter's rights'.

Although squatters paid no rent and were hated and berated by the popular press of the day, in truth, they often left properties in a better condition than they found them. The same response to the housing crisis doesn't exist today. Any legal loopholes involving squatter's rights appear to have vanished in today's landlord-friendly world. Homeless people are forced into shop doorways instead of having semi-legal access to houses left mostly neglected by absentee owners (or incompetent councils).

The house we shared was a slightly dishevelled two-up, two-down cottage. Furniture was begged, borrowed, stolen, or made out of old bits of junk. Beds were just mattresses on the floor or sleeping bags. There was power and water but no heating. It was rough and ready, but what we could do in these places was rehearse our bands without upsetting our near neighbours, who were squatters too, so they didn't care how much noise we made.

The house next door to us (and the freaky people in it) soon caught my attention. The back garden had giant marijuana bushes growing in it, some of which were so sturdy you could stand your bike up against them. Occasionally, women wearing nothing but mud and ethnic jewellery could be observed cavorting in the garden, accompanied by loudspeakers blaring out Fela Kuti or Kraftwerk records. The Slits and Rip Rig & Panic rehearsals took place there. Viv Albertine and The Pop Group/RR&P's Gareth Sager lived there. Ari Up, Sean Oliver, and Tessa Pollitt visited sometimes. I was really captivated by the music they made, which was definitely a step forward from the nihilistic amateurism of punk. The Slits in particular represented a new and entirely positive face of young women knocking down the walls of the patriarchal mores of the 1970s. They didn't give a flying fuck about what anybody thought of them, and they ended up producing some of the best music of the era. 'Typical Girls' they were not. They made an album called *Cut* with reggae producer Dennis Bovell—a total blast of fresh female energy. Rip Rig & Panic were really trying something new too. They almost singlehandedly invented punk-jazz.

I started to hang around other bands and tried to learn from them. I was a visitor to the Camden Town squats in Carol Street where Scritti Politti lived and worked. They started life as a somewhat cerebral and alternative band of self-taught musicians trying to find a new way and ended up (like the Thomson Twins) with the singer, Green, and the manager, Matthew, turning to pure pop. They abandoned their bandmates and went on to make hits on a global scale. Maybe this was an early manifestation of Margaret Thatcher's individualistic philosophy, which would eventually leave even the most rebellious and searching musicians either side-lined or selling their souls to the devil. I don't know. Maybe alternative music just gets to feel like a ghetto for some. I have remained friends with Scritti's extraordinary drummer turned group motivator and philosopher, the extravagantly dreadlocked Tom Morley, who has retained much of his pioneering punk spirit and channelled it into bringing joy to thousands in his inspiring drum workshops.

After living on Lillieshall Road for almost a year, I moved to a shared 'housing association' place in nearby Brixton. Houses in the area change hands for the low millions today, but in the early 80s it was a rundown part of town. Despite this (or maybe because of it), it was a magnet for musicians and artists who liked living alongside the West Indian population. Brixton, like West London, had been home since the 1950s to people whose parents had come to England on the

SS *Windrush* in the first wave of black immigrants invited to take up working lives in postcolonial Britain.

Reggae culture was everywhere, and it soon caught my ear in a serious way. I'd seen the Jamaican acts that Terry Collins reluctantly booked at the Roxy in Harlesden, and I had heard the *Tighten Up* LPs in the 1970s. But now, living in Brixton, proper reggae music was part of the ambience. It rattled out of houses and boomed out of independent record shops, taxi ranks, and barbershops.

I enjoyed the village-like atmosphere of Brixton, with its soft drugs, street food, and Caribbean music. I lived in the attic room of a five-storey house at 19 Effra Road. The rent was extremely cheap but the properties were sometimes semi-derelict. Believe in astrology or not (I don't) but there were actually ten Aquarians living in that house. If we water-bearers do indeed share any traits by accident of birthdate, one of them would definitely be *not giving a fuck about housework in any way whatsoever*. The communal areas of that house were dead zones, devoid of any decorative feature or sign of life. But the tenants' rooms were a hive of social activity. The beaten-up, overstuffed sofas were always perched on by housemates and visitors drinking endless cups of tea—those who weren't playing host to various itinerant partygoers and casual crashers wrapped in blankets until the late afternoon.

Three doors along, there was a better-appointed house that was divided into private flats. Into one of these moved Alan Wise—a notorious face in the alternative music scene in Manchester that spawned The Smiths, Joy Division, Factory Records, and the Hacienda—and his friend, the poet John Cooper Clarke. They were soon joined by The Velvet Underground's ice-goddess, Nico. A few of us from the Aquarian project at number nineteen would go and hang out at Alan's and smoke dope. Once, at a party, I was deep in conversation with Johnny when I noticed Nico sitting on the stairs in a tight-fitting black tracksuit, her head deep in a book, ignoring all around her. I didn't catch the name of the tome she was reading, but suddenly she looked up and stared across at us with those headlamp eyes. She enquired of Dr Cooper Clarke in the deep German monotone so familiar from the Velvets' records, 'John, vot's a strap-on?' I'm surprised she had to ask.

I also hung out with a Brixton band called This Heat, who I thought were amazing. They had a local studio called Cold Storage, which used to be a refrigerated meat warehouse, and were making the kind of atonal, searching, brutal music I could only dream about. Their drummer, Charles Hayward, is one of the most compelling live musicians I have ever seen. His kit was made up of bits of old car wheels and biscuit tins, as well as proper drums. The way the band attacked their instruments was truly thrilling. It seemed as if they were trying to reinvent music or play beyond physics. I once saw them do a gig where their guitarist, Charles Bullen, played with a broken right arm. He'd fallen off his bike on the way to the gig but still attacked his guitar like he was trying to damage it. The title song on their album *Health & Efficiency* makes the hairs go up on the back of my neck even now. It sounds utterly modern.

I also saw The Birthday Party, fronted by a young Nick Cave, play at the ICA in London on their first visit to England (with their original bass player, Tracey Pew, who died not long after). Seeing The Slits at an amazing gig in Finsbury Park with The Pop Group's drummer, Bruce Smith, was memorable too. This period of submersion in underground music confirmed me as someone who would be forever sceptical of the mainstream and happier to self-identify as an outcast.

Some say that your taste in music is formed in your late teens and early twenties and that what you like then always sticks with you. I think that's true, to an extent. Whatever work I have done since, in whatever style, has always been coloured by what I loved in the classic-rock era of the 70s and something of what I heard in experimental post-punk as well. It also left me with an enduring distaste for corporate pop. With the exception of American hip-hop, modern artists just don't seem to want to stick their heads above the parapet and protest about anything.

I liked it when bands read Franz Kafka and Jean-Paul Sartre, not *Hello* magazine and Twitter.

* * *

Oval Records supremo Charlie Gillett had accepted my need to reinvent my approach to music in the wake of Ross's death. He continued to support me even though he must have felt that my early stuff was more likely to find a ready audience.

I was devastated by the loss of my brother, and I just wanted to tear up the rulebook and start over. I ditched all the songs we had been playing and tried to reach a more primal place within myself. So it was that Local Heroes developed a sort of early Public Image-like sound, with cavernous shards of echo on the guitar and dubby drums and bass, with my reedy voice intoning juvenile anguish over choppy time changes.

I loved Kim's skippy, energetic style of drumming and Matthew's fat, lyrical bass lines. We made an album for Oval called *Drip Dry Zone* that continues to enthral about seventy-two people to this day. We recorded it all pretty much 'live', with a few overdubs and sound effects. Though we were thrilled to have a real album out, it wasn't quite the masterpiece that I'd hoped for, even if it does have character and show intent.

The band limped along, with Matthew Seligman returning to The Soft Boys and being replaced by ex-FBI member and influential Antiguan bass player Lennox Meade. I took Lenny around to my grandmother's house one time. Nana was a sweet old thing but a dyed-in-the-wool *Daily Mail* reader and therefore a little 'old-fashioned' in her views, shall we say. My provocative act worked wonders, though, as she was forced out of politeness to invite us in and give us tea and biscuits. Afterwards, she said to me, 'That chap Lenny is actually rather nice, isn't he?' To which I replied, rather passive-aggressively, 'Well why wouldn't he be, actually?' It was probably the first and only time my dear old nan ever met a black man who wasn't a bus conductor or a cleaner.

Local Heroes continued to make a name for ourselves around London. We toured Holland in my Transit van, smoking too much weed and sleeping on friendly girls' floors (and in their beds). We lived the dream until such time as the drummer and I nearly had a punch-up onstage at a London club because I ran out of patience with his excessive drinking.

When it came time to do a second album, the band was effectively over, so I put some tracks we had already recorded on one side of the album and recorded some more songs in a totally different style, completely alone, for the other side. For this reason, the second Local Heroes album has a double title, *New Opium / How The West Was Won*.

Nowadays it's very easy to make tracks on your own because of things like Garageband and Logic Pro. Everyone who's interested has some sort of music-making software on their laptop or even their phone. Drum loops that sound like hit records are available at the touch of a button, and readymade sounds and beats can be combined with great ease and no discernible talent. When I made *How The West Was Won*, however, there were no such gizmos available, so I had to do it all on tape, starting with nothing. I sat down at the drums and played a part for three or four minutes, trying to sing in my head what might go over the top. Then I played some bass overdubs and added guitars and sang. It was a very hit-and-miss, organic kind of process. I was trying to sound a bit like early-period Scritti Politti (when they were still a pseudointellectual squat-rock band and hadn't had any hits). I enjoyed being experimental and writing songs 'on the fly', and I definitely learned quite a bit about recording my own performances from those sessions.

On the 'band' side of the album, I also took the music a little further on from the trio we had been. For one song, the bombastically titled 'Age Of Oppression', I added vibraphone player and Local Heroes fan

Philistin D'Aroso (Tin Tin for short). Matthew had also introduced me
to a formidably serious young man with something called a synthesizer
who came and played it to great effect on a couple of the songs for the
New Opium side that we'd recorded at Eden Studios in Chiswick. He
added some really effective electronic textures and chords on a song
called 'Hippie Street' and another called 'Love Is Essential', which later
became the prototype for Bowie's song 'Outside'. This was the first
time the synth player—who called himself Thomas Dolby—and I
would record together. It was also the swansong for Local Heroes.

New Opium / How The West Was Won didn't sell but a few dozen
copies. Oval Records had sort of lost enthusiasm for my deliberate
attempts to be experimental, too. They wanted hits, hits, hits! Lene
Lovich did it for them with 'Lucky Number', and my pursuit of wilful
obscurity became a self-fulfilling prophecy. I was going to be wilful and
we were going to be obscure.

* * *

The period after the breakup of my band in 1982 saw me drafted into a
band called The Passions. I can't remember how we met, but somebody
must have suggested me to them. They'd had a bit of a hit with 'I'm
In Love With A German Film Star'. I was there to replace guitarist
Clive Timperley, who'd already left, so I never got to meet Clive at the
time, but I really liked the others: singer Barbara Gogan, drummer
Richard Williams (her partner), and bassist David Agar. My time with
them was characterised by laughter-filled evenings in their Shepherd's
Bush flat, animatedly discussing Irish Republicanism (they used to get
the banned newspaper *An Phoblacht* sent to them), tearing down the
Thatcher government's war in the Falklands, and taking a hell of a lot
of poor-quality cocaine. I played a few university dates with the band
and recorded the album *Sanctuary* with producer Mick Glossop at the
helm.

Mick was (and still is) Van Morrison's producer, and the album was a departure from The Passions' earlier work. They added a keyboard player called Geoff Smith, and he and his PPG Wave synthesizer sort of took over as the main influence on the sound of the record. It wasn't entirely an improvement on their earlier work, and the album performed poorly, though it does have its fans today. The Passions missed a trick when they departed from the dreamy, psychedelic, echo-guitar approach that Clive had brought to the band and went for a more 'current' sound. The band broke up when Barbara and Richard's relationship did. I think Barbara was looking for something entirely new in life, as she then went to live in France, followed by New York.

Fast-forward to 2015 for a moment. I am playing a Sunday afternoon gig in a café in Bexhill with a young soul singer I met locally. Normally, this is the kind of sleepy place that a few slightly bewildered pensioners frequent. A grey-haired gent and his partner are sitting at a table right near the front, and the guy is really concentrating on my playing. Afterwards, he approaches me and admires my vintage Fender Telecaster. He also has some intelligent observations about my pedal techniques and stuff. Eventually, a quizzical look comes over him as he asks, 'Wait a minute, you're not Kevin Armstrong, are you?'

I tell him I am, and he announces, 'I'm Clive Timperley. You replaced me in The Passions in 1981.'

We finally got to meet, a mere thirty-two years after I joined his old band, and we still see each other around today.

CHAPTER SIX

THOMAS
MORGAN DOLBY
ROBERTSON

§

THE YOUNG SYNTHESIZER WIZARD MATTHEW HAD BROUGHT ALONG TO MY LOCAL HEROES RECORDING SESSIONS HAD REALLY LEFT AN IMPRESSION ON ME. Thomas Dolby and Matthew were old friends (and die-hard Fulham FC fans) who had played together in Bruce Woolley's band The Camera Club. I thought Thomas was talented and really interesting. What he did on my record added something sophisticated and clever but very musical. With just a few electronic brushstrokes he transformed the recording into something that was much more subtle than what we'd started with. He was certainly a cut above any other studio musician I had worked with up until that point, so when he called me a few months later and asked me to add some guitar to something he was recording, I was very happy to oblige. It seemed to offer a way to continue to make music without the pressure of being the artist.

On the day of my first session for Thomas, I'd been to a kind of alternative fancy-dress party in North London with my new girlfriend and a few of her friends from St Martin's College of Art. Chief among them was the artist Caroline Johnson, or 'Wilma' as she styled herself, who was wearing only a Hell's Angels belt with a big brass buckle bearing the legend 'Born to Ride' positioned inches above her green-painted pubic hair. Some of these self-styled 'Neo Naturists' went on to have very notable careers. Out of the scene they created emerged people such as Boy George, Grayson Perry, Michael Clark, Derek Jarman, and many other artists, filmmakers, and musicians of significance.

When I turned up at the studio to play with Thomas, I was dressed in drag and quite drunk from the party. This didn't seem to faze him in the slightest. But what I wasn't prepared for was the way he wanted to work. The song he was recording was called 'Europa And The Pirate Twins'. The impression his technical skill had made on me at the Local Heroes session was no false one. All my studio time up to then had been about starting the tape, playing something, listening back in awe at the sound we made, and then going down the pub. Dolby opened my ears in a different way.

I played exactly what he wanted on the song, to very specific direction. He was very clear and easy to understand, but what he needed was a real stretch for me as a player. The thing that intrigued me was his insistence that I do forty-odd takes of the same bit. I'd never done that before, and at first I couldn't hear the difference between take three and take thirty-seven. After a while, though, I started to tune in to the fine detail he could hear, and, from that day on, I learned to listen to recorded performances in a new way.

Dolby has the most meticulous pair of ears of anyone I have ever worked with, and it shows in all his records. There are very few people who go to the lengths he will to realise what he wants from a recording. Latterly, I have heard him be asked the question, 'Do you ever listen to one of your old records and ask yourself what could have been improved upon?' His answer is always the same. 'Nothing.' I became a bit in awe of his technique, which was both a good thing and a bad thing. Good because there was so much I could learn about how to make records; bad because I had the nagging certainty that I would probably never attain the kind of skills and focus he had at his command. Anyway, he offered me more work, and soon Matthew and I became his first proper band.

I didn't look back. Local Heroes had run their course for me, and playing with The Passions was but a brief detour. Becoming Dolby's guitarist—and being paid regularly to perform at a new level—was a real novelty. At twenty-four years old, I felt like I was in school for the first time. If I kept my ears open, I might even improve as a guitar player.

Thomas's flat in Fulham was where he spent many hours alone, programming a giant, dining-table-sized metal box that was originally designed to run Tangerine Dream's light show. It was a custom-made computer that had been converted to output 'on' or 'off' signals to various electronic keyboards. When he played a 'sequence'—made by typing ones and zeros that appeared in rows on a flickering black-and-white screen—they bleeped and blipped in response. I listened to the robotic rhythms that he made with this mountain of gear and thought to myself, utterly wrongly, *This shit will never catch on.*

Of course, what Thomas was doing was experimenting with the very techniques that were about to transform the way music is made forever. He had his hands on the early form of half-homemade equipment that would lead directly to the digital revolution we are all so familiar with now. Remember: at that time, nobody even had a personal computer at home. They were rare and exotic machines that you didn't see every day.

Thomas was generously supportive of my own songwriting, too. When the opportunity was offered to collaborate with Tangerine Dream's Klaus Schulze at his studio in Mainz, Germany, Thomas invited me along. Klaus had found something better to do and didn't show his face until the last day of our trip, so Thomas used the time to produce two of my original songs, 'Samson And Delilah' and 'Master Of The Animal World'.

Dolby also taught me the basics of electronic synthesis—i.e., how to use and understand the elements that make up an analogue synthesizer. All of them are essentially a variation on one basic theme. First, there is a wave generator or oscillator from which you can select a basic signal, sine, square, triangle, or sawtooth; then filters, LFOs (low-frequency oscillators), and resonance shapers; and at the end of the chain, an envelope shaper that has four controls called ADSR (attack, decay, sustain, release). Finally, there are pitch and modulation wheels and tuning controls. For a while, I threw myself in at the deep end and learned how to try and make the sounds I wanted from these machines.

When we started playing gigs, I was in control of two keyboards and my guitar, and singing harmonies too. The band, with the addition of drummer Andy Duncan, filmed a thirty-minute concept performance video at Riverside studios called *Live Wireless*, and Thomas even let me include 'Samson And Delilah'. He made a 'projector breaking down' sequence that made my song collapse in the middle, though.

Grateful as I was for Thomas's patronage, there was no doubt that I had to decide between being a member of his band or pursuing my own artistic efforts. I couldn't really do both. I chose to put my own dreams aside for the time being, get my head down, and continue to learn what I could as a Dolby sideman.

A little funk workout of Tom's that we spent time jamming out in rehearsal called 'She Blinded Me With Science' sounded really good, and Matthew and I contributed a lot to the way it shaped up. EMI put it out as a single, and it became a bona-fide global hit. It's still, I think, Dolby's biggest moment.

* * *

Working with Thomas offered me a close look at the music business at a higher level. I thought about the ridiculous record deal that Fiver had with EMI in the early 70s, where we were nothing but props pretending to be a band and selling music made by a bunch of old hacks. It felt right to be part of something much more professional. My own playing was valued, and I was part of the action.

Thomas was clearly in control of his deal with EMI. They even let him revive the old Harvest label just for fun. I was getting a glimpse of what it felt like to be a successful musician in the real world.

To prepare for some dates in Europe, we closeted ourselves in the tiny village of Nievre in the Loire Valley in France. The Chateaû de la Valotte would later lend its name to an album by Julian Lennon, but back then, when we rehearsed there, it was a converted cowshed on the grounds of a crumbling manor house. Our hostess, Princess Mimi de Crôy, was a member of the dispossessed Belgian aristocracy and a very odd fish indeed. She lived in what can only be described as splendid squalor, drinking endless bottles of red wine from her well-stocked cellar while writing impenetrably terrible songs. She would record her wobbly falsetto and inept fumblings on the guitar with a cassette-based Portastudio on which she would overdub the sounds of her pet donkey braying and the birds tweeting in the garden (I shit you not), then play the embarrassing results to us at dinner. We would smile weakly, nod politely, and say, 'Very nice, Mimi.'

Mimi used to say things like 'You are good boys . . . and I have had *hundreds* of boys,' which was a bit of a conversation stopper. She surrounded herself with boozy middle-aged men with huge moustaches called things like Hervé and Gaston who would do her bidding, day or night. Her 'special friend' was a guy named Bérnard-George who was about thirty years her junior. She would take us aside and whisper, 'Please don't drink wine with Bérnard-George. After a bottle or two, he talks to the stones.'

At Valotte, we slept above the rehearsal space in the cowshed on mattresses in the rafters. I had obtained some enormous homegrown sprigs of weed from somewhere (I suppose I must have brought them from England) that were too fresh to smoke and in need of drying out, so I had pinned them to a low wooden crossbeam in the kitchen area. One day, during an evening meal, we found ourselves playing host to the local *capitaine* of the gendarmerie. He had obviously come knocking to check up on the sightings of strange-looking young men buying Rizlas and beer, which must have been reported to him by the villagers. As he stood and introduced himself to us, we chatted to him nervously in our somewhat inadequate French while trying not to eye the giant bunches of drying marijuana leaves that hung inches from the top of his hat. Seemingly satisfied that we weren't any kind of threat to the natives, he and his constables bid us adieu and, to our great relief, withdrew into the night.

We worked hard with Thomas to rehearse a live set. Matthew and I were like a pair of multitasking octopi, swapping from guitars to synths as we followed Thomas's automated sequences and drum machines. We returned to London and played a successful three-night residency at the Marquee Club in Soho and a bunch of other shows around the UK.

I really enjoyed the recording sessions for Thomas's second album, *The Flat Earth*. We set up in ex-Telex synth guy Dan Lacksman's home studio in Brussels. I shared a beautiful Art Deco apartment on the edge of the city near the Atomium with newly hired percussionist and programmer Clif Brigden and bassist Matthew Seligman. Clif and I had actually been at St Olave's together, but while we recognised each other's faces we didn't get to know each other properly until he joined the band. We quickly became quite close friends. After the daily sessions at Dan's, we would hit the bars and nightspots of the Grôte Markt and the Rue des Bouchers in the oldest part of Brussels.

Thomas would stay late at the studio, where he and Dan would be bent over a huge and terrifyingly technical instrument called a Fairlight that looked like a keyboard attached to a self-service checkout. It was one of the first such rare beasts in Europe and represented a huge leap forward in recording and arranging music electronically. Sampling technology was still in its infancy, but of course Dolby wanted to be out there on the leading edge.

The basic principle of the Fairlight was that you could record any sound as a source, then turn it into a playable instrument by pitch-mapping it across a keyboard. You could make any number of layers of your instruments into a sequence that would play back what you told it to in response to a timecode fed from a track on tape. So, you could record everything else, like singing or guitars, on the other tracks on the tape and the Fairlight would play along in time. It was possible to turn a sheep bleating, a car horn, or a fart into a fully pitched playable instrument if you wanted (and many did). Basically, it was a less sophisticated forerunner of GarageBand, except it cost £25,000—about ninety grand in today's money. That—plus the fact of it being the size of a small car—put it out of reach of the average Joe. Dan and Thomas spent almost a week figuring out how to synchronise the Fairlight with multitrack tape machines via some code-generating wizardry so that we could pull together Thomas's sequences and our live performances.

Outside the studio, the band had more prosaic fish to fry. One night we found a cosy little bar and chatted up the Irish barmaid who, depending on my patchy memory, was either on the run from the IRA or an IRA member on the run from the British authorities. We started drinking a black beer called Trappiste, obviously made by monks. I had about ten of them, then stupidly drove across the unfamiliar city and somehow located our apartment. The next day, I had a horrible dream that I was sitting on a toilet, hunched over a pair of vomit-covered feet, and it wasn't until the dream had continued for a while that it began to dawn on me that these were in fact my feet and I was in fact awake. The day was spent massively hung over, taxi-riding to various car pounds and police stations, trying to discover the whereabouts of my impounded car, which I had parked at a rakish angle over someone's driveway.

Later, when I finally turned up at the studio, still feeling shaky and white as a sheet, Thomas, Matthew, and I recorded an acoustic version of Dan Hicks's gorgeous song 'I Scare Myself' over Clif's Roland TR-808 drum-machine beat.

'It could do with some trumpet,' I boldly affirmed. 'And I will play it.'

Only one vanishingly insignificant hurdle presented itself. I had never actually touched a trumpet in my life. Nevertheless, my still-pissed-from-the-night-before, totally inept attempt to 'blow some mean horn' proudly exists on the record for anyone to marvel at.

I think Dolby enjoyed throwing us in at the deep end. Despite his obvious technical perfectionism, he still sometimes displayed a counterintuitive, almost punk mentality, my trumpet take being one such moment. At least the acoustic guitar isn't too bad. Landscape's Pete Thomms played some proper trombone later, in London, which certainly added a bit of much-needed class to the brew.

Thomas's preparation for *The Flat Earth* was meticulous and, like everything he did, utilised our abilities to the best effect. While Clif, Matthew, and I spent evenings in Brussels partying and pursuing women, Thomas was pulling together his masterpiece in Dan's front-room studio. *The Flat Earth* was a boundary-defying record that still has a loyal army of admirers and is a testament to Thomas's gifts and our willingness to contribute to his vision. If you've never heard it, you should give it a listen. It remains an outstanding piece of work. Arguably Thomas Dolby's best.

My guitar playing took an upgrade just by virtue of learning how to play the difficult parts Thomas wrote and translate them to something that would be physically comfortable (or even possible) for the guitar. The song 'Screen Kiss', for example, opens with a delicate, sparkly Stratocaster sound and has echoey arpeggios throughout. This was entirely Thomas's creation, and I had to tie my fingers in knots to try to make it flow for the guitar. I've never seen anyone else play it correctly.

Matthew later reminded me that one of the major influences on *The Flat Earth* was Marvin Gaye's *Midnight Love*—the album with 'Sexual Healing' on it, which was also made in Belgium, as it happens. The 808 is heavily featured because of it. Japan's *Tin Drum* album also gave inspiration, prompting Thomas and Matthew to feature a mellifluous fretless bass on 'Screen Kiss'.

Once our Belgian odyssey was concluded, we met up back in London. The final sessions for *The Flat Earth* were recorded at Pete Townshend's Eel Pie studio on the Thames, near Twickenham, with Thomas occasionally commuting from Fulham to the studio on a small motorboat he had bought. Many of his fans will be aware that Thomas is a keen sailor and that nautical themes occur frequently in his work. He left the boat moored on an island jetty in the middle of the river and had a small inflatable dinghy to ferry him to the shallows near the shore.

One day at Eel Pie, Thomas didn't have use of the dinghy but wanted to recover the boat from its mooring. Displaying way more mouth than trousers, my inner idiot rose to the challenge. I offered to swim out to the boat (some fifty yards) to retrieve it. All was going well until I got about halfway there and realised that, in a contest of strength with the River Thames, I was not going to win. It just took me sideways on the tide and I wound up deposited in a muddy reedbed, several hundred yards downstream. The trudge back through the well-heeled streets of Twickenham in soaking shorts and T-shirt was only slightly less humiliating than the gales of raucous laughter that greeted my bedraggled appearance at the studio.

Of course, this was the day that Pete Townshend himself had decided to drop in on us. He no doubt enjoyed the spectacle, and as consolation he lent me one of his vintage Les Pauls, which can be heard on the song 'White City'. New Yorker Adele Bertei's wonderful high vocal choruses for 'Hyperactive' were added at Eel Pie too. Though she says she is decidedly gay, Adele and I had a brief and very sweet romance.

Before the album's release, Clif and I drove to a llama farm in Snowdonia for the cover shoot. We took a lot of mushrooms and pretended to be goldminers in the Old West. It's our silhouettes on the back cover.

CHAPTER SEVEN

ALIEN EXTREMES AND SHATTERED DREAMS

MY MUSICAL LIFE TOOK A CONTRASTING TURN WHEN I HOOKED UP WITH SOME OLD FRIENDS FROM THE PUNK ERA WHO ASKED ME TO PRODUCE AN ALBUM THEY WERE MAKING. Alien Sex Fiend are a married couple, Nik Fiend and Chris (aka Mrs Fiend), and their guitarist, Dave, who went by the name Yaxi Highriser. Nik had given me my first production gig some years earlier when his punk band, Demon Preacher, cut a single called 'Little Miss Perfect' for the indie label Small Wonder.

Nik is a Norf Laandon geezer with a bottomless appetite for cups of tea and mood-altering drugs. He has a real gift for painting (usually psychedelic/gothic representations of drug trips, corpses, and graveyards) and laughing like a drain. When he and Chris moved into a new flat, the first thing they did was paint the windows black and sit watching old horror movies and episodes of *The Munsters*, all the while drinking tea, eating toast, and chain-smoking 'orrible soap-bar hashish.

Although he is the sweetest and nicest of guys, Nik Fiend is possessed of a face that could scare small children out of their skins. Imagine a cross between Nosferatu and a possessed pantomime horse (or just google his picture). With or without makeup, the effect is the same. I always thought he would have made a great Joker in the Batman films. The band have distinguished themselves heroically among all the people I've ever worked with by never having learned a single new thing about music during the thirty years or so since they've been a band. Nonetheless, Nik's unhinged, tuneless, psychotic ramblings and screams over crude electronic drumbeats and slabs of wild, distorted guitar noise have proved to be a winning formula.

The sessions for the album *Acid Bath* took place mostly at night and involved the ingestion of large amounts of amphetamine sulphate, cigarettes, and currant buns. I immersed myself in the task of creating order out of chaos. We spent many nights chopping up tapes with a razor blade and experimenting with ever more outlandish effects gizmos in the studio. An unhealthy cycle of nocturnal living—and overuse of stimulants—resulted in the album being finished and me being finished too. I loved the Fiends for their innocent creative efforts and dedication to their limited oeuvre, but I knew that involvement with them was a diversion for me, not the totally immersive lifestyle it was for them.

I still sometimes write anonymously to their website. Stuff like this:

To whom it may concern. On purchasing a concert ticket, because I had heard of the song 'New Christian Music', my wife Norman and I were very much looking forward to the performance by Alan & His Six Friends. Imagine our horror, therefore, on being confronted with the bizarre and degrading ritual offered to us by such creatures from the pit, the like of which we have never before encountered, save in our most extreme nightmares.

Well, they get a kick out of it. I still like their Christmas single, 'Stuff The Turkey', too.

A couple of years ago, a cardboard box arrived on my doorstep from deepest rural Wales containing five kilos of home-grown potatoes and an enthusiastic description of the kitchen garden lovingly tended by Mr and Mrs Fiend. They're still out there, being fiendish, growing veg, and selling merch online to the Japanese. Bless their gothic cotton socks.

* * *

Late in 1983, I decided to try and get back into the fray as an artist. I started a band with the brilliant drummers Martyn Barker and Steve Monti. The bassist was still Lenny Meade, and we found a young talented pianist and Hammond organ player called Seamus Beaghen— the same Seamus who would later play in Iggy's band. With that, Bush Telegraph was born.

Thomas Dolby's manager, Andy Ferguson, had brokered a deal for me with EMI records and agreed that his company, Cracks 90, would manage me. Andy and his partner, Nancy Phillips, are the kind of people you rarely encounter in the music business—that is, they're honest and decent. I would come to rely on them for wise counsel and emotional support for a long time.

Soon we had a very large cheque in the bank and were on a boat on the Thames, celebrating signing with an EMI record-company beano attended by all the A&R staff and management. We were thoroughly entertained by my good friend Lu Edmonds's fake Balkan wedding band, The 3 Mustaphas 3. I don't think I was quite 'on-message', though. When I was introduced to the visiting head of EMI South Africa on the boat, I looked him in the eye and enthusiastically declaimed, 'I will donate all my royalties in South Africa to the ANC.' This was years before the end of apartheid and a decade or more before the release of Nelson Mandela. Needless to say, it went down like a cup of cold sick.

Despite my gaucheness, EMI decided I would benefit from a trip to New York to attend something called the New Music Seminar. They flew me business class on Pan Am, and when we landed company lawyer Martin Haxby suggested we take the helicopter shuttle from JFK to the top of the Pan Am tower in the centre of Manhattan, back when you could still do such a thing. My first view of New York, therefore, was the famous skyline looming out of the early morning mist from a large, twin-rotor helicopter. It nearly knocked the breath out of me.

I had been allocated a deluxe room at the Parker Méridien hotel in the swanky Upper West Side and spent ten days charging around New York, packing in all the naughtiness I could. Hyperactive singer Adele Bertei and I rekindled our intimate friendship there. I don't know why but I've often been attracted to gay women and have had a number of lesbian or bisexual girlfriends.

New York in the mid-80s was an inviting playground for young English musicians. It was very easy to run amok. Opening your mouth was enough to get you in anywhere, get you high anywhere, and get you laid anywhere. One day I was in a massive vintage clothes store called Cheap Jacks and I met a beautiful young Italian American woman who worked there called Linda Geraci. (She went on to become a hatmaker to the stars.) We spent a few hot and sweaty nights together in her apartment in the East Village.

One morning, I picked up one of my socks off the floor and about five huge cockroaches scuttled off in all directions. *Bloody hell*, I thought to myself, *I'm actually in one of those Henry Miller novels I used to read as a teenager.* Linda had a good friend called Marci Webber who worked for the William Morris agency. Marci knew everyone in New York and could get us on guest lists anywhere. There were amazing parties every night.

The hip-hop scene was just starting to seriously register. Breakdancing and boomboxes abounded, and there was quite a crossover with pop and rock, too. Clubs like Area and Danceteria were like nothing else on Earth. I nearly tripped over a prone Green Gartside in the dark bathroom at Area but was caught by Joey Ramone. I partook of some illicit, nasally ingested pharmaceuticals with him in a toilet cubicle, despite never having met him before or since.

I got taken to a Tina Turner gig in New Jersey and got introduced to her backstage for a brief moment by an EMI staffer. I talked with Nona Hendryx from LaBelle there too. Well, I say talked: she had just had surgery to remove nodes from her vocal cords, so I talked and she wrote things down on a pad. Andy Hernandez (aka Coati Mundi from Kid Creole & The Coconuts) invited me to watch as he conducted string arrangements for Kid's album at Electric Ladyland. I got into a party at Trump Tower one night, met a nice girl called Donna in the elevator, and was having sex with her ten minutes later. I was totally off the chain and having the time of my life, a jumped-up English wannabe consuming everything and everyone around me.*

I came back from my record company-sponsored beano feeling energised and ready to take on the world, although the world had other ideas. Bush Telegraph recorded our album at Marcus studios in West London, with Bros producer Simon Humphries at the controls. Back then, in my somewhat damaged way, I was still partial to promiscuous sexual encounters and regular drug abuse. Some of the invoices we sent to EMI had considerable amounts of money budgeted to a 'Mr S. Norting of Tooting' for 'technical maintenance'. Snuff, Muff, and Puff were everywhere. Never before or since in what's starting to feel like a long life have I indulged in so much self-absorbed immaturity.

During the album sessions, I was visiting British reggae giants Aswad in the other studio (mostly to score weed). I had become a fan after seeing them rehearsing in the days of the Roxy Theatre in Harlesden. Brinsley 'Dan' Forde, Tony 'Gad' Robinson, and Angus 'Drummie' Gaye were a fantastic band. Long before more commercial songs like 'Don't Turn Around' scored them a hit, they had been a backing band for Burning Spear and other visiting Jamaican heavyweights and had established themselves as the UK's best live reggae band. Their Notting

---

* A few years later, NYC had become a little more jaded. Merely having a British accent and an attitude no longer had the clout it once did. I suppose the invasion of so many young and slightly predatory musos like me, rampaging through the city as if they owned it, eventually wore a bit thin on New Yorkers.

Hill Carnival album, *Live & Direct*, remains an electrifying record and a British reggae classic.

I decided to offer Aswad's amazing horn section the job of arranging parts and playing on the Bush Telegraph album. I played the tracks to trombonist Vin Gordon and struck a deal worth several thousand pounds with him to provide arrangements for my songs and do the sessions with his players.

The horn section was Michael 'Bami' Rose (alto), Eddie 'Tan Tan' Thornton (trumpet), George Thompson (tenor sax), and token white guy and eccentric trumpet wizard Dave Defries. On the day they were due to record, they arrived two hours late and started to set out the music on stands. I was thrilled to have the authentic horn sound from some of my favourite reggae records on my album. These guys had attended the famous Alpha Boy's School in Jamaica, which under Sister Mary Ignatius's stern hand had turned out the cream of reggae musicians in the 60s and was highly influential in the island's musical history. They all had reputations as badass players, then, but this wasn't a smooth ride. They started to warm up but then, for the first hour, sounded like a bunch of distressed cattle, out of tune, messy, and unfocused. After several cans of Red Stripe and a bag of weed had been consumed, however, the situation drastically improved.

We started to get the tracks down, but whenever I wanted to make a change to an arrangement, I noticed that it was Dave DeFries who whipped his pencil out and altered the scores on everybody's music stands. After a while, I twigged that Vin Gordon had asked Dave to write the parts I paid him for but kept the lion's share of the money himself while paying the players peanuts.

This was an awkward situation that would require careful handling. Though I was in awe of this Jamaican gent, I did in the end pluck up courage enough to confront Vincent on the second day and insist he distributed the fees fairly. He was a little confrontational at first but eventually he saw the fairness of my position (and that he had been rumbled), and all was corrected. Apologies were made and respect was restored.

I met some of the horn players again, years later, on the other side of the world, when I was playing with Sinéad O'Connor. They had found a home in their later years, along with trombone legend Rico Rodriguez, in Jools Holland's Rhythm & Blues Orchestra. Sinéad loved it when I introduced them to her as she was familiar with their work too. We all ate together in the gardens of the old asylum at Point Nepean on the southern tip of Australia.

* * *

In 1984, Bush Telegraph toured university campuses around the UK as support for Aswad, and we started to sound pretty decent as a band. Our single 'Turn Those Guns Around' was released by EMI, and—as was becoming the custom more and more—we were told we had to make a video to promote it.

That's how I found myself at Blackbush Airport in Hampshire, in the middle of the night, with a whole film crew and a hundred extras. A mock-up of the Berlin Wall had been constructed, complete with military checkpoints and yards of barbed wire. All for me, and all paid for from my future royalties. (NB: there weren't going to be any.) I was in my trailer, about to go and mime my song for the cameras in this artificial warzone, to sell myself to the world. I smoked a joint and had a hash-induced fit of paranoia—a crisis of confidence that shook me to my core. I realised that this just wasn't 'me' anymore. I was going to choke.

I don't know why it happened then, but right at this moment I was gripped with doubt about the record and my fitness for the role of frontman. The whole direction of travel of my music seemed, to me, to have been taken over by record company men, video directors, stylists, lawyers, and accountants, and I just couldn't reconcile with it emotionally. I was told what to wear, even taught how to walk, and given a script that had been prepared by a well-regarded director who I had never met. Looking at the video now, I just cringe at how terrified I look in it. I was having a proper meltdown.

I got through the filming, but I wasn't a happy bunny. It was dawning on me that I wasn't going to succeed as an artist if I didn't have full confidence to stand up and say, 'This isn't right, I don't like it.' It was all getting away from me, and I couldn't stop it. EMI even had famous recording engineer Michael Brauer over to mix the record. Because he had engineered a few big hits, it was presumed he could make us one. I have no personal beef with Michael, but I absolutely hated what he did with the record, yet I had to just shut up and accept the result. I felt he had done a slightly cursory, take-the-money-and-run job on it, driving a coach and horses through everything I even vaguely liked about the record. I had taken the industry sixpence before I was truly ready for the challenge. It was clear that something had to give, and that something was going to be me.

Staff changes at EMI meant we weren't going to be given the kind of resources that would keep the band afloat for very much longer. It was becoming apparent that we were a low priority even before the release of our album. Andy Ferguson made the strategic decision to negotiate our way out of our EMI deal and try and retain control of the album masters. Thanks to his leverage as manager of Thomas Dolby and The Undertones, plus his excellent business skills, it worked. He pulled off the withdrawal agreement. And, for a moment, this looked like a good idea.

We had a London gig planned at the Station Tavern in Tufnell Park, opening for The Higsons. Every A&R person at every major label accepted Andy's invitation to come and snap up a deal with Bush Telegraph. After all, we were an up-and-coming band with a bit of a buzz about us and a readymade album in the can. What's not to love?

The gig was not only a great opportunity but also a make-or-break situation. Our set started well enough in front of a crowd of people who were plainly there just to see the main band. Then, however, one or two hecklers started to barrack me; I got rattled and nervous and started trading insults back and forth with them. Big mistake! Cans began to fly. We lost the crowd and had to limp on and finish the set to an indifferent and partly hostile reaction. I came offstage with the certain knowledge that every record company scout had left the building after about four songs. We wouldn't get a single offer from anyone in the wake of such a disastrous performance.

The next day I awoke with the knowledge that it was curtains for Bush Telegraph. Curtains, too, for my ambitions to be an artist. I have rarely felt such a sense of utter dejection in my life. My feelings of failure were complete when I was told we had to sell all the band's equipment. I found myself living in a rented room alone for the first time in three years, unsure what the next day would bring.

Before life would improve, I had one further piquant humiliation to suffer. The flat I had a room in was owned by one Celestino Coronado, a very camp Spanish man who'd had an auspicious past as a prominent member of Lindsay Kemp's famous mime company (another connection to David Bowie's early life). He had a habit of appearing in my room uninvited and somewhat the worse for drink. He wore nothing but a silk dressing gown and started performing what he must have thought were seductive, swirling movements designed to allow his robe to flap open. I was always embarrassed for him and a bit revolted by this, but being his tenant put me in a very awkward position. I didn't feel I could get angry and tell him to fuck off, so I just firmly refused to notice his ridiculous and clumsy advances until he gave up and retreated.

One morning, after a night on the tiles, I awoke with a raging thirst after hitting the vodka pretty hard. I looked in the fridge for the litre of pineapple juice that I had put there the previous day. It was not there. I silently cursed Celestino and, since I knew he was out, stuck my head cautiously around the door of his room. There was my juice carton on his bedside table, and it was still half full, so I tipped it up to my parched lips and took a giant swig. I'm sure some of you can guess that it wasn't until I'd swallowed a few good glugs that I realised that, yes, I was chugging Mr Coronado's stale piss. I just about made it to the kitchen sink before violently throwing up all over his dirty dishes. I moved out the same day.

They say you sometimes have to hit rock bottom before you can come up again, and I really felt lost for a while. Fortunately, rescue was at hand—in a spectacular way.

CHAPTER EIGHT

A DATE WITH DAVID BOWIE

§

ONE DAY, EMI A&R MAN HUGH STANLEY-CLARKE CALLED ANDY FERGUSON and made it known that a certain Mr X (who could not be named for legal reasons) would require a guitar player to be at a session at Abbey Road studios next week, and might Kevin be available?

Kevin was most definitely available.

'Tell him to take a guitar along,' he said, 'and he can thank me later.'

I've been thanking Hugh for nearly forty years for guiding me through that pivotal moment in my life towards what would be a new dawn—an event that would transform my life.

On arrival at Abbey Road Studios in the spring of 1985, I was shown upstairs to Studio 3. This was not the famous large studio in which The Beatles had worked but a later addition. We were directed up to a smaller suite at the top of the building, designed for demos and overdubbing. There was a control room and a glass-partitioned band room where we set up. Also present were my old buddy Matthew Seligman on bass, Roogalator keyboardist Nick Plytas, and Prefab Sprout drummer Neil Conti.[*]

As we readied ourselves with our instruments and gear, we speculated on who we were there to play for, as we genuinely didn't

---

[*] It occurs to me now that the three drummers I had worked most closely with were called Barti, Monti, and Conti.

know. I think somebody did suggest David Bowie as a *possible*, but it still caused a frisson of excitement when he breezed in and cheerily introduced himself.

'Hi, I'm David,' he said, rather ridiculously. My attention was drawn to the strange ovoid plastic instrument he was carrying under one arm. It looked like something out of *Star Trek*—something that might be played by a miniskirted alien girl leaning against a polystyrene rock. Turns out it was called an Omnichord: an electronic thing with chord buttons on it and its own speaker. He had brought it with him to show us the chords of the song we were there to help him demo.

He explained that the music was for the upcoming film adaptation of Colin MacInnes's book about urban London in the 1950s. The film, *Absolute Beginners*, was to be directed by Julien Temple and would feature Bowie's acting and music. The song he wanted us to record was called 'That's Motivation', a sort of cheesily ironic clarion call to action and entrepreneurial success. Was it a thinly veiled critique of contemporary Thatcherite Britain, perhaps? You'd have to ask Julien Temple.

We could easily have learned the whole song structure in one gulp, but David wanted to work in a different way. He set about getting the band to learn and record just the first few bars, then stop the tape, learn the next few bars, then start the tape again, dropping in to record where we'd left off. Once we'd done that (and got it right), we'd learn the next slice, then repeat the process. This was a somewhat tortuous, halting way of recording, and it gave a slightly disjointed feel to the playback. But hey, this was David Bowie, and if that's what he wanted, that's what we would do.

When we took a break, David came and sat next to me and whispered in my ear.

'Can you get me a gram of coke?'

I don't know why he singled me out, but I told him I would make a call. I went out to the corridor and used the payphone to call someone in Shepherd's Bush that I thought might be able to help. I asked him to deliver to Abbey Road as soon as he could.

A little later, my old mate called me back.

'I've got your gram. You'll never guess who I scored it off: Angie fucking Bowie!'

My jaw dropped.

'You'll never guess who it's for . . . David fucking Bowie!'

I returned to the control room and rather unwisely told David about the incredible coincidence.

'Whaaat?' he said, looking alarmed. 'That bloody witch can't know it's for me. You didn't say who it was for, did you?'

'Er . . . of course not,' I lied.

The package duly arrived and, fortunately for me, the moment was forgotten. Even more luckily, it led to no other adverse consequences than the realisation that I am a loud-mouthed twat who probably shouldn't get involved in scoring drugs for rock gods.[*]

Near the end of our Abbey Road session, David looked at the clock and said, 'Well, there's another hour of studio time left, and we've done what I came here for. I do have this idea for another song for the movie, but it's unfinished.'

I grabbed a guitar and asked him to show me what he'd got, and he played the chords that were the start of his theme song for 'Absolute Beginners'. I took the bull by the horns and started tentatively suggesting how it might be arranged and what it might need, identifying some sections that could be repeated or lengthened and where the turnarounds should be.

After twenty minutes of trying various things, we had a structure and shape that seemed to please him. He took a pen and paper and started jotting down lyrics. We recorded the whole thing in one or two

---

[*] Over the ten-year period we worked together, I never saw David indulge in anything stronger than a can of beer, so I suppose it's possible that our interaction was the last time he ever partook of the Devil's dandruff. I like to think so, anyway.

takes, and it sounded fucking amazing right off the bat. David seemed really impressed and asked me, Neil, and Matthew to be ready to do the real session in a week's time at Westside Studios near Ladbroke Grove.

'Oh, and I need to find a girl singer who sounds like a shopgirl,' he said.

'My sister Janet sings a bit, and she works in Dorothy Perkins,' I ventured.

'Great,' he laughed. 'Get her in.'

This was no idle comment. He really meant it. That really is my sister Jan harmonising sweetly above Bowie on 'Absolute Beginners'.

As if this wasn't mind-blowing enough, before he left, David pulled me aside and said, 'Kevin, would you be interested in helping me put a band together for a charity thing I've been asked to do by Bob Geldof?'

'You're kidding me,' I said. 'I'd be happy to.'

With that, the session was over, and David left. Actually, he didn't leave the building but went to another session downstairs to collaborate with Muppetmeister Jim Henson on the *Labyrinth* soundtrack. It was just another day at the office for a global superstar.

And me? I'd gone from zero to hero in one astonishing session. Though it hadn't sunk in yet, in those six hours that I first worked with David Bowie I'd rescued my music career from disappearing down the crapper.

I thought about my late Bowie-obsessed brother, Ross, on the way home. While I felt elated by what the future might hold, I was also terribly sad that I couldn't share it with him. It would have made him so proud of me. He would have loved it beyond measure.

* * *

A few days later, I got a phone call from David.

'I've got an idea for something extra for this charity show,' he said. 'Come and meet me at about 9pm at this place in Wardour Street. And bring a guitar.'

I turned up at the address of a film-editing suite he'd given me. I was let in and shown down to a tiny basement office. I sat there, nervously perched on one of two small sofas next to a giant fake pot plant, tuning my guitar and waiting for David Bowie.

After twenty minutes, just as I was starting to wonder if anyone would show up, I heard a door swing down the hall. Looking up, I had to draw breath and try and keep my cool. Walking along the corridor toward me was David, but who was that strangely familiar, lanky dude by his side? Yes, it was unmistakably Mick Jagger. A week or two ago, I was homeless, my career in ruins.

Pinch me, I thought. *Now I'm rehearsing with Dave and Mick like it's normal.*

David's idea was to work out an arrangement and key for the Martha Reeves & The Vandellas classic 'Dancing In The Street' and tack the recording of it onto the end of the upcoming 'Absolute Beginners' and 'That's Motivation' session. I can't remember a lot about the actual process of sitting between these two legends and strumming away in that tiny office. It's a blank in my mind, possibly because I was in a state of shock. But I do remember them laughing a lot together. At one point they talked about calling 'Sharon' for some reason. I later learned that they were talking about Sir Elton John.

In another twenty minutes we were done. David asked me to teach the song to the band at the end of the planned session at Westside but not mention that Mick was coming. *Good move*, I thought.

The following Saturday, I arrived at Westside Studios and was introduced to producers Clive Langer and Alan Winstanley. Clive is a softly spoken, bespectacled, slightly collegiate man with a very dry sense of humour. He made his reputation in the band Deaf School and subsequently as the producer of all the Madness records, as well albums by Elvis Costello and Nick Lowe. He also wrote the song 'Shipbuilding' with Elvis, as so brilliantly sung by Robert Wyatt.

Clive's impeccable musical taste is what drives the Langer/

Winstanley partnership. His partner, Alan, is a large and serious guy and clearly 'the technical one'. Alan is a recording engineer to his roots and someone who has the stamina and focus to spend countless hours at the SSL console that spanned almost the entire width of Westside's enormous control room. So, Clive never touched a fader but had all the ideas, and Alan didn't make too many musical suggestions but knew a whole lot about where to put microphones, frequencies, and reverb tails. These two were at the peak of their powers in the mid-80s.

The studio was buzzing with activity that day. When I arrived, I watched Jerry Dammers (ex of The Specials) and his band—including a large brass section of maybe sixteen to twenty players—lay down his music for a riot scene in the movie. Amazingly, my old school friend, Frank Zappa and *Penthouse* mag enthusiast Phil Butcher, was playing upright bass with Dammers' band. It was the first time we had seen each other in the ten years since I left school, and it was to be a proper renewal of our friendship.

Also present was American jazz legend Slim Gaillard, then in his late seventies. I had read about him in Jack Kerouac's *On The Road* and was familiar with his work in old Hollywood movies like *Hellzapoppin'* and *Planet Of The Apes*. I had also heard that he had been the inspiration for Little Richard's early work.

Slim had 'invented' a sort of comic nonsense language in the 1930s that ran through many of his songs. A lot of it was based around the syllables 'Vout-o-reenee', and he was sometimes known as McVouty. One of his early records, 'Opera In Vout' (as Slim & Slam with bassist Bam Brown), is the funkiest thing you can ever imagine—and it's from 1937! Little Richard's 'A-wop-bop-a-loo-bop-a-lop-bam-boom' was clearly copied from Slim's made-up *lingua franca*. Slim, a native of Detroit, appeared to have settled in London, and he appears in *Absolute Beginners* with the song 'Selling Out'.

Also there that day at Westside, as the arranger for the Bowie session, was another senior jazz maestro, Gil Evans. Gil had been Miles

Davis's producer and arranger on *Porgy & Bess* and *Sketches Of Spain*. Gil was accompanied by a good-looking Greek boy who couldn't have been more than seventeen or eighteen years old. His function was to hand Gil his scores and his glasses, and who knew what else? (One could but guess.) At one point, Gil said, 'They think I'm this sweet old guy, but I've got three joints down my sock, and'—nodding toward his young assistant—'we can still party like a motherfucker!' To watch him routine a big band that day was incredible. The sound of it was awe-inspiring. It was like something out of a dream.

The rest of the band arrived, and then Bowie, accompanied by his PA, Coco Schwab, and Yes piano legend Rick Wakeman. I felt so excited to be among such an amazing maelstrom of talent. I was way out of my depth but felt that somehow it was the right place for me to be and that I would try and earn my place there and give it all I'd got.

We recorded 'That's Motivation' first. The song had been transformed by Gil Evans's arrangement from the awkward demo that we'd made in small sections at Abbey Road to a massive big-band jazz extravaganza. The scene in the film in which it appears sees Bowie and Eddie O'Connell leaping balletically over a gigantic typewriter.

After we recorded 'Absolute Beginners' as planned (the guitar riff I played for the intro of the song is the very first thing you hear on the movie soundtrack), I taught the band the arrangement for 'Dancing In The Street'. I enjoyed the astonishment on their faces as Mick Jagger bowled in with daughter Jade on his arm.

There was a real contrast of styles when it came time to record the vocal performances. Although they both worked very quickly, Bowie was meticulous as he redid things and talked with Clive about nuances and detail between takes, as well as entertaining us with a host of impressions of other singers. There is a bootleg cassette going around of him doing Marc Bolan, Bob Dylan, Bruce Springsteen, and so on. Jagger just did his thing, once, and that was that. He seemed easier and more relaxed with himself than Bowie was.

The atmosphere in that studio that day crackled with so many brilliant people working together. I've never really seen anything like it in all the years I've been playing. By the end of the day we had worked our socks off, but more fun was to come. We were all invited to go to Docklands to witness David and Mick filming a video for 'Dancing In The Street'.

Yes, *that* video. To this day, one of the most embarrassing and camp pieces of footage of rock stars poncing about that has ever been seen. Well, it was for charity.

CHAPTER NINE

LIVE AID

§

THE TV NEWS HAD BEEN FULL OF NIGHTLY HORROR STORIES FROM ETHIOPIA. The heartbreaking sight of women and children starving to death in squalid and overcrowded refugee stations in Tigray and Wollo affected everyone who saw it. Four hundred thousand people had died in that awful confluence of natural and political disasters.

Implausibly, Boomtown Rats singer Bob Geldof had discovered his inner crusader, and, along with Ultravox singer Midge Ure, had decided to try to move mountains. Everyone they reached out to in the music biz was keen to get involved, and Christmas 1984 saw the huge success of the 'Do They Know It's Christmas?' single. Band Aid, as Bob and Midge had called it, was already having a real impact on the situation in Ethiopia with the money it was raising. The idea for a mega-concert called Live Aid the following summer was a natural development. They were trying to redesign the way in which charitable help was delivered into a more direct, less bureaucratic model that might see more of the money donated actually reach its target, instead of finding its way into the pockets of corrupt officials and warlords.

David Bowie's band for Live Aid was to be me on guitar, Thomas Dolby on keys, the omnipresent Matthew Seligman on bass, Neil Conti on drums, and Pedro Ortiz on percussion. My ex-girlfriend, Clare Hirst from The Belle Stars (with whom I had squatted in the house next to Bowie's birthplace in South London), had been invited to play tenor sax. Backing singers Tessa Niles and Helena Springs completed the line-up.

Thomas was already working with Neil in his role as Prefab Sprout's producer. I had also played a little on the *Steve McQueen* record at Thomas's invitation. Neil and Matthew had been on the *Absolute Beginners* soundtrack with me, as well as 'Dancing In The Street'.

There may have been some confusion in later years about who was actually asked to assemble David's band for Live Aid. For clarification, I should refer people to the after-show interview with Bowie and Dolby that MTV did and leave it to David to explain (spoiler: it was me).

We had started out rehearsing at the famous NOMIS studios near Olympia in West London. On one occasion, David asked me if I would give him and Coco Schwab a lift to their hotel. I don't know why. Maybe he just didn't have a driver that day, or maybe his sense of mischief just fancied an interesting drive through London traffic in the back of my beaten-up yellow Vauxhall Cavalier. At almost every traffic light, people would stare, do a double take, then freak out when they realised who my famous passenger was. We had quite a tail of sightseers by the time we reached the Dorchester.

Rehearsals moved to Bray film studios in Berkshire, where we could set up in a space comparable in size to the Wembley stage. We rehearsed a number of songs that didn't make the final list on the day. 'Loving The Alien' was in there, and we ran through it at Bray a few times. I have read that we prepared 'Five Years', too, but I don't remember that.

During a break one day, I was wandering around between the film lots and soundstages, looking for a cup of coffee, when I noticed a rubbish skip outside one of the buildings. I peered in and saw several Gerry Anderson character puppets from *Thunderbirds*, just tossed away and lying there. I think one of them was Lady Penelope's chauffeur, Parker. There may have been a Virgil Tracy, too. I was quite surprised at how large they were. I don't know who put them there or why. Life seemed so stratospheric at that point that I didn't really register that they might be worth recovering, so I just sort of noticed them with casual interest and left them lying there in the trash. Lordy, how I wish I'd rescued them!

In the run-up to Live Aid, I had a recurring nightmare. The day comes and I go onstage and don my guitar. Neil counts in the first number and *BOOM!* I go blank and can't remember how to play a note. My stomach turns to jelly, and I double over in pain, only to be taken away by two roadies and ejected from the building, a permanently disgraced and vilified figure.

I've always suffered from these kinds of disastrous premonitions and anxiety attacks. It still happens today and is nature's way of making sure I prepare properly before appearing on a stage. A little fear isn't a bad thing—it keeps you on your toes, I reckon.

David had said that it was 'just a charity concert', but I hadn't fully grasped the implications of what we were preparing for until the actual day of Live Aid itself. Maybe he hadn't, either.

* * *

July 13, 1985, dawned warm and bright. I woke up in my Streatham flat on the third floor of Angus House and turned on the TV to see what all the fuss was about. The unnatural absence of traffic was a sign of how much impact it was going to have. It would be a day when everyone remembered where they were and who they were with—the kind of historic occasion that only happens every few decades.

Usually, this kind of mass attention on one event is only shared so widely because of a crisis or a disaster like the Kennedy assassination, the death of Princess Diana, or the destruction of the Twin Towers. In complete contrast to those other events, Live Aid was an entirely positive and joyful experience—one that has only good memories attached to it. In that sense, it remains pretty unique for our generation. Geldof's vision had made it happen, and on that day we really believed we could come together and have an effect on something that normally made us feel numb or powerless.

I smoked a joint and made sure my suit and shoes were in good condition. We had been asked to turn up at Battersea Heliport on the river at 2pm. I think the helicopter company was owned by the extravagantly mulleted Radio One DJ and latterly gameshow host Noel Edmonds. A small number of fans were pressed up against the fence at the perimeter of the heliport. When Bowie arrived, he got out of his car, went straight over to them, signed autographs, and chatted for a few minutes. Then it was time to go.

I was lucky enough to join Bowie aboard chopper number one for the hop to northwest London. Fear of flying was something Bowie suffered from all his life, but on that day he kept it well hidden, and he seemed to enjoy the ride over the west of the city. We landed on a school playing field after passing directly over the packed stadium. A bus with blacked-out windows accompanied by police outriders whisked us through the streets of Wembley and into the stadium's backstage area.

Bruce Springsteen had played at Wembley Stadium the previous week and had donated the backstage facilities erected for him to the Live Aid event. A corral of Portakabins with doors all facing each other (now so familiar to me from the hundreds of big festivals I've played) was arranged so that it was possible to meet every other performer on the day and mix in the central area. Bob Geldof and Paula Yates mingled with Queen and Status Quo. Mel Smith and Griff Rhys-Jones (in police uniforms) chatted with Princess Diana. We humble band members milled about, taking it all in and snapping photos.

A three-part revolving stage ensured that smooth setups and breakdowns could happen and the show could flow without gaps between the acts. An army of technicians, support staff, film crews, caterers, and drivers all worked like stink for forty-eight hours or more, without pay. The whole crowd stood and cheered everyone to the skies on that unique day, and it felt as if we really might change the world, or at least make a genuine difference.

It's very hard to imagine nowadays, how an event that would galvanize such energy on such a huge scale. I know that the BBC's *Children In Need* telethons raise a lot of money every year and are watched by millions, but this was truly global, and I don't think it has ever been equalled for the kind of impact one single event could create.

Queen took the stage at 6:30 and raised the stadium to new heights. At that point, Freddie Mercury had spent some time carving out a career away from the band, and they hadn't played together in some while.

Queen started the day as a band in a bit of a decline but ended it as solid-gold legends. I'll never forget watching Freddie take that crowd of seventy-four thousand in his hands and just rule it. He was a man on fire—a guy who was, at that moment, at the absolute peak of his abilities as a performer. Pure electrifying talent. I've since seen the filmed dramatisation of that performance in *Bohemian Rhapsody*. It's very good, but it doesn't come close to capturing the incredible surge of love that Freddie created that July day.

Just after 7:15 in the evening it was our turn. The adrenaline rushed through me as we ran onto the stage with Bowie and heard the roar of recognition from that stadium crowd. I strapped on my old Fender Stratocaster and we were off. The band rather raced through 'TVC15' and 'Modern Love' and into 'Rebel Rebel'. Looking at the video clips now, the tempos seem way too fast, but I'm guessing we were all experiencing a similar rush of nervous energy. David wore the light blue suit from his *Young Americans* period, and I remember how pleased he was that he still looked so good in it.

'Fuck me,' he said to us in the dressing room, 'I can't believe this still fits me.'

It was a real education to be around David that day. He had no ego. Even though he was surely one of the biggest names there (if not *the* biggest), he was relaxed and funny and behaved like a real team player. Though he surely didn't have to, he introduced the whole band by name during the intro of '"Heroes"'. There was one small mishap, though. When it came to introducing the backing singers, he blanked for a second and said 'Helena and Teresa Springs' when he should have said 'Helena Springs and Tessa Niles'. Tessa of course took it with good grace, but David was mortified. The second we came offstage he looked really upset and apologised profusely for fluffing her name. The fact that he'd agreed to drop a number so that the poignant film of the child over the Cars song 'Who's Gonna Take You Home?' could be shown, then introduced all of his musicians and showed his concern for Tessa's feelings, gave a real insight into his character. The most flamboyant and self-referential artist of our age was clearly a very empathetic and generous person. A proper gent, in fact.

I don't know why but I had left the building by the time the 'Feed The World' finale happened. It just felt like overload at that point, and what I needed was quiet. A few of us from the band spent the evening at China White in the West End, watching the American half of the concert live from Philadelphia. It was a big deal over there too, but not a patch on London for sheer atmosphere.

Few things in life have given me more of a sense of accomplishment than playing in David Bowie's band for Live Aid. In the aforementioned backstage MTV interview with Bowie and Thomas Dolby just after the gig, he publicly thanked me again—straight from the horse's mouth, so to speak!

It had occurred to me later (with a frisson of smug satisfaction) that all my old teachers would have been watching Live Aid. The one I hoped had seen it more than any other was the deputy headmaster of St Olave's, Jack Hawkins, who had once told me unequivocally that my 'guitar-swinging escapades' would go nowhere and would, more than likely, 'lead me on a path of folly and destruction'.

CHAPTER TEN

SPROUTS, SHARKS, AND PROPAGANDA

THE AFTERMATH OF LIVE AID SAW MY MARKET VALUE RISE SOMEWHAT— perhaps not surprisingly, after playing the biggest gig in history. We did it for the cause of famine relief, of course, but it didn't exactly hurt anyone's career—with the possible exception of Adam Ant. He was the only one who didn't quite understand the 'global jukebox' idea and instead decided that it was an opportunity to play some new material. Silly sausage.

A series of live dates with Prefab Sprout was my next job that summer after the rush of Live Aid. I had met the Sprouts late in 1984 when I was invited to contribute some guitar overdubs to the sessions for their second album, *Steve McQueen* (or *Two Wheels Good*, as it was called in the States). Thomas Dolby was in the production chair and had asked me along to play.

Prefab Sprout are from Consett, near Newcastle. They all have that lovely northeast accent, although I'm not sure people from Consett are regarded as proper Geordies. The band is eccentric songwriter, guitarist, and singer Paddy MacAloon; his brother and bass player, Martin; and London drummer Neil Conti; with Paddy's girlfriend Wendy Smith providing the super-breathy, ethereal backing vocals. Keyboardist Michael Rose and I were additional musicians, not official band members.

I had been a fan of their first record, *Swoon*, when it came out in March 1984, and I was immediately struck by Paddy's extraordinary gifts as a songwriter, 'Don't Sing' being the first ear-pricking thing I heard. Paddy's songs are a curious hybrid of English folk strained through yearning blues. They also showed a melodic sophistication closer to the style of Cole Porter and Burt Bacharach than most modern songwriters ever dare go. They have complex structures and lush chord sequences that represented a real challenge for me to learn. Paddy writes beautiful, heartfelt, intelligent lyrics, too. I learned tons from him about guitar voicings and the kind of harmonic subtleties more usually found in jazz and film scores. The level of musical depth was, at once, deeply unfashionable and utterly compelling.

Paddy and Wendy were a couple at the time, and their love for each other was clearly the fuel for a lot of Paddy's songs. They had a kind of 'Tweedledum and Tweedledee' relationship that sometimes resulted in matching sweaters and jeans, which could be a bit cringemaking for the rest of us. As a couple, they were so close that you could feel you were intruding just by being around the kind of intense romance they were having. They were really sweet, though, and I have nothing but affection for my time as an honorary Sprout.

Paddy MacAloon is one of those sensitive people you sometimes come across who are simply too good for this bland and cruel world. He could be ball-achingly funny, too. Rehearsals for the UK tour took place in a room in Greenwich with large windows overlooking the river. The place was owned and run by Billy Jenkins, the guitarist from the band Burlesque, who had shown me a thing or two when I was a teenager back in Bromley.

One day, we had been out for lunch and got completely soaked in a London downpour. Paddy removed his sodden trousers and continued to rehearse with his thin white legs protruding from under his Paisley Fender Telecaster. He started playing a version of The Rolling Stones' 'Paint It Black', substituting the words 'up my nose' for the title phrase every time it appeared until he was unable to sing anymore from pissing himself laughing.

I did get asked to join Prefab Sprout as a full-time member, but I turned it down on the grounds that I wanted to try to carve out a reputation as a record producer. But I was still content to be a jobbing guitar player. I probably would have made a good band member as I was so into the songs and Paddy's enormous talent, but I felt that I had other fish to fry. Also, I was aware of Paddy's shyness and emotional fragility (despite his obvious comedic talents in rehearsal), which I thought might be an obstacle to their future long-term touring prospects. As it is, Paddy has become something of a reclusive figure since the early 1990s and rarely travels far from his eyrie in the northeast. But he still writes incredible and beautiful music. Check out *I Trawl The Megahertz* from 2003 if you want a dose of his unreconstructed genius, or later songs from his cupboard like 'Grief Built The Taj Mahal'. It makes me cry to hear such beauty go so criminally under-recognised.

* * *

My manager, Andy Ferguson, started out in music with a record stall in Nottingham Market. He went on to manage those loveable, spotty Belfast teen idols The Undertones. Andy helped them establish themselves in the post-punk years as real indie favourites after BBC legend John Peel named 'Teenage Kicks' as his 'favourite record ever made'.

Andy formed his management company, Cracks 90, in 1979, and I had been with Cracks since meeting him through Thomas Dolby in 1981. After The Undertones broke up, Andy carried on managing the various spin-off bands, like That Petrol Emotion and Scary Thieves, and the solo career of singer Feargal Sharkey.

Feargal had gone from Parka-wearing, acne-riddled, teenage Ulster misfit to smooth and sophisticated 80s pop guy (now wearing Armani and Anthony Price) in a couple of smart moves. With the release of 'A Good Heart', 'You Little Thief', and a successful collaboration with pop synth genius Vince Clark on 'It Never Happens To Me', Andy had kicked off Feargal's bid for stardom in style. Now he wanted me to join Feargal's band for a quick promotional jaunt around Australia, where 'A Good Heart' was number one. Some gigs and TV appearances were scheduled around Europe, too.

I had bumped into Feargal a few times at Andy's office in George Street, which his acts often visited for a cup of tea and a kind word. Andy's partner, Nancy Phillips, was a big draw for the Cracks 90 gang, being one of those smart and engaging women who make the whole music business function in spite of the idiots that it is mostly populated with.*

Nancy and Andy had been a couple at one time, but they continued to work together after their relationship ended, and they made a fantastic team for several years. Feargal Sharkey, meanwhile, is a brash and outspoken character with a razor-sharp intelligence. He talks very fast, suffers no fools, and takes no prisoners. At the time I toured with him, he was at the zenith of his solo career, and he had rather embraced the celebrity lifestyle. He spent a lot of time hanging out with people he thought of as his peers—Jack Nicholson, Keith Richards, Eurythmics' Dave Stewart, and so on—but despite being accepted by this coterie of A-listers, I don't think he realised that he wasn't quite in the same league when it came to the resources required for full-time membership of that particular set. Feargal had hooked up with a very beautiful young Brazilian woman called Rebecca, and together they lived, for a while, like real celebs. She was clearly a creature of expensive tastes, and where she went Feargal and his money followed.

On the English leg of the tour, Feargal's brass section had ex-Blockheads man Davey Payne on saxophones. Yes, saxophones: like Rahsaan Roland Kirk and Terry Edwards, Davey could play two horns at once. Davey hadn't toured for a while, though, and his overexcitement on the first night led to a furious drinking binge that resulted in him

---

* After leaving Cracks 90, Nancy went on to successfully manage The Spice Girls and also handled some of their individual solo careers.

vomiting enthusiastically out of the window of a moving tour bus.

We schlepped around rainy and dank England from Liverpool to Cornwall, but soon it was time to fly south. The flight to Australia is long and boring, so I decided to challenge trumpet man Dave Plews to a 'who can stay awake the longest and drink the most' contest. We were doing okay until near the end of the journey, when Dave started to go a bit rogue. Drummer Geoff Dunn had knocked a drink into Dave's lap by accident and covered his crotch in red wine. He finally lost his temper in the queue for immigration and some inept fisticuffs ensued, resulting in the drummer—who was sober—dodging Dave's rather woeful attempts at punches and leaving a wine-stained and fuming trumpet player sprawled on the floor, flailing his limbs about like a stranded beetle. Strangely, the immigration officers didn't bat an eyelid. I guess they had seen musicians come off those very long flights in all kinds of bedraggled and messed-up conditions, so they let it go and ushered us through. Feargal and Rebecca just thought it was funny.

At that time, all the bands that toured Australia stayed at the Sebel Townhouse in Sydney. After-show parties were held there, or at a tiny private club whose name now eludes me, where you had to know someone to get in. When you knocked on the door, a little flap would open, and you would either be admitted or told to 'Do one!' depending on your cred with the doorman. It was there that I met the blonde and alluring Monica. I soon realised she was handing out lines of coke to the band, but I got caught up in the moment and ended up partying quite hard with her for three days. The rest of the band left me there, and I managed to postpone my flight to visit another girlfriend in Bondi. It was only when Monica asked me for the $900 the band owed her for drugs that I decided to show Australia a clean pair of heels. When she went out for more supplies, I threw my stuff into my suitcase, double quick, and skedaddled for the airport.

* * *

In 1985, I saw a concert by the German industrialist-pop combo Propaganda, one of the products of Trevor Horn's ZTT stable. Their dark, bombastic electronic music was the brainchild of Michael Mertens, and the pretentious, Faustian lyrics were written by Düsseldorf bank clerk Ralf Dorper. Propaganda were fronted by two striking women, Claudia Brücken and Suzanne Freytag. Claudia sang and Suzanne recited. I joined the live band along with the original bassist and drummer from Simple Minds, Derek Forbes and Brian McGee. I say 'live band', but in fact it was an early manifestation of something much more common today: a 'half-live' band with a good deal of pre-recorded sound involved. Nowadays, this would be taken care of by computer sequences seamlessly woven into the live setup (usually via a click track fed to the drummer), but in '86 it was literally a guy in the wings hitting play on a tape recorder and everybody hoping for the best.

Michael Mertens and ZTT's star engineer, Steve Lipson, had made very polished and complex productions for the records in SARM West Studios, which was consistent with everything that came out of Trevor Horn's stable. But Propaganda's sound was so reliant on huge layers of multi-effected, highly crafted, synthesised sounds and electronic percussion that it would have been expensive and difficult to reproduce accurately in concert using real people. The solution was to have Derek, Brian, and me play along with the tapes and march up and down in a vaguely Teutonic way, wearing long black coats, either side of Claudia and Suzanne. Michael was onstage too, miming along behind a marimba (a sort of giant wooden xylophone).

The Scottish contingent in the band were very fond of hashish, and it got to be a twenty-four-hour pastime. This was the only tour where I have been stoned out of my mind onstage. Once, on a transatlantic flight on Pan Am, we shared a sort of bullet-shaped sniffing device full of cocaine (carried by a reckless Aussie sound guy named George) with one of the stewards, who was as a result very attentive with the drinks and snacks.

Mostly on that Propaganda tour we were a happy bunch, but complications crept in when Derek paired up with Suzanne and I with Claudia. The difficulty arose because all of us were in other relationships. When the two girls' partners joined the tour—one of whom was a senior guy from the record company—you could have cut the atmosphere with a knife.

On-the-road affairs rarely make it past the end of the run, but the atmosphere changes and the bubble bursts pretty quickly when partners arrive during the tour. This is true whether there are shipboard romances going on or not. The intensity of band relationships can be overwhelming in the cocoon of a rock'n'roll tour, and the damage can be lasting if you let yourself get swept away by fleeting emotions and desires. The old epithet 'what goes on tour, stays on tour' is a lame excuse for sure, but a lot of homes have been wrecked by attachment to temporary passions that may have been sweeter if left on the tour bus with the backstage passes.

Tour manager Andy Corrigan, an ex-member of The Mekons, made a spectacular booboo on that Propaganda tour. We were checking in at the Gramercy Park Hotel in New York when he put down his briefcase in the lobby and walked away from it for a couple of minutes, only to look around and find it had been spirited away—along with tens of thousands of dollars in cash. Needless to say, that didn't go down too brilliantly with the band or the management.

On another occasion, in Rome, we turned up to the venue to find that the promoters had moved the gig to a larger place because they had sold many more tickets than anticipated. They had relocated the show to a *teatro tenda*—a giant marquee—and were now earning considerably more out of the gig than had been expected. Derek and Brian showed their true Glaswegian mettle by insisting that we remain on the bus unless they came up with an extra million lire each in cash. *Double the dough or no show!* I thought this was madness and that we might get run out of town at gunpoint, but, sure enough, a wheelbarrow of paper money duly appeared, and therefore so did we. Somehow we all survived intact, although some of the aforementioned members' relationships with their long-term partners didn't last very long.

After the tour, several weeks had gone by, and my messages to Andy Corrigan's office, reminding him to pay me, were being ignored. I got really angry when they finally sent me a cheque and it bounced back from the bank, unpaid. I went to his office in Notting Hill and bounded up the stairs. I told the secretary that I was really pissed off waiting for my money, and she sort of scoffed at me in a dismissive way, as if I were the least of her problems. I hate to say it but the old red mist descended very fast, and I hulked out in an explosive and uncharacteristic manner. The poor girl was left quaking in a chair in the corner while I made quick work of piling every stick of furniture into a disorderly heap in the centre of the room and chucking her bike on top for good measure. My fee was paid in full later that same afternoon.

My display of psychotic temper at the tour manager's office, though completely out of character, didn't seem to bother Propaganda's manager, Keith Boughton. He asked if I would appear on *Top Of The Pops* with Public Image Ltd and pretend to be Steve Vai, or at least make a fist of miming to the American guitar god's parts on the song 'Rise', which was steaming up the UK Top 40. My second encounter with Johnny Rotten was about to happen.

An imaginary band was assembled for the BBC show. This one and only line-up of PiL consisted of Hugo Burnham (Gang Of Four) and Bruce Smith (The Pop Group, The Slits) as the double drummers; Deon Estus, who had played on Marvin Gaye's 'Sexual Healing', on bass; and well-known photographer, DJ, and chronicler of punk, Don Letts from Big Audio Dynamite, on pretend keyboards. Then there was multi-award-winning TV composer and violinist Jocelyn Pook, John Lydon, and me in a rather fetching little Scottish hat called the Foldfelt Bonnet, which I had borrowed from my mate Phil Butcher.

Johnny didn't remember that we'd met before when the Pistols were rehearsing back in '77, but he was nice enough to me, even though he behaved abominably all day at the BBC. He was perfectly convivial to the band, but when he turned his attention outwards to anyone else, he became a one-man festival of narcissistic rudeness. He covered the dressing room mirrors in giant scrawl using his wife Nora's lipstick, writing 'I'M BORED' in two-foot-high letters. The act of scrawling was accompanied by his unearthly, high-pitched, quavering voice. It wasn't dissimilar in style to a number of PiL songs.

'IIIII'MMM BOOOOORRRED!' he keened loudly, for ages, so that everyone right along the corridors could hear.

Johnny never tired of being comically objectionable to nearly everyone who came near him and took obvious delight in making a scene in the BBC canteen. When people steered clear of him, he stood up on a chair, arms outstretched, and shrilly enquired of the entire room, in a scathing half-scream, 'What's the matter with everyone? Am I black or something?'

That same week, a remix engineer of my acquaintance had been asked to put together a version of 'Rise' for a twelve-inch release of some sort. He told me that he'd been working on the mix for a while when Lydon unexpectedly visited the session. He came into the control room at the Townhouse and stood silently on his head for a while at the back of the room. The engineer kept working on the mix, despite feeling a little unnerved by Johnny's presence. Finally, after about half an hour, Johnny came over to the engineer's chair, bent over, and leered into his ear.

'Oi, mate, put something on my voice that makes me sound popular with the kids!'

CHAPTER ELEVEN

BLAH BLAH BLAH §

UP UNTIL NOW, I'D NEVER THOUGHT OF MYSELF AS A 'PROPER' SESSION GUITARIST, but I was more than happy to get the kind of calls from Clive Langer, Ronnie Wilson and Dennis Charles, or Gary Langan that would see me playing on dozens of records over the next few years. Some of these sessions were just a revolving door affair where you turned up and played a few overdubs. I never met the artists (and often never got a credit), I just turned up for an hour or two, went home, and threw in a large invoice.

There are a few very good players from that era who went on to have amazingly prolific careers as session men, but I wasn't really cut out to be one of those. For a start, I wasn't really good enough, technically, back then. I think people hired me because of the people I had worked with before (mostly Bowie, of course). I wasn't super-well equipped like some of the really long-term pros, even though I could hold my end up most of the time. At the height of the excessive 80s, I could charge a grand a pop just for showing up and twiddling over somebody else's record for half an hour. It was, frankly, money for old rope.

The session work ebbed and flowed while I made vague plans to start up something of my own again. My old gothic punk buddies Alien Sex Fiend invited me to their new base in Cardiff to help them work on a record. 'Sample My Sausage' was one title I remember. Before I could get too drawn into the project, though, one day Nik handed me the phone and said, ''ere, Kev, it's that David Boowie for yer!'

The familiar posh-cockney drawl greeted me once again.

'Hi, Kevin. How would you like to come to Montreux and make a record with Iggy Pop? Could you come tomorrow?'

Despite being high as a kite at the end of a long day's recording with the Fiends, I said my farewells and jumped into my rather knackered Triumph 1300 for the wobbly drive back to London to pack a bag.

The following afternoon, I boarded a flight to Switzerland with my Stratocaster slung over my shoulder and a few Boss pedals in my bag. I couldn't know it then, but the direction of the rest of my working life was being gifted to me, once again, by David Bowie.

* * *

Arriving at the Montreux Casino, I was shown to the flat on the lower level of the complex where I would be staying. Upstairs, a small door in a faceless concrete building led into the control room of Mountain Studios. This was the room where Queen made records, and where Bowie had made his *Lodger* album. Here, David welcomed me warmly and introduced me to his engineer, David Richards.

'And this,' he said, 'is Iggy Pop.'

Iggy was smaller than I had imagined, but sinewy and tough looking. There was no mistaking that handsome, slightly simian face, at that time topped off with shiny black hair, or those huge blue eyes.

'Call me Jim,' he said.

I don't know if I expected him to bite the head off a live chicken or something, but Iggy was the essence of charm and decorum and suggested taking me out for a boat trip on Lake Geneva. He piloted the boat around the island that supports the medieval prison and fortress, Castle Chillon (that had been a hangout for Lord Byron), and we got to know each other a little. I told him I had actually been to his hometown of Ann Arbor, Michigan, with my first wife in 1976, at the age of eighteen.* She was from Ann Arbor too, and we had married so she could stay in the UK. It seemed to impress him that an English boy like me would know anything about familiar places from his youth, like Ypsilanti and of course Detroit. We talked about the MC5 and John Sinclair and the White Panthers and the little I knew of his era growing up there, so we got on pretty well.

Blah Blah Blah was made at a time when Iggy Pop didn't have a record deal. Bowie and he had written the songs while Iggy stayed as David's houseguest. David was the producer, and he was probably funding the recording from his own pocket, too. Turkish multi-instrumentalist Erdal Kizilcay had been brought in to program drum machines and play almost everything on the record. He had just worked with Bowie on the music for Raymond Brigg's post-apocalyptic love story *When The Wind Blows* and would go on to join the Glass Spider tour the following year.

My job on arrival was to rough up the guitars a bit and sing some backups. Every morning, David would appear with a list of tasks for the day. Regular engineer (the late) David Richards, who had recorded all of Queen's stuff, and bright young tape-op Justin Shirley-Smith would go through the list, and we assembled the album over a few weeks, almost like building a kit of parts.

I remember the day Bowie wanted a special effect for the song 'Blah Blah Blah' itself. He asked me to show him how to operate an Akai S900 Sampler, which was a revolutionary piece of technology at the time. I started to talk him through the workings of this grey box, with its small blue screen and array of white buttons, as I had recently taught myself how to use one in my home studio. He lost interest in about three minutes flat.

Dave Richards had a simpler alternative. He showed Bowie a

---

* My chaotic four-year marriage to Camilla B began two days after my eighteenth birthday. It would take another book to go into the ups and downs of my significant relationships, and I'm not ready to write that one yet!

'sample and hold' guitar pedal that could capture fragments of sound and spit them back out at varying speeds. It was a much cruder device with absolutely no learning curve, and it better suited David's purpose than the more technical Akai. Bowie had the pedal mounted on the desk and did all of the vocal effects for 'Blah Blah Blah' with the heel of his hand, rapidly mashing the switch, sampling bits and twisting the speed knob, chucking back fuzzy little chunks of Iggy's vocal at different pitches. It was one of those times when you could clearly see that vision and limitation went hand in hand when an idea collided with open-minded talent. *Can't do it this way? Fuck it, we'll do it that way, and make it better.*

On sunny days we would open the door of the control room and David, Iggy, and I would chat to the local girls who hung out in the car park outside. That door is blocked up now and covered in Bowie and Queen graffiti. I had a fling with a very beautiful Swiss-Italian girl called Ambre and spent a few extremely pleasant afternoons in the flat with her.

Julien Temple visited the *Blah Blah Blah* sessions too, as did Sean Ono Lennon on his summer holidays. One day, David was out there smoking a cig, looking out over the parapet at the side of the car park onto the auto workshop below. He noticed a stunning, silver E-Type Jaguar being restored down there and shouted down, 'How much do you want for it?' At the end of the day, he drove it back to his house in Lausanne. Fuckin' rock stars!

What *Blah Blah Blah* lacked in spontaneity, because it wasn't really a band record, it made up for in producing the hit song 'Real Wild Child' ('Wild One'), a cover of a song by the Australian rocker Johnny O'Keefe from 1958.

After a couple of weeks, the album was done, and Iggy asked me to think about helping him form a band to tour when it got released. A&M America signed a deal with Iggy, so David presumably recouped his investment almost immediately. Not long afterwards, I set my sights on touring the world as Iggy's latest bandleader. I was asked to hire the other band members, and I immediately thought of my old freaky school friend, Zappa aficionado Phil Butcher. Phil and I had lost touch for many years until we met again briefly at the 'Absolute Beginners' sessions in '85. Until then, I'd never known he had become a musician, let alone that he was accomplished enough to be Jerry Dammers' bass player.

When I called Phil for the *Blah Blah Blah* tour, he naturally jumped at the chance. Bush Telegraph keyboard player Seamus Beaghen would join too, doubling on rhythm guitar, and we would audition for a drummer. We went through a dozen hopefuls, including Karl Hyde from The Fall, who had taken a train down from Manchester with just his drumsticks in his back pocket. He had the right story but his drumming wasn't quite what Iggy needed at that point.

I can't remember how we were introduced, but in the end we hired the highly accomplished drummer Gavin Harrison. Something about Gavin didn't quite sit right with me, but I couldn't put my finger on it right away. There was no doubt about his amazing level of skill, but I hadn't yet made the kind of distinctions that I'm better at now when choosing bandmates. In hindsight, the Patrick Swayze mullet and the double bass drums with fifteen tom-toms should have rung alarm bells.*

We began rehearsals at Nomis in West London. Iggy's career at that point was something that had to be built up from scratch again, and the first date we did was literally in the back of a fish restaurant in Santa Barbara, with a chalkboard sign outside that read, 'Tonite: Fresh Halibut ... and Iggy Pop!'

I can't remember much about the first gig as I was recovering from a stupid self-inflicted injury. I had dived headfirst into an eight-foot-deep pool at the El Prado Motor Inn, only to discover, very suddenly,

* Gavin Harrison has since become a legendary technical genius drummer with Porcupine Tree and later King Crimson.

that it was really only four feet deep. Iggy was poolside, on the phone, doing an interview, oblivious to my blood-drenched form being dragged from the water only feet away. He may have turned at one point and said, 'Hey, keep it down, will ya?'

The *Blah Blah Blah* tour was my first experience on a real American tour bus. In the USA, tour buses are only single-decked, unlike modern European ones, which have an upper deck. This is because road bridges in America are too low to cope with tall vehicles. The bus had a proper custom paint job, with flames licking down its flanks and a giant eagle on the back. It once belonged to Jimi Hendrix, so we were told, although I would hazard a guess that it's one of those ubiquitous stories the tour bus company always trot out, just to make you feel special.

Either way, touring the States by bus is an amazing thing to do. The bus had a kitchen, rows of bunks in the centre, and lounges at the front and back where you could watch movies or listen to music. The endless highways through deserts, across mountain ranges, and over vast prairies, accompanied, always, by the roar of the huge diesel engine and the low hum of the generator. Socially, though, it does have its challenges. Young men sharing a small space for long periods have to be careful not to seriously piss each other off. Colonising too big an area with their personal belongings, eating super-smelly food, or inviting overly flamboyant groupies onboard can all be a problem. Even leaving a dirty sock in the wrong spot can lead to friction. Don't make a mess, don't be late, try not to forget your stuff…

All of these unspoken rules are of course flexible, given the dynamic between the individuals, but I'm sure everyone inside or connected with the music business knows that there is one commandment of bus life that you must cleave to at all costs, and breaking it is a hanging offence. In all the bands I've ever been in, the one absolutely sacrosanct law that must never be transgressed, and there's no easy way to say it, is NEVER DO A SHIT ON THE BUS! If you do this even once, you will never not be reminded of it for the rest of your professional career.

Musicians you have never met before will come up to you backstage at a festival in Sydney, ten years later, and say, 'Oh, right, you're the guy who did a shit on the bus!'*

At the start of another leg of that US tour, I'd eaten some dodgy pink chicken at a restaurant in Heathrow and picked up a very nasty dose of the food poisoning bug campylobacter, which was engaged in a rampant assault on my immune system by the time I was asleep in a Virginia hotel. I spent half the night violently evacuating my bowels and vomiting. (Luckily, we weren't on the bus yet.) I phoned the hotel reception in the wee small hours and groaned, 'Please call a doctor, I've got food poisoning.' The night manager seemed more interested in establishing liability and avoiding a lawsuit for his employers than doing anything to help me. Once he was finally satisfied that I hadn't eaten at their restaurant, he called an ambulance. I spent the next day—the day of the show—on a slab in a West Virginia emergency room, being intravenously rehydrated. I did the gig, despite feeling like a wrung-out sponge. It felt like the whole world had fallen out of my bottom.

We continued to plough around the Southern states of America in a replacement bus after the Jimi Hendrix one broke down. Somewhere along the way we had become attached to The Pretenders, and now we were opening for them in large arenas and sports halls. Chrissie Hynde was a huge Iggy Pop fan. The Pretenders were much bigger than Iggy in the US at that time, so these were her crowds. She would come on after us and say, 'Let me kiss the stage that Iggy Pop has walked on.' Then she would kneel down and do just that, hopefully avoiding the pools of gob that Iggy had a habit of expectorating all over the place.

It was Chrissie who, as a private joke, gave us the band name that we adopted for the tour: The Nerds. Seamus, Phil, and I were all skinny white blokes with thinning hair and specs. In some places in the States, people thought Iggy's band must be some sort of Hare Krishna cult

* I never did this, by the way.

because of the un-rock'n'roll image we projected. Chrissie hit the nail on the head.

The gigs got better, but as the tour and the months wore on, personal relationships in the band began to show signs of strain. First, there was Gavin's decision to build a physical barrier between his kit and my amps. In hindsight, it could have had something to do with the fact that I hadn't really got a clue what I was doing, as far as the geeky world of guitar tone goes, and Iggy is one of the only people I have ever played for who likes the guitar volume set to 'stun'.

'Turn it up, motherfucker,' he would bellow encouragingly (and still does). It's likely that my lack of expertise at this point meant that the quality of my guitar sound (or 'core tone') was, not to put too fine a point on it, fairly rubbish. It was how I learned the hard way that sheer volume doesn't improve a shit sound. It just becomes a louder shit sound.

Gavin had clearly had enough of being subjected to the tinny harshness emanating at face-melting decibels from my Marshall stack. That's why he had gone to great lengths to set up a wall of Perspex screens stretching out from his hi-hat into my stage space. I didn't take too kindly to his unilateral move to erect partitions on the stage. My nose was put out of joint, and my confidence took a knock. It wasn't until after a lot of neurotic experimenting over many years that I would be even halfway happy with my guitar sound. Even now, I still tinker with it all the time. It took ages for the penny to drop for me. I learned that you can't really buy a good guitar sound straight from the shop. It's something you have to craft for yourself. Equipment is only a small part of the story. It comes from a deeper place. I have got closer to it now, and I get many compliments, but I envy those players who had it down when they were younger. It took me decades, and it still keeps me up at night. Anyway, it was clear that Gavin didn't like my over-processed sound very much, or me for that matter.

Early on in the *Blah Blah Blah* tour, Iggy would sometimes tap on my door and cop a smoke off me. I was still a habitual hash smoker back then and I would happily share a joint with him. In truth, I should have given up smoking dope years earlier, because it tended to make me a bit paranoid and antisocial, as well as causing me to over-examine myself and find everything wanting. It was an energy-sapper, too.

Iggy seemed to be rethinking this habit as well. Very soon he realised that, if he was going to sell his album as hard as A&M wanted to sell it, he had to be in a condition to meet various local radio and press people nearly every day—characters a lot like Artie Fufkin from the *Spinal Tap* movie—shaking hands and 'making nice' with them after each show. He had got to the point where smoking dope just put him in a catatonic state, so he quit altogether.*

I'd never been to New Orleans before, and it didn't disappoint. We stayed right in the French Quarter, which is a mind-blowing place to walk around. Young black street musicians in small ensembles play rough-and-ready ragtime blues and compete for attention with scantily clad whores and hustlers of one kind or another. An old man on a street corner sings 'Ramona' at the top of his lungs for small change. A marching band with members aged from ten to eighty moves along to a snare drum, rattling out that distinctive creole shuffle as the raw sound bounces off the houses and bars. A crisply dressed card sharp keeps up an endless stream of smooth patter as he rinses money out of punters who walk away cursing their luck. All this happens through clouds of kitchen smoke smelling wonderfully of blackened Redfish. Baskets of flowers spill from ornate wooden balustrades, while voodoo fortune-tellers ply their trade below. Wandering into a bar and drinking a cocktail, you might see a shit-kicking zydeco band or a blues piano legend, or meet friendly drifters from out of state, each with a

---

* Thinking about it now, I may have been close to each of them when both Bowie and Iggy decided to give up drugs permanently. I was probably there to witness Iggy's and Bowie's very last vestiges of naughtiness, before they grew up.

fascinating drunken story to tell. We drink it all in. New Orleans is the Cradle of Rock'n'Roll.

Roadie Jos Grain had the habit of carrying a video camera on his shoulder, and he seemed to effortlessly attract all manner of wackos to disport before him. Perhaps it was his broad Yorkshire accent, his rippling arm muscles, his dyed blond crop topped with a military peaked cap, or the chains he wore hanging from his belt. I don't know, but in New Orleans he captured some memorable footage as an overweight woman strutted around, waving her arms, possibly high on something, then walked up to him preaching hellfire and brimstone in a Southern drawl.

'Sin is everywhere! Where are our morals? Only Jesus has the fire! We are all Soldiers of Christ. You've got to use your shield and your sword as offence.'

She stressed the 'off' of 'offence', then came in close and tilted her head as her eyes squinted toward a small badge on Jos's lapel bearing the charmless slogan, 'If You Don't Fuck, Let's Suck.' She read this aloud, took a minute to consider, then her eyes widened and she half-smiled and said to Jos coquettishly.

'We could do that ... you and me.'

One minute she's a firebrand street preacher, the next she's propositioning a stranger. Such things are not so unusual in the Big Easy.

* * *

We did so many shows on that tour that they all seemed to blur into each other. A few do stand out in my memory, though.

When we reached New York, our gig at the Ritz was to be filmed for MTV. The 'Real Wild Child' video features black-and-white footage from that show. I am wearing my Alien Sex Fiend T-shirt, and it was at that show that I fell into the crowd and got hauled out by Jos.

Bowie showed up at the after-party and held court. I spent the night getting high with two professional strippers at the Waldorf Hotel—well-heeled college graduates who got into stripping as a side gig to make ends meet.

Before 'leg two' began, Gavin Harrison quit to pursue his career as a drummer's drummer. I was relieved, as I never thought his style suited the music. New blood arrived in the form of Andy Anderson, ex of The Cure, who was a total breath of fresh air. He had a feel that was more Ringo Starr than Billy Cobham. He was much easier to play with and gave the band a beating heart and a rhythmic drive that pushed it to new heights.

Going out to eat together somewhere in Alabama, on our second go-around the Bible Belt, we got a reminder of the dark side of the South. We found a good old American log-cabin diner with geraniums in pots outside and red-and-white gingham tablecloths and curtains. Country music played on the jukebox. Chicken and biscuits with collard greens was on the menu. Outside in the parking lot, we admired a stunning 1950s Mercury that had been lovingly restored and pimped: dark gold metallic paint, a giant silver grille that look like whale's teeth, blacked-out windows and no door handles, just solenoids that popped the door when you stuck your foot under the side.

We sat down in the restaurant and waited for service for ages, but none came. Eventually, a large, snaggle-toothed guy in a giant checked shirt and cowboy boots sauntered up to the table and said something I thought I'd never hear outside of a John Houston movie.

'I reckon you boys should up and leave quietly, like.'

We couldn't figure out why we should until it dawned on us that Andy's skin colour seemed to be a problem. To this day, in parts of America, de-facto segregation still exists. There are places where blacks and whites just don't mix. We naively assumed that everywhere was like New York, Chicago, or Los Angeles. This was our mistake. We had entered the fucking twilight zone. It seemed inadvisable to get involved in a row with the diner people. Nowadays, we might have spoken up, but there are places in America where it's risky to be 'liberal', and this may have been one of them. Back then, in the Deep South, you never knew who was carrying a gun or how much of an altercation it would take before they might whip it out. The only difference now is that the guy in the check shirt would have had better teeth, and, because of the 'open carry' laws, he'd probably have his AR15 slung over his shoulder instead of under the seat of his pick-up.

Andy Anderson was a real character. Despite being a shit-hot rock drummer and a lovely bloke, he was also a complete space cadet. On days when we were all there with our luggage packed, ready to catch a plane, he might arrive in the hotel lobby dressed for a gig with a pair of drumsticks protruding from his back pocket. Or he might turn up with all his bags packed when we were on the way to a venue for a show. On one occasion, nobody could raise him by calling his room. We waited until the decision was made to enter with a passkey. A hotel security man eventually found him blissfully asleep under a hedge in the grounds. Andy was a gentle, kind, and funny soul, who left this world early in 2019 and will be sadly missed.

A gig we did in Long Beach, California, at Fender's Ballroom, was exciting for a number of reasons. Hell's Angels had turned up in numbers and did that old trick of 'providing security'. They lined up both sides of the corridor as we left the dressing rooms and proffered hunting knives, tipped with amphetamine sulphate, for us to snort on the way to the stage. Ninety-nine percent of the audience seemed to have ingested something weird. They were high as kites. There must have been a run on some mind-bending, locally made hallucinogen that week. People made absolutely no sense when they spoke to us. Their mouths moved and noises came out, but that was it.

The layout of the venue was an accident waiting to happen. Too many people were crammed into the place, and some of them had started to climb the girders and beams that spanned the pitched roof. That meant they could crawl along above the stage and drop down, or hang from the crossbeams. The PA speakers were poorly secured, too, so Iggy's habit of clambering on the equipment resulted in one side of the PA all but collapsing onto the crowd.

At one point, I couldn't believe my eyes as the whole audience seemed to be heaped up in a pile that started low in front of the stage and raked upward toward the back. People must have been crushing each other to death under there. It was like a warzone. Things were stolen from the dressing room, too, and the vibe felt really edgy and genuinely dangerous. After the show, we sat around in a state of exhausted shock at having witnessed so much mayhem and destruction. All of us except Iggy. He just swigged a bottle of water, poured some over his upturned face, and remarked, 'Well, that was cool!'

Sometimes, after a show, a crazy fan would rush the bus as we were boarding and hurtle toward Iggy, arms and legs flailing, shouting and screaming in excitement. When this happened to other artists, as I'm sure it did, there would be someone employed to deal with what could be perceived as a physical threat. Old fashioned muscle, perhaps, or someone like Bowie's guy, Jerry Mele. Iggy seemed to possess a unique ability with these crazies, though, and he never had a bodyguard or a heavy around. He would let them come right up close and just say, 'Calm down, it's okay,' while resting a firm hand on their shoulder. Often, they would go completely limp immediately, as if Mr Spock had administered a benign version of the Vulcan Death Grip. I think they just got dazzled by getting near him. Mostly, they just wanted an autograph or to give him something—a drawing, a letter, a cassette of their band—or just to kiss him.

* * *

Another line-up-change came in 1987 when my old friend Phil Butcher decided to quit the *Blah Blah Blah* tour band. He was involved in building a recording studio in the basement of a boutique called Demob in London and was also modelling in Tokyo for Yohji

Yamamoto. On a break in the tour, I went to Demob in Beak Street to check out the studio Phil was building with the shop's owner, a Welshman called Chris Brick. I got introduced to a young and very talented American singer and asked if I could road-test the studio by recording her. This was Gail Ann Dorsey. We'd never met before, and neither of us had a clue that she would go on to become such a brilliant foil for David Bowie for such a long period.

At that time, Gail was a struggling singer/songwriter and bassist, just arrived in England, trying to cut it on her own. I produced a song called 'Wasted Country' for her, and I think it played a part in getting her signed and going on to record with Nathan East. The studio at Demob was a short-lived project, however. Eccentric proprietor Chris Brick deliberately set fire to the window display with a joint during a row with his wife, reportedly just to scare her. The fire spread to the whole shop. The building was gutted and the studio, though undamaged, was rendered unusable. That was the end of Demob. After a short time on remand, Chris managed to avoid jail time before running away to New York. Phil managed to salvage some of the studio equipment and relocate it to Gee Street Records near Moorgate. He went on to produce demos for acts like PM Dawn and a few others, then joined the Tiger Lillies as bass player.

One of the last appearances Phil made with Iggy's band was on the British Saturday morning kids' TV show *Number 73*. Broadcast entirely live, the ITV show was a bright and breezy mix of cartoons, music, interviews, and features about things to make and do, aimed at kids aged between about eight and fourteen years old. Iggy had a hit with 'Wild One', so off we went. We played in the studio, on a set that was made to look like a basement rumpus room, full of bikes and toys and stuff.

Surprisingly for such a show, we did actually play live. All was going well until the last chorus of the song. A young female presenter on roller skates with multi-coloured ribbons in her hair came down the stairs halfway through the performance. Iggy reacted with a display of typical alpha-male behaviour. He cast around for a suitable prop with which to entertain her and found a very large teddy bear at the back of the set. After enthusiastically punching it in the head and then strangling it, Iggy flipped it over and gave it a right old seeing to up its furry backside. Cameramen, sensing some action, zoomed in on this act of wilful teddy-buggery, and it went out on live TV to all the little kids of Britain.

I was concentrating on my guitar at the time. I was behind Iggy, and the plushy assault took place during my solo, so I didn't really notice what had happened. In the green room, when we came off the set, roadies and managers were pissing themselves laughing. A line producer came in and reminded Iggy of the inappropriateness of abusing stuffed toys in such a manner on a live broadcast. Iggy seemed genuinely nonplussed. 'Oh, I'm sorry,' he explained, 'I didn't realise what I was doing.' The slightly fuzzy clip is still on YouTube.

It's a shame that such an epic failure to protect our youngsters from such degradation occurred, but it's still as pant-wettingly funny today as it was then. The Sunday tabloids were great the next morning, too. 'Must We Fling This Filth At Our Pop Kids?' and so on. Well, if you will book Iggy Pop on a kids' show . . .

Ex Magazine member Barry Adamson came in to replace Phil in Iggy's band and brought his big, heavy bass sound to the party. My own role in the group was still secure, but I was doing my best to undermine it with some prima donna behaviour and increasing tension with Seamus.

It would be fair to say that the folly of youth played a part in the situation. We were young guys jostling for position, all with something to prove. Though I was nominally the bandleader, I still had a long way to go personally before growing into any kind of responsible adult. If truth be told, I was being a bit of a prick. You read a lot about the stresses of touring and the mental health problems that youngsters can suffer on the road, but these are not an excuse for being an arsehole.

The seeds had been sown at a Texas hotel, where I got drunk and a nameless roadie had the truly terrible idea to obtain Seamus's room key under false pretences. This crewmember and I systematically removed every stick of furniture—the carpet, the TV, the minibar, even the lightbulbs—from his room and place them in a fire escape stairwell. We thought it was fucking hilarious. Needless to say, Seamus was not terrifically amused when, at 2am, he put his key in the door and found the results of my boorish practical joke. Unsurprisingly, things deteriorated to the point where, if I walked into the back lounge of the bus, Seamus would immediately walk to the front.

While personal interaction degraded, paradoxically the music we made onstage just got tighter and better. By the time we got to play the European festivals, we were on fire as a band. Iggy had dropped some of the *Blah Blah Blah* songs and substituted more Stooges stuff—songs like 'Dirt' and '1970'. If Iggy wanted to routine something new, we would convene in a hotel room, Andy belting the *Yellow Pages* with drumsticks and the rest of us playing guitars unplugged. I used to record these sessions for reference, and on one occasion I captured a 'hotel room run-through' of the song 'I Need Somebody'. It sounded so good that I played the cassette to everybody on the bus. It vanished soon after. Iggy may have taken it for his own archive, though I have never asked him if he did.

The intensity of nearly two hundred shows and two years of circling the globe was proving too much for my fragile psyche. It had been my first real taste of the intensity of touring at that level. An endless whirlwind of travelling, relentless gigging, drinking, getting high, and getting laid. By the end, I felt hollow and depressed and didn't know what to do with myself.

A few months after the end of the tour, I ran into a roadie in the café of a North London rehearsal studio.

'Hi Kev,' he said. 'I hear Seamus is going to New York to record with Iggy Pop and you're not. What's that all about then?'

I couldn't answer. His words just cut me in half. Years later, Sandie Shaw told me that for performers and musicians to survive for long in this industry they had to 'learn to deal with humiliation'. At the time I didn't know what she meant, but now, looking back at the *Blah Blah Blah* tour, I realise exactly what she was on about.

There were some amazing times on that first Iggy tour, but I still didn't really know myself well enough to be comfortable in my skin. I am, at heart, an introvert, and somewhat prone to bouts of depression. This is not such a problem for me now, as I understand a little more about inner confidence and making time for others. But this was the first time I'd come across that feeling common among high-level touring musicians of being a VIP one day, with zero responsibilities, and then an ordinary guy returning to a tiny flat another day, with no decompression time in between.

I'm happy to say that touring with an older, more experienced bunch of people is very different now than it was when we were younger. We're all a little more secure, we have good homes, and we're happier with who we are. If someone goes off the rails today—and they do—there is more support and kindness on offer. In general, too, I think that men have learned a little more about how to dial down the macho crap. We share problems and care for each other better, which is no bad thing. Maybe it was there back then, but I was just too young and silly to see it clearly.

CHAPTER TWELVE

NOTHING LESS THAN BRILLIANT

§

FOR DECADES, *LATE NIGHT WITH LETTERMAN* **ON CBS WAS ONE OF THE MOST POPULAR CHAT SHOWS IN AMERICA.** David Letterman's easy-going and sardonic style attracted top-line guests, and the show had a killer house band under piano man Paul Schaefer, who was a good straight man for Letterman's waspish banter. I got to play on the show once, sitting in with Schaefer's band for 'Real Wild Child' in 1986. In the middle of the tour, we flew into New York from Tempe, Arizona, to do the show, then back to Denver the following day.

A couple of years later, British TV producer Alan Marke and young presenter Jonathan Ross based their own show, *The Last Resort*, on the *Letterman* format. Channel 4 saw the potential and bought it. It was the same mixture of chat show and musical guests. Steve Nieve, the piano player from Elvis Costello & The Attractions, was hired as the bandleader, along with drummer Pete Thomas. American bass player Steve Fishman was added too, and they asked me to play guitar. This was a great offer after my exhausting time on the road with Iggy.

We were billed as Steve Nieve & The Playboys and dressed in shiny blue suits, tailor-made for us by Anthony Powell. The band rehearsed every week at Nomis Studios in Olympia to prepare for Friday night's show. It was broadcast live—not 'as live' or 'pre-recorded' but well and truly live. We would gather at a TV studio complex in Wandsworth and spend the whole of Friday routining the show until it went out in front of a studio audience at 9pm. We'd get to hang with the celebrity guests who'd come to chat, as well as the musical ones we backed.

It was also our job to play some intro music for the guests as they walked on, and sometimes our sense of piss-taking mischief got the better of us. When Carrie Fisher (Princess Leia from *Star Wars*), appeared fresh from her divorce from Paul Simon, we played 'Fifty Ways To Leave Your Lover'. When Ronnie Wood displayed his rock portrait paintings, we struck up the *Vision On* gallery theme.* The final straw was when we heralded Brigitte Nielsen, the massively surgically-enhanced, Amazonian ex-wife of Sylvester Stallone, with 'I've Got A Luvverly Bunch Of Coconuts'. After that, the killjoy producers said we had to stick to a short sting adapted from the show's theme tune (written by me!)

The night Ms Nielsen was on the show, there was an afterparty at Madness singer Suggs's house in Camden Town. We joined a frenzied and frankly dangerous car chase, as a convoy of tabloid paparazzi hurtled across London, pursuing Brigitte's limo and trying to get one decent shot of her.

Another time, we played the outro theme to the show on small toy instruments in the pub next door to the studio. George Harrison had been a guest, and we ended up having a cosy pint with him and Radio One legend John Peel as they heartily disagreed about the quality of a recent Bob Dylan gig they'd both attended. Peel dismissed Dylan as a mumbling has-been, but George thought he was amazing and sang like Bessie Smith. George seemed like a really great bloke. He was very relaxed and 'real'—somewhat in contrast with my upcoming experience with another member of The Beatles.

Another week we were backing Roy Orbison, and, in the build-up, we were invited to a secret gig at the Mean Fiddler in Harlesden, a small club that held only two hundred people max. It was utterly

---

* For those too young to remember, the iconic vibraphone tune was used to present children's drawings on the BBC in the 60s and 70s.

superb, every tune as familiar as an old sofa. To witness his deadpan delivery and to hear those heartrending songs made flesh was truly awe-inspiring. When we got to the rehearsal day at Nomis, however, The Big O couldn't make it, so we practised without him. During lunch break, a tousled blonde mane appeared around the door of the canteen, followed by a long pair of blue-jeaned legs, and, fuck me, Robert Plant—for it was he—ambled in.

'Hey guys, what are you doing?' he inquired. After we explained that we were practising to play with Roy Orbison, he said he knew all the songs.

'Why don't you sing one with us?' I asked.

To my amazement, Robert walked up to the mic stand and stood in for Roy. What a good omen for the show, we thought. I remembered the last time I had seen him, at thirteen years old, resting my arms on the front of the stage at Alexandra Palace, gazing up in awe at the mighty Led Zeppelin. I never dreamed I'd ever play with him, even if it was just for half an hour in a rehearsal room.

Although the signs were good, it was a different story when Roy Orbison appeared on show day. The producers had decided on a retro sci-fi theme for *The Last Resort* that week. There we were, about to accompany a twenty-four-carat solid gold legend while dressed in silver sparkly onesies and white *Star Trek*-style wigs. Though this was an indignity in itself, the first song, 'In Dreams', didn't go too badly. In between songs, Jonathan Ross had taken my Stratocaster to do a painful routine where he tried to learn the riff from 'Pretty Woman'. I picked up my spare guitar instead, but it had suffered a tuning mishap under the lights. When we played the intro, it all went a bit Pete Tong.

Dah-dah-dah-dah Clang!

Orbison, behind the blackness of his shades, remained unphased by the hideous disharmony of my contribution to his multi-million-selling classic. Afterwards, a huge Texan roadie came up to me, put his pockmarked face right up in mine, and drawled, 'Well, I checked it mahself, boy, an' it warn't Roy's geetar that was out o' toon!' The clip still exists on the unforgiving, eternal shame bucket of the internet, should you want to share my cringing embarrassment.

The show also played host to Marc Almond, Was Not Was, Mick Hucknall, Alexander O'Neal, and many more. One day, the late British comedian Frankie Howerd of *Up Pompeii* fame was a guest. It was true what they said about him. He prowled the dressing rooms for half-dressed young men and blatantly propositioned several of us.

A memorable *Last Resort* day was spent with *Blue Velvet, Twin Peaks*, and *Eraserhead* director David Lynch and his then partner, the staggeringly beautiful Isabella Rossellini. Mr Lynch said he loved the sound of my '62 Stratocaster and asked if I would be interested in doing some music for an upcoming rockabilly-based film he was planning. On the strength of our conversation alone, I assembled my studio gear in a Brixton attic where I had lived some years earlier. Pete Thomas, Steve Lawrence, and myself, along with Winkies singer Philip Rambow, recorded some shit-kicking, 50s-style twelve-bars and sent them to Lynch's agent in LA on a cassette. I never heard back, but I believe the movie *Ronnie Rocket* is one of those 'never realised' projects that Lynch always wanted to do and that all auteurs must have up their sleeves. The cassette still sounds like a long-lost Johnny Burnette album, though, and I love it anyway.

* * *

The final *Last Resort* show of the season was to be with Paul McCartney. The first live TV he had done in twenty years. He came on set in the morning and we played together for a couple of hours before settling on 'Don't Get Around Much Anymore', 'I Saw Her Standing There', and the Little Richard tune 'Lawdy Miss Clawdy'. Macca played guitar but gave me the solos, and I made a pretty good fist of it. My old Strat burned and sang that day, and he seemed impressed. I only noticed later, watching the clips on YouTube, that as I played, literally touching him, back-to-back, my leg was pumping up and down in exactly the way it had when I was six years old in my mate Andrew's house, wearing a plastic wig and fantasising about being a Beatle.

I must have done something right that night because, a week later, I got a call from one of Paul's people, asking me to clear my diary and prepare to be his guitar player for an album and a world tour. Just as the series ended, I seemed to have won the lottery—what a gig to get offered! Not only did it come neatly at the end of a series, it also enabled me to dodge an approach from Level 42—a close shave indeed.

McCartney's Hog Hill Mill studio is near the East Sussex village of Icklesham, halfway between Rye and Hastings. A small bungalow was rented for me in the village.

My first mistake was to install my bulky, eight-track recording equipment in the house—as if being McCartney's guitar player would allow me time to continue to work on anything else. I don't know what his assistant would have told him when he visited and found me moving furniture around to accommodate all the gear and wiring, but I can only imagine that it didn't go down that well. I still seemed to be working the old self-destruct button as hard as I could in the face of massive good fortune.

McCartney's studio is in a converted windmill, and the first day was full of surprises. The album *Flowers In The Dirt* was, at that phase of its development, a collaborative effort with Elvis Costello. Elvis appeared to be in charge of the production, although it later became clear that other producers had been at the helm before, and others would follow after his tenure. As I had just done the season of *The Last Resort* with two members of The Attractions, we had something in common, and I felt we had a good rapport. He'd seen me play with Macca on *The Last Resort*, too, and asked me, 'What was all that leg-pumping stuff, Kev!?'

With McCartney himself, though, I never felt relaxed. He had a myriad of personal assistants to do his bidding and seemed constantly to hold court with somewhat tedious anecdotes about The Beatles.

You'd think these would be amazing, but they had no real punch lines or point to them. He also played us a selection of his personal demos, which he called *Drones and Workers*. To me, they just sounded like aimless electronic doodles, mostly made with one synthesizer, and I couldn't believe why he would waste his time like that.

Of course, everybody paid close attention to Paul, but the atmosphere was always a bit tense and weird around him. I was nervous and guarded and felt like I was there on trial. We worked on the songs 'My Brave Face' and 'So Like Candy', and Elvis seemed to be going for a kind of early Lennon/McCartney 'homemade' approach to the sessions. Drummer Chris Whitton was banging on cardboard boxes, Ringo-style, and the vocal arrangements sounded very much like early Beatles, the timbre of Elvis's voice being somewhat similar to Lennon's.

Hog Hill studio was like a museum. The Mellotron used on 'Strawberry Fields' was there.* That iconic Hofner Violin Bass, with the last ever Beatles set list still taped to it, sat on a guitar stand along, with loads of instantly recognisable bits of vintage hardware from Abbey Road.

One morning, two Japanese gents—vice presidents from Roland Corporation, I soon learned—flew in from Tokyo to present Macca with a personalised Roland Synth-Guitar. He kept them waiting in the kitchen for an hour before he eventually went in and shook hands with them. He took the instrument and turned on his heel, leaving them to return from whence they had come, with only a two-minute audience with the great man and a hastily taken photograph to prove they were ever there.

At the beginning of another day, an assistant asked me to go and see Paul upstairs alone. I went up to the large loft space where he had his personal den. He was on the phone and motioned for me to wait. Looking around, I started to play an old, gold-finished double bass

---

* A keyboard instrument where every key activates a loop of tape to play a pre-recorded, orchestral sound.

with white binding that looked familiar. When he finished his phone call, he said, 'Oh, you like that, do you? If you think you've seen it before, well, you have. It was Bill Black's bass when he backed Elvis Presley in 1956.'

I carefully let go of the priceless relic and sat on a sofa opposite him.

'I just called you up here to share this with me,' he said, whereupon he lit up a small joint of neat grass, took a draw, and handed it over. I hadn't smoked weed in a good while but, not wishing to be impolite, I took a hit on it and passed it back. Very quickly, my tongue began to swell, and a buzzing noise rang loudly in my ears. Time slowed to a crawl, and I could hardly speak.

Without warning, McCartney stood up, pointed a finger at me, and headed out of the door and downstairs with the words, 'And that's you stoned!' Still to this day, I've absolutely no clue what on earth the point of this was or why he would want to test me like that. Did he just want a friendly joint with a fellow musician? Was it an experiment to see how I would react to the powerful shit he smoked? Was he looking for a smoking partner for the upcoming tour? I'll never know, but back home in London, during a break in recording, I got a call thanking me for my time and asking me not to return. He gave me three weeks' pay as severance.

I found out years later, when I ran into Elvis Costello, that my principal 'crime' was to have announced that *The Rutles* had been on TV the night before. *The Rutles* is Eric Idle and Neil Innes's affectionate movie pastiche of The Beatles' career, complete with very clever and funny songs, all paid for by George Harrison. According to Elvis, he knew my P45 was in the post as soon as I even mentioned it in The Presence.

For whatever reason or number of reasons, I had failed spectacularly to seize the opportunity given to me by Paul McCartney. I guess some people just don't click with each other. My admiration for him as an artist remains undimmed by my unfortunate and brief experience as one of his musicians. The *Ram* album is something of an overlooked classic in my view. As far as I know, *Flowers In The Dirt* moved on to pastures new, and, when it was released, I couldn't detect a trace of the versions of the songs we recorded at Hog Hill Mill during my three-week stint there. I've no idea if anything I played made it onto the album, but I suspect not.

* * *

Newly unemployed, I went to visit Steve Nieve at his flat in South Kensington to try to inveigle myself back into the *Last Resort* band. I was desperate, and I knew that once the McCartney money ran out, I'd struggle to pay my bills. As I entreated Steve to let me back in the band, his kids were pricking me in the arms with sewing needles they had got hold of, just to add to my sense of utter humiliation. He'd already promised my old gig to another guy, and he wouldn't budge.

Once again, I was experiencing the wild fluctuations that had dogged my whole career as a musician. Now, however, the arrival of my first-born daughter Beatrice meant that I had new priorities. It was time for another rethink.

My introduction to Sandie Shaw may have come about because I used to ring Clive Langer occasionally to remind him that I was still alive and in need of some work. There are certain musicians who might frown upon hungry behaviour of this kind. It's a very British thing to suffer in aloof silence. You never want to seem desperate, but there are always a few good souls who understand. Clive was definitely one of those. He must have recommended me to La Shaw, and I was duly hired to play for her at Westside Studios on a cover of the Lloyd Cole song 'Are You Ready To Be Heartbroken'.

Sandie was experiencing an upswing in interest following her collaboration with The Smiths on 'Hand In Glove' and Morrissey's very public gushing about her. I'd probably had my very first stirrings of preadolescent longing watching Sandie on *Ready Steady Go* when I was about ten years old. With her high cheekbones, silky black bob, and those elegant bare feet that shocked and terrified a nation, she looked amazing. I loved her work with Chris Andrews, too. 'Girl Don't Come' and 'Always Something There To Remind Me' were flawless pop records.

By the time I worked with her, Sandie was in her mid-forties. She was still very attractive. We got on well, and she took to me as a musician and a person. At that low point in my life, after the twin disappointments of Iggy and McCartney, plus losing my TV gig, I felt that I'd let myself down. Sandie sensed my low confidence and saw something of a project in me. It was her natural inclination to try to reach out and help people, so she took it upon herself to steer me inexorably toward the practice of Nichiren Buddhism, something to which she has dedicated much of her life.

During sessions for her Rough Trade album *Nothing Less Than Brilliant*, she would take me to visit Hugh Burns at his flat, where they would perform something called Gongyo together.* This consisted of chanting long verses of the Lotus Sutra in classical Japanese, offering incense, ringing bells, and so on. I was entranced by the sound and the sense of purpose and calmness it seemed to engender. For the next nine years, I practised it fully and completely. I really enjoyed being involved in a Buddhist summer concert at Taplow Court, with Herbie Hancock and Wayne Shorter heading a bill that also included Kid Creole (fronting Richard Niles's Bandzilla). Eager Buddhist members had thrown everything into organising the event. We even scored a free helicopter ride so that one of the performers, rapper JC-001, could get from the Reading Festival to Taplow in time to appear.

The magical day wasn't even spoiled when Herbie Hancock's assistant went to check the piano half an hour before Herbie was due to play. He hit two notes and said, 'Nope!' The Steinway had been sitting

---

* Hugh is a very seasoned and gifted session guitar player with everyone from Wham to Placido Domingo.

in the sun for hours and had drifted out of tune. Frantic phone calls were made and a local piano tuner duly arrived and patiently tuned the piano onstage until such time as Herbie's guy was happy. The plangent sound of Wayne Shorter's soprano floating across the Buckinghamshire countryside at sunset is something hard to forget.

That was probably my best day with the Buddhist organisation, although my diligent practice caused me to be given responsibility after a few years as a so-called 'district leader'. This meant I was responsible for supporting a few dozen members locally in the Notting Hill area. One of these was a guy who was introduced to me as Raymond. An older gay man with long grey hair tied back, Raymond would turn up to meetings with an enormous pair of scissors tucked into his voluminous yoga pants and was often accompanied by his young lover, Diego. He was outspoken and abrasive and could be quite disruptive and unpleasant at meetings. Raymond could seemingly argue with a lamppost and often had a real attitude for no particular reason anyone could identify. Maybe he was drunk or stoned.

As district leader, I took it upon myself to visit the tiny housing association flat Raymond and Diego shared, to chant with them and just offer friendship and support for their Buddhist practice. Eventually, someone revealed to me that Raymond used to be better known as Ossie Clarke, once world-renowned as dressmaker to the stars. He had fallen on very hard times and had clearly made a few poor choices. As it turned out, one of these was Diego, who in 1996 stabbed him to death with a breadknife and half sawed his head off. I was due to visit and chant with them that very morning but was met with police tape at the entrance to their landing. Diego was jailed for six years on the grounds of diminished responsibility.

* * *

In 1990, a tour of Japan that was partly to do with Sandie's status as an important cultural ambassador for the Soka Gakkai International (the Japanese organisation at the heart of Nichiren Buddhism) was undertaken with Andrew Paresi on drums, Andy Metcalfe on keyboards, and Philip 'Soul' Sewell on bass. It was partly a music tour and partly a pilgrimage for me, the wide-eyed new acolyte keen to know about the history and culture of my recently found spiritual discipline. The bubble didn't even burst when Sandie had a blazing row in a swanky Tokyo restaurant with somebody very senior from the cultural arm of the Soka Gakkai. She flounced out in a great huff, leaving us all sitting there awkwardly, continuing our meals and not knowing what to say to our embarrassed Japanese hosts.

On another trip to Japan, under very different circumstances, I finally decided to cease my Buddhist practice, partly based on my experience there. What had started as a genuine quest for enlightenment—or at least trying to climb out of a bit of a hole—had left me a bit jaded after seeing the public squabbles between the Japanese priesthood and the ordinary members. On one visit to a Gakkai Welcome Centre in Tokyo, I was urged to watch secretly shot footage of priests consorting with Geisha girls in restaurants, filmed from behind some large indoor foliage. I later went to another meeting in London that consisted of leaders planning to stalk visiting priests around the city and spy on them as they tried to set up rival temples.

When the disputes spilt over into this kind of blame culture, with leaders taking sides and factions splitting off, I realised I'd had enough. I have lost contact with those who chose to regard my lapsed Buddhist practice as a challenge or a threat. I remember from the inside how members regarded those who had stopped practising. This strange mixture of pity and fear made me uneasy to meet up with Buddhists who had the subliminal agenda of reanimating me as a member.

I don't think Nichiren Buddhism is a cult exactly, but it does exhibit certain cultish characteristics. It views the world in terms of those who are okay because they are 'inside' and engendering anxiety about the world 'outside' the practice. People like me, who stopped, are referred to by a Japanese word that translates as 'asleep'. The Japanese word for the non-Buddhist world translates as 'chaos', so you might easily conclude that there is a subtly manipulative mindset at work.

Some people I knew from that world literally didn't mix with anyone outside the SGI. When that happens, you know it can't be healthy. I never got to that point. I always had plenty of friends and colleagues who wanted nothing to do with organised religion, and that suited me fine. As with any passionate spiritual community, there are good and bad people involved. Although I no longer practice Buddhism or call myself a Buddhist, I don't regret my time with it. It's right for some people some of the time and others all of the time, but I rest in the knowledge that 'It pleases The Buddha to see a bodhisattva seek enlightenment, even for a short time.'

TOP In the crowd at the Ritz, NYC, 1986—a foolhardy move that didn't end well. **ABOVE** Cruising in LA in a Chevy Impala on hire from Dreamboats. Iggy so wanted to ride with us but he had other fish to fry. In the car with me are Seamus Beaghen, Phil Butcher, and Gavin Harrison. *Both photographs by Paul McAlpine.*

OPPOSITE PAGE, FROM TOP Bowie looking nervous on the ride from Battersea Heliport to Live Aid; our first look at the Wembley Stadium crowd; David and Freddie, smokin' fags backstage.

PREVIOUS PAGE Paris, 1986: Iggy's winning smile on display. *Paul McAlpine.*

TOP Looking for inspiration during the *Blah Blah Blah* sessions at Mountain Studios in Montreux. **ABOVE** Mick Jagger, myself, and David at Westside for the 'Dancing In The Street' session. Helena Springs reads a magazine in the background. **RIGHT** Erdal Kizilčay, me, and David sing backups on Iggy's 'Isolation' at Mountain.

RIGHT David and I share a brotherly clinch after a show at the Ritz. *Paul McAlpine*. **BELOW** Melissa Hurley smiles and David writes a postcard as Reeves Gabrels looks on outside Compass Point Studios in Nassau. **BOTTOM** My sister Janet and David sing 'Absolute Beginners' at Westside. Whenever I hear the song I think of his awful shirt, and now you can too.

RIGHT The *Last Resort* band: Steve Fishman, Pete Thomas, Steve Nieve, and me with guests Mel Brooks and Ronnie Wood.
BELOW The Iggy band with Metallica before a show in Mexico City, 2018: Mat Hector, Lars Ulrich, Seamus Beaghen, James Hetfield, Kirk Hammett, myself, Robert Trujillo, and Ben Ellis. They were so loud, my left leg fell off.

ABOVE Me, bassist Phil 'Soul' Sewell, and a young Sia Furler at a late-night shebeen in Notting Hill. RIGHT Me with Telecaster aloft at Colchester Arts Centre, playing some Lou Reed and channelling Robert Quine.

RIGHT Me with my Custom Les Paul. BELOW Mr Hudson, Mike Garson, Alan Childs, Sass Jordan, me, Corey Glover, Carmine Rojas, and Gerry Leonard taking a bow at the Bowie Celebration in London, 2019.

PREVIOUS PAGE Me and Iggy at Portland Pabst Festival, 2017. *Paul McAlpine*.

ABOVE I felt the urge to kiss John Waters when we met at the Burger Boogaloo in Oakland. I don't know why. I just thought he deserved it. LEFT At Wishing Tree Studio, where I spend many hours playing and writing.

CHAPTER THIRTEEN

LAYING LOW
AT LAYLOW

§

MY MOVE TO NOTTING HILL IN 1987 BEGAN WITH THE NEED FOR A WORKSPACE IN WHICH TO SITE MY GROWING COLLECTION OF STUDIO GEAR. I struck up a friendship with Brian Curran, the owner of a café on the corner of Portobello Road and Cambridge Gardens. He agreed to let me beaver away in the basement in return for some time with the gear for himself and his own musical efforts.

Though he was a lovely guy, gentle Geordie Brian's behaviour soon became rather erratic. One day I arrived to find him sitting in the studio, showing it off to a BBC film crew and being interviewed by Emma Freud about *his* music and *his* studio. I thought that maybe it was time to move. Luckily for me, the guy with the shop next door, a distinguished community filmmaker named Barney Platts-Mills, had a bigger, better basement and was willing to let me rent it.

Laylow Studio was duly born at 307 Portobello Road, and there it continued to exist for nearly ten years. The name Laylow is how locals referred to the Ladbroke Grove area. As it turned out, that very basement had an auspicious musical history. It had once been the rehearsal space for King Crimson and many other bands. I'm not a believer in Feng Shui, but there was something about that room that seemed to coax good music from the walls.

I met engineer Rod Beale when I worked with him on an album for Virgin Records by Californian singer Ashley Maher (her second album, *Pomegranate*). Rod's history included work with Peter Gabriel at his Real World Studios and on Youssou N'Dour's album *The Lion*. Ashley's album was a great learning curve for me as a producer, and Rod and I made a great team. We decided to become partners and pooled our resources to seriously upgrade the equipment at 307 and build proper cabling into the floor and walls. We spent nearly three months building a patch bay, prepping wires, squirting them with Hemmeling Oil from a plastic bottle to soften the ends, adding rubber sleeves and copper tips, and then soldering hundreds of connections. We shredded our fingers with the gruelling work. When it was finished, though, it had a thirty-two-channel Soundcraft desk and lots of cool outboard hardware, and it looked really professional. We were still in a location where the occasional junkie would be found in our toilet, or where people would randomly ring the bell and swear they had 'a great idea for a house tune, man', but Rod and I played host to some truly great musicians and artists in our time there.

On one occasion, Jimmy Helms from London Beat was singing on a session when he said, 'I'm going to bring my friend here to record something.' His friend turned out to be Ike Turner, who showed up with his young blonde Texan wife (number thirteen, as it happens) and beat the living daylights out of the piano for hours (just the piano, thankfully). When asked how the recently released biopic of Tina Turner, *What's Love Got To Do With It?*, had affected his reputation, he simply shrugged and said, 'Frankly, I was glad when O.J. Simpson came along and the world had a new black bogyman!'

Laylow Studio soon became the venue of choice for local record companies and artists to make demos or to record 'mid-range budget' projects. One such company was Jago Management. The folks at Jago were responsible for breaking All Saints, Don E, Ronnie Jordan, and Mark Morrison (of 'Return Of The Mack' fame). Their offices were in Notting Hill's famous 'frontline', All Saints Road, which had been the centre of the influx of Caribbean immigrants in the 1950s—the backdrop for *Absolute Beginners*, in fact—and still wore its West Indian heart on its sleeve.

Jago was run by a coterie of local faces, including Jamaican musician Michael Palmer, Rasta Johnny Laws, and producer and larger-than-life Svengali figure Ron Tom. Jago put a lot of work my way until one day, when I went to collect on a studio bill they owed, instead of the rows of good-looking girls seated at iMacs and the sweet smell of ganja emanating from Johnny's office, I found a locked building and nobody there. Peering through the glass doors, I saw that all the furniture and office equipment had vanished overnight. It seemed as though whoever had been bankrolling the company through its early successes hadn't been seeing the return they'd hoped for and had unceremoniously pulled the plug.

I never got the £800 I was owed, but I did run into Johnny several months later. He was sitting on an upturned crate, smoking a big spliff in the doorway of the People's Record Store, opposite the scene of his former empire. We greeted each other in the usual laid-back and friendly way. I knew there was no point in asking what had happened. I'd seen it all before.

Another local big-shot, DJ and remixer Steve Jervier, had done a similar thing. He based himself on the top floor of a studio in Fulham for a whole year and divided his time between developing pop stars for Sony and hosting epic all-night parties. After producing a couple of hits, he moved into a large building in Hammersmith where several writing and recording suites quickly took root until, one day, boom! The locks were changed, and all the gear and the money vanished.

I don't think guys like Johnny Laws or Steve Jervier were crooks, just chancers. They had a good go at succeeding and even produced a few hits, but their putative empires were always built on sand and bullshit. None of them really had the chops to become a Suge Knight or a Berry Gordy. Perhaps, as black entrepreneurs, the odds were stacked against them from the start.

Soul legend Chaka Khan lived in West London at this time. I had met her sister, the wonderfully named Taka Boom, and we wrote some songs together. She introduced me to a Korean bloke called Sangki Yu. Sangki had but two things going for him: loads of money and an obsession with Chaka Khan. He had seemingly made a fortune by running pachinko parlours in Japan. These places are often owned and run by Japanese Yakuza or Koreans. The fact that they deal in piles and piles of unregulated cash makes them a magnet for organised crime.

Sangki gave Taka and me good dirty money for a demo that we'd made and promised to release it on his indie dance label. I visited his offices once, and everything about the setup seemed slightly wrong. The 'label' was more than likely a front for drug dealing and money laundering. Before our record ever came out, poor Sangki came to a sticky end, piling his Mercedes into a pillar on the M1 at a hundred miles per hour while ferrying two American DJs to a club gig up north. All three were killed, and that was that.

On another occasion, Youssou N'Dour came down to record at Laylow, accompanied by Peter Gabriel. I played nylon guitar on the song 'Don't Walk Away' from his album *Joko* (*From Village To Town*). Legendary Sly and the Family Stone drummer Andy Newmark did some sessions there too, as did Sugarhill Gang members Skip Jackson and Doug Wimbish, with drummer Keith LeBlanc. We even hosted the never-released solo album by Howard Donald of Take That. Gary Barlow came and hung out at a couple of Howard's sessions and complained about the quality of our studio sofa, which was admittedly held together by gaffer tape and carpet tacks.

Shara Nelson, the singer on Massive Attack's 'Unfinished Sympathy', passed through for a writing session, which I engineered. During a break, I picked up a guitar, she sang over what I played, and the song 'Inside Out', from her album *What Silence Knows*, was written in about five minutes. Shara called me again to accompany her as a duo, and we performed the song on a very early Jools Holland show in

1993, sandwiched between the band Jellyfish on one side and Leonard Cohen, looking on benignly from about six feet away on the other.

A lot of local artists and managers booked our studio for its easy-going vibe and great atmosphere, and life settled into a rhythm of constant studio work under the street in Portobello. My second child, Olivia, had just been born, so I made renewed efforts to put food on the table and try to behave like a grown-up.

* * *

The post-punk pop band Transvision Vamp had a hit with 'Baby I Don't Care'. Their producer, Duncan Bridgeman, was one of the first people I met on Portobello Road. He had a similarly sized basement recording studio very nearby. When the band were recording their album *Velveteen*, he asked me to come in and play guitar. I spent a week at the Townhouse in Shepherd's Bush, grinding out power chords with a Les Paul and a Marshall amp. Bandleader Nick Christian Sayer, who was supposed to be the guitar player, rocked up at the studio in the evenings. He was always in a vodka- and weed-induced stupor. I was never credited as guitarist on the *Velveteen* album as it would have damaged the band's cool reputation to admit that they weren't quite good or sober enough to play on their own record.

Transvision singer Wendy James was having a passionate affair with comedian Rowland Rivron for a while, or at least seemed passionate until Rowland was unceremoniously dumped when Wendy got bored. For years afterwards, I would see Wendy around Notting Hill, and depending on her mood she would either greet me with a smile and invite me for coffee or I'd inexplicably get blanked in the street as she pretended not to see me. By all accounts, I wasn't the only person who had this kind of experience with her.

Following fairly hard on the heels of Transvision Vamp in 1988, the Bowie hotline rang once again. Never a day goes by when I don't thank heaven for that excellent man and his faith in me.

CHAPTER FOURTEEN

TIN
MACHINE

§

SOMETIME IN 1987, DURING HIS *NEVER LET ME DOWN* TOUR, Bowie had come up with the idea of forming a good old-fashioned hard rock band with his new friend, guitar maverick Reeves Gabrels. Reeves suggested they hook up with brothers Hunt and Tony Sales, sons of US comedy icon Soupy Sales and the rhythm section on Iggy's *Lust For Life*. Reeves had come to Bowie's attention through his wife, Sara, who worked as a publicist on the tour and had become a trusted confidante after Bowie was falsely accused of assaulting a woman in Texas. She offered calm wisdom and support after the furore caused by the allegation and introduced David to Reeves when he was visiting her on the tour.

I think it was Sara who gave Bowie a cassette tape of her husband's band, and it really piqued his interest. By the time they met, Bowie was already fully aware of Reeves's prowess as a guitarist. Reeves is a quietly spoken, intensely bright guy with a playful but very skilled approach to music. He became the sort of guitarist for Bowie that I could never be. I am more of a 'musical glue' all-rounder, but Reeves, a Berkeley graduate, is a howling monster of a player, in complete contrast to his self-effacing and shy personality. Bowie started collaborating closely with him soon after they met and would continue to do so for the next ten years.

I'd long been an admirer of the Sales brothers' work with Iggy

Pop. The famous big-band drum intro to 'Lust for Life' tells you everything about Hunt's swagger and style as a drummer, and Tony's thunderous bass style was also great. Not only that but the pair of them could really sing, too. Listen to 'Here Comes Success' from *Lust For Life* album and you get their vibe. They were funny, smart, and a little dangerous. I quickly became very fond of them after we met at Mountain Studio in Montreux, where I'd been for Iggy's *Blah Blah Blah* record three years earlier.

The dynamic tensions in Tin Machine were evident from the start. Tony Sales had been in a coma and nearly died in a drug- and booze-fuelled car crash in Los Angeles some years before. No wonder he had something of the ex-drinker mentality that could make him reluctant to be around any consumption of alcohol. His brother, Hunt, had a somewhat more ambivalent approach to sobriety. In fact, he had an insatiable appetite for stimulants of any kind—in large quantities and often. Hunt also had his father's habit of putting out piss-taking jokes and one-liners that never stopped.

It was literally chalk and cheese with these brothers, who had both been through the mincer in their own different ways. It therefore fell mostly to Reeves to be the mediator between these fractious siblings, as well as a creative muse for David Bowie. The atmosphere in Tin Machine was sometimes a little prickly but by no means unpleasant. I had no axes to grind with anyone, so I never got involved in the power struggles that went on.

Bowie enjoyed the interpersonal tensions, I think. It was a very 'male' energy, and there was plenty of laughter and general bonhomie to alleviate any bouts of bickering that occasionally erupted. As an experiment, I reckon Tin Machine was only a partial success for David. The band recorded a lot of songs for that first album. Some of them were mothballed for future Bowie projects, and I'm pretty sure he had the final say on those that were allowed through. David always said publicly that the band was a democracy, and that may have been the way he wanted people to see it, but I don't think anyone was really in any doubt about who held the reins.

By the time I joined the group as sort of fifth member, the album was already more than half-formed and growing every day. British engineer/ producer and all-around good egg Tim Palmer occupied the studio hot seat, pulling it all together. In the vast room that was the main part of the Montreux Casino, Tim had erected a platform six feet up in the air on which to mount Hunt's Slingerland drumkit. Other rooms up and downstairs at Mountain took the guitar amps and so on. The drum sound on that record is humungous, with ambient microphones placed around the enormous space much further away than is usual.

On the day I got there, I was pitched straight into this cavernous space where we were all thirty feet apart from each other, with David singing unseen in an upstairs room. We cut the opening song on the *Tin Machine* album, 'Heaven's In Here', my rather fetching swoopy, tremolo-arm chords providing a contrast to Reeves's Stevie Ray Vaughan-like flights of mad bluesy lead. The track gets wilder and wilder until it ends up with Hunt and Reeves conjuring the sound of a building being inexpertly demolished with jackhammers while several baskets of cats die horribly in a fire. *This'll be a refreshing challenge after the melodically polite songs of Paul McCartney*, I thought.

Bowie's bodyguard, Jerry Mele, was an ex-Navy Seal. Until his death in 2016, he was U2's guy too, and many other 'high net worth' famous types had trusted him with their lives. His job was to be somewhere near David but to be almost invisible unless there was a direct threat to his safety. In Montreux, Bowie was rarely if ever hassled. The locals were accustomed to rock gods coming and going at Mountain Studio, so Jerry had time on his hands. To find something useful to do, he had taken it upon himself to try and improve the general fitness of the Tin Machine band members. This involved morning calisthenics and lectures about what we should and shouldn't be eating. Now, Jerry was a dear soul, even though he could probably kill you with his little finger while smoking a cigar. His earnest efforts to improve our lives were coming from the right place. Most of his sound advice was completely wasted on the lazy, drink-addled, drug-taking, and slightly overweight musicians he had as raw material. He tried, though, and we played along.

One day at Mountain there was a disturbing incident involving a fan, just when it happened to be Jerry's day off. David had arrived at the studio mid-morning and was sat drinking coffee and reading the *New York Times* in the control room. Tim Palmer was setting up the desk, and I was there changing some guitar strings. Without warning, a guy appeared in the room, stood over David's chair, and started to talk to him.

'You never responded to my invitation to dinner. Why not?'

His tone was aggressive. For a moment we didn't know what to do, as David was answering him calmly—as if he knew the guy—but when he continued to press Bowie for an explanation, we twigged that this might be a harmful situation. The guy was a fan with some emotional issues and not someone David knew at all. I think it was Hunt and I who stepped in and ushered the bloke out, pretty quickly.

David was a bit shaken and told us that since John Lennon's murder he had been forced to adopt a much more vigilant attitude to fans who might be a danger to him. If he received a letter from a group of fans living together, for example, it might be the usual adoring praise, but then the questions would start. *What exactly did you mean by 'A cop knelt at the feet of a priest?' or 'Stands ensealed by his cabinette?'* While these questions might be tedious, they are quite normal for the nerdier Bowie obsessive. If the letters continued and had return addresses that got geographically closer to his, a red flag would go up. One day he might get a letter from the same group that says, 'We love you David, and we don't hold you personally responsible for Robert's death, but we feel as if your lyrics may have contributed and that some retribution is in order.'

'If you get one like that, you have to move house,' he explained.

I didn't totally warm to the sound of Tin Machine, to be honest. I thought it had a bit too much 'muddy hair' on it. Bowie's songwriting was at the core of the record, but he seemed happy to let the band dictate the direction of the sound. I even got a song on the album. 'Run' is an old tune of mine from 1980, originally called 'Babylon Bridge'.

I have a habit of playing old songs and favourite guitar riffs at soundchecks and sessions, and the riff for 'Babylon Bridge' is very much a product of my personal guitar style. Other players have difficulty copying it. It wouldn't be the only time David had tuned in to something of mine, he had a very keen musical antenna. 'Run' rests on my original riff, but he took it somewhere entirely his own.

A lot of the time, Tin Machine was like a sonic wrestling match. The one time I really *felt* the music was when we were recording in the Bahamas, at Compass Point Studios. Robert Palmer had lent Bowie his place opposite the studio, and the band stayed there. The house was small, modern, and somewhat characterless. I, on the other hand, was installed in a beautiful colonial-style chalet on the beach nearby. It had a white wooden veranda and was nestled on the sand under waving coconut palms. I couldn't believe it! The others were sharing a cramped house, but I had this wonderful place all to myself. I could get up in the morning and go snorkelling with dolphin rays and sand sharks before breakfast in the crystal blue Caribbean Sea right outside my bedroom window.

One night in the studio, somebody called us outside to witness a proper tropical rainstorm. Sheets of water fell from the sky and the roads briefly ran like rivers. When it stopped, a thousand frogs appeared on the lawns and started singing in the twilight. We reconvened in the studio and started playing 'I Can't Read', which was a magical moment in the humid atmosphere after the storm. It was a one-take deal that finally sounded like a band gelling together and properly listening to each other. Along with 'Prisoner Of Love' I think it's the best song on the *Tin Machine* album. I like the double entendre in the payoff line, too. Does he sing 'I can't reach it anymore' or 'I can't read shit anymore?' You decide.

David was considering marrying Melissa Hurley, who had been a dancer on the *Glass Spider* tour, and she accompanied him part of the time in the Bahamas. The general feeling was, 'Nice girl, but was she right for him?' There were a couple of jaw-dropping moments that answered the question. Melissa persuaded David to wear some very un-Bowie-like apparel. One such item was a very small black leather cap in which he looked slightly ridiculous.* Another time we were on the beach when he appeared, sauntering along, hand-in-hand with Melissa. He was sporting a minuscule thong that barely covered his tackle and had just a string at the back that disappeared alarmingly up his bum crack. It's an image that, once seen, cannot be unseen.†

We very much enjoyed the company of Status Quo, who were in studio two at Compass Point for much of our stay. Happy hours were spent playing table football with them and sharing stories and bottles of wine. Quo's Francis Rossi is a seriously good table football player and could thrash anyone anytime with a flick of his wrist. I visited their sessions and talked guitars with the late, great Rick Parfitt, too. One day I picked up his famous white Telecaster, and he said, 'Go on then, try and bend a string.' His strings were of such a heavy gauge that they were like telephone cables. It was virtually impossible to bend one as they were designed just to go chunka-chunka-chunka-chunk and never play anything like a solo line.

Status Quo were all wearing T-shirts bearing the legend 'I've Sat On Rick's Boat'. Francis used to say, 'We're just a Butlin's band that got lucky.' They had a microphone set up in their control room at bum level attached to a digital DAT recorder. Every time one of them felt the need to pass wind (which was quite often) they would sit on

---

* I have a photo to prove it!
† No, I don't have a photo!

the microphone and press record for the split second it took to relieve the pressure. At the end of the day, they would play back the resulting ten-minute audio clip of continual horrendous staccato farting, accompanied by the sound of muffled *awww*s in the background. It shouldn't have been funny, of course, but it was. Oh yes it was.

I soon discovered why I had been favoured with the best accommodation on the island. After a few days of recording, David came to the bungalow in the evening alone and sat on the veranda with me. The sun was setting and the yellow moon was reflected on the water. He opened a bottle of white rum and poured us two glasses. He said he had something important on his mind. Without much hesitation or small talk, he told me that his strategy for the band revolved around the four-piece—i.e., himself, Reeves, and the Sales brothers—and would not, therefore, include me as a full member. I would be credited fully for my contribution and indeed go on to tour with the group, but all interviews, photos, publicity material, et cetera would not include me.

I had been brought in after the band's inception, it's true, but this definitely felt like a bit of a blow at the time. I asked David if I had fallen short in any way or disappointed him musically, but he was adamant that his decision was only to do with the image of the band and nothing more. I guess my face didn't fit, or maybe he thought it was stronger to build it just around the four. Whatever his reasons, I had no choice but to accept it with good grace. Unlike some others, at least, he had been very honest and upfront. He dealt with me personally, and with great kindness, so I took it for what it was. Journeyman again!

In fact, when Tin Machine did interviews on camera, I was often there and often included. David took the time to speak about me in glowing terms on more than one occasion. He was always aware of how much it meant to give a shout-out to the people around him, and I am truly grateful to him for thinking of me when it mattered. I'm sure I'm not alone in getting far more out than I put in when it came to working alongside David Bowie.

One day, after a session at Compass Point, David suggested we go and play at a bar in Nassau town. There is nothing else at all written down or recorded about this as far as I know, but it really happened. We went into a tourist place where a Goombay-style dance band was playing and borrowed some gear from them, then did three or four songs to an audience of bemused Americans. I can't remember much about it except that it was so incongruous that David Bowie had turned up to play for free in front of a handful of people that they didn't quite believe it was really him they were seeing—or seem much to care, for that matter. It was Tin Machine's first live appearance, and it was as obscure as it's possible to be for a David Bowie gig.

Tin Machine's first real public performance was at the International Rock Awards at the Armoury in New York on May 31, 1989. We had been in the city for a couple of weeks, rehearsing on the upper floor of a disused hotel in midtown Manhattan. Various English and American DJs, journalists, and TV crews had dropped in on the rehearsals to get a first glimpse of Bowie's new project. The band was so fucking loud at those rehearsals that David was going hoarse trying to be heard above the squalling storm whipped up by Hunt and Reeves. Some of the journalists looked like they were going to shit themselves at the sound levels we generated. It was quite physically tiring after a couple of hours, but we did it for seven or eight days straight.

Interviews were conducted with the band present, and sometimes I was included and sometimes not. There is a nice clip going around of Bowie bantering with the band at those rehearsals. That was when he took time out to introduce me. 'Kevin does what I pretend to do,' he says of my guitar playing. 'Kevin's a proper musician!'

On the day before the show, David gave us all a thousand dollars in cash and told us to go and buy the smartest suits we could. I ended up with a very nice double-breasted, chocolate-brown Italian number. It was stolen from a dressing room a few years later, ironically at a Buddhist event.

I breakfasted at the Mayflower on Central Park West on the morning of the show before turning up at the Armoury. Backstage, everywhere you looked, there were icons: Keith Richards here, Eric Clapton and Alice Cooper there. I was standing with David and Reeves when Grace Jones appeared next to us in a dress that was really just a few leather straps stitched together in a very loose lattice of large rectangles, leaving her undergarments totally visible.

'Hello, you look like a six-foot sandal,' I ventured. Possibly the worst chat-up line in history, but it worked! She looked at me like a spider examining a fly and then, with a broad grin, took hold of my tie and tried to lead me into a nearby bathroom. She might have succeeded but a firm hand appeared on my shoulder.

It was Bowie.

'Come back, son, she'll eat you for breakfast,' he said, poking his tongue out at Grace and steering me away.*

It was at that awards show—my first proper live performance with Bowie after Live Aid—that David did his pre-show warm-up with us. Getting into some sort of intense huddle just before hitting a stage is a common ritual for many bands. We all stood in a tight circle, facing each other. Bowie looked at us intently for a second and then pointed a finger at each of us in turn with the encouraging words, 'Don't fuck up! Don't fuck up! Don't fuck up! Don't fuck up!' Of course, we all burst out laughing, which was entirely the best way he knew to crack the tension before our live televised debut in front of a waiting world.

Tin Machine's first mini-tour was designed to cause a few ripples, as it was Bowie's wish to play very small venues. The opening night was June 14, 1989, at the World in New York. Then it was off to California. The night before the LA gig, we held a sort of preview party somewhere in Hollywood, possibly at the Viper Room. I was standing with Hunt Sales when he noticed Paul Young across the bar.

* This wasn't my only slightly weird encounter with the divine Ms Jones. More of that later.

'Hey Kev,' he said. 'Wanna know something about Paul Young? His nose has no cartilage left in it!'

'Really?' I asked.

'Yeah, really, man, he did so much blow that it's all gone! Follow me I'll prove it to ya.'

With that, Hunt charged across the club and greeted Paul Young with a smile and a hug. He then took his thumb and literally flattened the unsuspecting singer's boneless nose into his face while looking back at me, grinning. I'd never seen anything like that before, and I'm not sure I ever want to again.

Holding a David Bowie gig in a small club like the Roxy was a great idea on paper, but it came with a few challenging security issues. One of which was that several thousand people showed up trying to get into a place that only held five hundred. Girls were climbing up the drainpipes and tumbling in through bathroom windows on the upper floors. Motorcycle cops were dealing with traffic chaos near the venue. It was great! Bowie added a second night to cope with demand, but in truth, we could have done three weeks.

The Tin Machine shows were all a bit like that, from the Paradiso in Amsterdam to the National Ballroom in Kilburn London. Crews were often paid to pretend to be the band with blankets over them, piling out of a rear door after the shows and being driven around until the paparazzi and fans gave up the chase.

During a sound-check at La Cigale in Paris, I started playing the riff from my song 'Love Is Essential', from the second Local Heroes album. David sidled up to me and asked, 'What's that you're playing, and can I have it, please?' It got worked into a song called 'Now', which we performed a couple of times with the band. The song would go on to have a better future, though, as David turned it from a good piece by me into the title song on the album *1. Outside*, which wasn't yet even a twinkle in his eye.

CHAPTER FIFTEEN

THE REMIX
BANDWAGON

§

AFTER THE TIN MACHINE WHIRLWIND, I WAS BACK IN THE STUDIO IN PORTOBELLO, LOOKING FOR NEW WORK. DNA's recent reinvention of 'Tom's Diner' by Suzanne Vega had married hip-hop-style beats with the original recordings and given her a huge hit. As a consequence, A&R departments around the world demanded more. I started to get asked to remix rock records for the dancefloor, as did every other jobbing producer in the business. I had literally no knowledge of how to do this, so I drafted in a couple of DJs I'd met in local record shops Honest Jon's and Vinyl Solution for advice and input.

Mostly, the technique involved stripping down the mix to just the vocal and spinning breakbeats from records alongside the original until the resulting mash-up sounded a bit funky. The new sampling technology, which had begun on a large scale with the Akai S900 machine, meant that you could chop up and rebuild a record out of any chunk of sound from the original or, indeed, anywhere. This meant that a lot of those 1990s remixes were nothing more than drumbeats with fragments of vocal hooks flown over the top and bore no resemblance whatsoever to the original song.

While the subgenre gave us the great Fatboy Slim hits, there were so many other records where the results were frankly pointless. I was willing to take the shilling at the time, though, so I jumped on the remix bandwagon. I did remixes for Gang Of Four, The Railway Children,

Aztec Camera and Mick Jones, That Petrol Emotion, and a few others I can't remember. These were all pretty awful records, frankly, but at least I learned a fair bit about sampling and mixing while ruining perfectly good songs for money.

It was during this time that I became aware of the potential tensions that could arise between musicians and DJs. Since the latter were becoming so powerful and influential, there was definitely a feeling that DJs didn't deserve the attention and huge earnings they received as they were, after all, only playing records made by musicians. Once, I hired local celebrity DJ Phil Asher to contribute to a remix and manually spin some vinyl breakbeats over a track by Ashley Maher that I'd been given to remix. There was no doubting the skill he had on the decks, or his good taste.

I was impressed seeing Phil's technique up close and it made me realise that being a successful DJ wasn't as easy as it might appear. Phil got paid and all seemed well, but Virgin Records somehow overlooked printing his credit on the record cover. Despite my apologies to him and my protestations that I had supplied the correct info to the company, I don't think he ever quite forgave me.

* * *

A lot of the sessions that came through Laylow emanated from the West London DJ and dance music scene. House music had been big since the early records out of Chicago reached London, and now seemingly everyone was a dance music expert.

I also recorded with Joey Ducane, a Nigerian public schoolboy with a high-born Yoruba background who had been sent to England for his education. Instead, he had dropped out of school to try and be a rock star. I didn't realise it at the time but the much older girlfriend Joey brought along with him was Anita Pallenberg. She had clearly fallen on quite hard times having hooked up with Joey, who, despite his charm and good looks, was an absolute no-hoper as a musician.

But Joey had an interesting friend who had hero-worshipped him when they were at boarding school together and who harboured similar dreams of making it.

I first spotted Joey's mate, Keziah Jones, when he was busking in Portobello Market. He was smacking seven bells out of a tatty nylon guitar and singing his own unusual-sounding songs. Like Joey, Keziah was a Yoruba princeling from Lagos, sent to England to be expensively schooled. He looked like a male supermodel, tall and thin with wide shoulders and high cheekbones. But, unlike Joey, he was clearly talented.

Keziah had something of a Hendrix or Richie Havens-like quality about him. Entirely self-taught, he made up strange chords that shouldn't exist but did because a) he had very long fingers, and b) he refused to acknowledge the rules of harmony or the laws of physics. Keziah had invented a profoundly strong rhythmic, slapping right-hand style that made him sound like no one else. He also had a rich and clear tenor voice that could range up to a Prince-like falsetto. The guy had a unique way with words, too. He was widely read and had a passion for everything from feminist theory to his own Yoruba tradition and culture, by way of the politics of the African diaspora, the civil-rights movement, the subjugation of Nigeria under colonialism, and superhero comics.

Keziah (real name Olufemi Sanyaolu, or just plain Femi) and I got on very well and quickly became friends. His personal style was immediately striking—a sort of 70s hippie charity-shop chic, but effortlessly cool. Lots of crushed and beaten-up hats and dark-coloured velvet, always accessorised with natty, distressed footwear. Keziah had real charisma, too, and women flocked around him. He looked like a rock star in waiting. Pretty soon, a passing A&R man called Colin Barlow found a budget to put him my way. The demos we made were something special, and they attracted interest from WEA (Warner Bros), who called him in for a meeting and offered him a large advance. What they failed to see was that he wasn't going to do what they wanted—that is, become a Lenny Kravitz clone.

A more sympathetic French label called Delabel soon got to hear about Keziah and signed him up. Something in the French psyche loves left-field African artists, and there isn't the same barrier to mainstream acceptance that there is in some other European countries. Maybe it's tied up in France's relationship with its colonial past. The influx of Arab and African artists who came as immigrants after the war seem to find eager audiences in Paris and further afield, looking for new musical horizons.

I found Keziah an ace rhythm section, namely my bass-playing buddy Phil Sewell (or 'Soul', as he would thereafter be named) and drummer Richie Stevens, son of well-known British jazz legend John. These two became Keziah's first and by far his best band, and his gigs that year got really good.

By the time we came to make Keziah's debut album, *Blufunk Is A Fact*, he and his band had a proper flow and chemistry. All I had to do in the studio at first was be there and watch them play. I contributed extra guitar parts, Rhodes electric piano, and Hammond organ, too. The album was produced by me and engineered by my studio partner Rod Beale, but I hadn't been the first choice. Before I took the reins, Keziah had been packed off to Woodstock, New York, to work with Simply Red producer Stewart Levine, which must have seemed like a good idea in theory.

Levine recorded the band in a very austere way—just bass, drums, and Keziah's nylon guitar—and left it at that. The results sounded like unfinished demos, and they weren't well received by the company. They bowed to Keziah's wish to come back to London and record with me.

Rod Beale and I rescued the situation. My more interventionist approach and Rod's flawless recording technique were going to make *Blufunk* an exciting record. From the off, I had the idea to take Keziah shopping for an amplified nylon guitar rather than continue with the crappy old Spanish one he had been using on the corners of Portobello Market. When he played his old guitar with the band, it just sounded like rubber bands popping. Classical gut-string guitar was never supposed to be set against a drumkit and electric bass, and this is part of the reason why Stewart Levine's recordings had not turned out well.

Having settled on an expensive Gretsch Chet Atkins solidbody, which looked great on Keziah, we stuffed a Fender tweed amp in a cupboard under the stairs in the tiny Soho studio and cranked it up. I got him to double-track all the guitar parts. We put them up left and right in the speakers against the bass and drums. Bingo! It sounded amazing. It was still Keziah's nylon-string style, but very powerful and full. I hadn't really heard that done before, and it created a signature sound for him.

Despite the risk of making Keziah uncomfortable, I added keyboards, cellos, and some brass parts to the album, as well as my own (tastefully buried) electric guitars. I took care not to dilute the purity of the band's sound but added just enough to spice up the arrangements. If he ever got too twitchy about what I was up to, Keziah would leave the studio for a few hours and let me get on with it. He didn't much like the idea of me adding other musicians to the record, but when he returned he almost always liked the results. Thus, we developed a real brotherly trust and creative energy, which became the pattern with a lot of the work we did together.

During the sessions, I got asked by Bowie to re-join Tin Machine for a second album and tour, but I felt—for the only time in my life—that I had to turn him down to pursue my path as a producer. I took Keziah along to meet him at a Tin Machine rehearsal that was happening nearby in Soho. We had lunch with the band and hung out for a bit. Bowie was his usual charming self and was very sweet to Keziah, showing much apparent interest in what we were doing.

Blufunk gave Keziah a bona-fide hit in France, and you can still find his song 'Rhythm is Love' on any French jukebox. It remains his biggest hit. I was convinced that my production career would take off after that. I expected offers of work to flow in from France, but the French music industry has a way of ignoring anyone outside of its own, so it didn't happen. I never felt as if I got much respect from Delabel or its mercurial boss, Emmanuel de Buretel, and the strong creative relationship I had with Keziah didn't stop the record company from looking for someone else to produce his second album. The follow-up, *African Spacecraft*, is okay, but although it was made by a 'name' producer—Red Hot Chili Peppers guy Ron St Germain—it didn't do as well as *Blufunk Is A Fact*, or sound as good. Richie and Soul always referred to the second album as 'African Handicrafts'.

* * *

Along with real talent like Keziah, a whole host of no-hopers and ne'er do wells crossed the threshold at Laylow during the time it was in Portobello Road. One such character, who called himself Bugsy, came along and asked for us to work on a girl band he was 'developing'. They had good looks aplenty but zero talent. We had to baby them through the recording process, micro-editing and pitch-correcting every note just to try to achieve any result that wasn't totally embarrassing. All the while, Bugsy would pace up and down, shouting into his brick-sized mobile phone. He was oblivious to the fact that anyone could hear him or that we were actually trying to record music. 'Not naah doll!' he would snarl down the brick at some hapless female. 'Aah'm acthally workin' wiv artisses, don'cha geddit?'

One day, Bugsy got pulled over by the cops, who found a massive bag of coke in his car. That was the last we saw of the guy in the camel coat, the talentless teens, the black Range Rover, and the envelopes of dodgy cash.

It wasn't all music at Laylow. One day, I got a call from a local filmmaker called James Le Bon who said he wanted to book some sessions in the studio on a regular basis for several weeks. This sounded great until I asked him what the project was. He said he was starting a 'telephone-based service' and wanted to record dozens of women reading 'scripted material' that would be available to 'subscribers'. I figured out that it was a sex-chat line and turned it down. I needed the money, but I would have lost the will to live.

For a few years we did amazing work at Laylow, but the times they were a-changing. The relentless march of cheap recording technology meant that there were fewer bread-and-butter sessions to help us pay the rent. After a while, Rod and I found ourselves working harder and harder with people we didn't really want to be working with, just to cover expenses. Meanwhile, our own projects would routinely fall to the back of the queue as we struggled to keep the studio business afloat.

CHAPTER SIXTEEN

STEPHEN PATRICK MORRISSEY

SHORTLY AFTER THE SMITHS BROKE UP, BACK IN 1987, I had a call from someone at Rough Trade asking me to go to their headquarters in Kings Cross to meet Stephen Patrick Morrissey. I loved The Smiths and had bought the amazing 'This Charming Man' as soon as I heard that signature skipping guitar intro, which seemed to be a cross between indie pop, African highlife, and I don't know what, I became an admirer. Great songs like 'How Soon Is Now' and 'Last Night I Dreamt That Somebody Loved Me' had touched the same nerve in me that it had in thousands of other determined miserabilists, and Johnny Marr had influenced my playing in a way that few modern guitarists ever did. To hear guitar parts that were unafraid of harmony was very refreshing, after all the greyness of the post-punk wannabees and pretenders.

The call from Morrissey was another one of those moments I have experienced throughout my life, where I felt a mixture of elation and nervousness. I think they call it impostor syndrome. The feeling that it must be some mistake and that I couldn't possibly be the person they are looking for. Anyway, on the appointed day I was ushered into Morrissey's presence at Rough Trade's offices and offered tea and digestive biscuits. He was indeed a charming man, and we talked about Bowie and Iggy and his love for them. He finally got around to asking me if I would like to be The Smiths' new guitarist. I was not expecting that, and I was taken aback. I asked him if he was really sure about continuing The Smiths. I told him that I thought he and Johnny Marr made a unique partnership and it didn't make sense to me, but he was adamant that The Smiths would go on without Johnny. I said that he reminded me of the Black Knight in *Monty Python & The Holy Grail* with all his limbs cut off, shouting, "'Tis but a scratch!' and 'Come back, it's only a flesh wound!'

What made me so bold as to challenge Morrissey like that? I can only think that my recent experiences with Bowie and Iggy had given me enough confidence to be completely frank with him. He was making a mistake to think anyone could fill Johnny Marr's shoes and carry on calling it The Smiths. I left, feeling confident in myself for refusing his offer.

In 1990, after the Smiths had indeed been left to die a natural death and Morrissey had had some solo success with *Viva Hate*, I got a call from Clive Langer, asking me to play on a second solo album with Morrissey.

Now you're talking, I thought.

The recording sessions were to be at Outside Studios in Berkshire. Hook End Manor is a rambling medieval mansion that had once been home to Pink Floyd's Dave Gilmour. Clive Langer and Alan Winstanley had acquired it and refurbished the studio in a huge outbuilding that was built by Ten Year After guitarist Alvin Lee in the 70s.

For the Morrissey sessions, my old friend Matthew Seligman was on bass and the drummer was Andrew Paresi (aka Andrew McGibbon), who had played on *Viva Hate*. We recorded a very odd song called 'Ouija Board Ouija Board' and a B-side cover of Herman's Hermits' 'East West', for which I did my most convincing chiming, arpeggiated Johnny Marr impersonation. Morrissey seemed happy enough, and we got called back a few weeks later to record some more songs. This time bass duties were taken over by original Smiths member Andy Rourke. He wrote the song 'Yes I Am Blind', which was the first thing we recorded, and it turned out magnificently in my opinion. Over a moody ballad in 6/8 time, the lyric has Morrissey having a pop at people in love, Christians, and meat-eaters—that is, anyone happier than him. I was really proud of the guitar part I came up with. Andy really loved it and told me so. I think it's one of Morrissey's best solo-period songs.

I spent time before the sessions writing some guitar instrumentals and throwing them at Morrissey and Clive Langer. I always thought Smiths songs sounded like finished pieces of guitar music that would have worked whether Morrissey had sung over them or not. That was my technique for writing with Morrissey in mind. He picked three of my songs to write lyrics to and record. The first thing of mine that we recorded didn't make it onto what would become the *Bona Drag* album. Instead, it would resurface years later on a reissue. It was called 'Oh Phoney' and featured the immortal line, 'You can make Hitler seem like a bus conductor.'

Another of my tunes, 'He Knows I'd Love To See Him', did make the cut, and the third one, 'Piccadilly Palare', became a single, featuring a cameo voiceover from Madness frontman Suggs. We also recorded a song called 'November Spawned A Monster', which was about the hopeless search for dignity for a severely disabled child (not exactly standard *Top Of The Pops* fare).

Morrissey was a great admirer of the brilliant album *Miss America* by Canadian singer/songwriter Mary Margaret O'Hara, and she arrived at his request to spend a couple of brooding, awkward days with us. He asked her to contribute a vocal impression of the child in the song (i.e., the 'monster'). We couldn't quite believe what he was asking her to do, but she tried her best to please. Basically, she sounds like she's drunk some bleach after choking on a fishbone.

Sire Records boss Seymour Stein came to visit us at Hook End for a couple of days with a young assistant or 'teenage rebel of the week', as Morrissey archly put it. *Carry On* actress Joan Sims stayed over too. She was somebody who Morrissey, with his love of all things British from the 50s and 60s, was profoundly in awe of. We actually conducted a Ouija board séance in the medieval dining room at Morrissey's suggestion. He had a genuine belief in and fear of ghosts and had convinced himself that the master bedroom in which he was staying contained a disturbed spirit. I thought it was all bollocks, of course, but I kept this trenchant view to myself, as Moz seemed happier if everyone was caught up in his haunted-house narrative.

After a month's break, we reassembled at Hook End Manor for more sessions with Morrissey. The single 'Ouija Board Ouija Board' had been released in the meantime, but the general reception from the music press had been one of mockery. It seemed amazing to me that Morrissey was so easily upset by what some tosser wrote in the *NME*. A bad review could knock him off balance to the point where he would retreat to his room for two days and not speak to anyone. *How could he be so fragile?* I thought.

A constant presence was Morrissey's mysterious mate from Liverpool, Peter Hogg, who has become the subject of some conjecture by Moz watchers over the years. You don't often meet men who are simultaneously camp and physically intimidating. Hogg's job was 'personal assistant' and gofer to Morrissey. It always felt like he had an eye on you, and if you crossed him or upset Morrissey, he gave the impression he would take you around the corner and beat the shit out of you.

Weekdays were spent working on recordings with Clive and Alan, but at weekends everyone cleared off home, leaving Morrissey and Peter Hogg to pursue what (and whom) they wanted. I had thought that working in a residential studio with Morrissey meant we would eat well, given his passionate advocacy for a meat-free world. He hired a cook who worked for Princess Margaret but, even though the meals were vegetarian, they weren't what you might call healthy. An awful lot of pastry and cream was used in the pies and soufflés that were dished up. Morrissey eschewed the fancy menu and instead preferred to subsist largely on toast and tea.

My first of only two experiences with Ecstasy took place during those sessions. Andy Rourke was an old hand at 'getting on one' and was clearly caught up in the whole Madchester vibe of 808 State and The Happy Mondays. Beanie hats, huge baggy trousers, and taking pills at every opportunity were the order of the day. Andrew Paresi and I invited two women we knew from London to come and visit us at Hook End one night. We all took E, danced in the studio to Black Box's 'Ride On Time' (another Morrissey fave), played a lot of pool, and ended up having stoned sex until dawn.

Another memorable outing with Andy Rourke involved going to a bowling alley in Reading while sniffing rather a lot of amyl nitrate from a brown bottle. Amyl produces a manic rush of short-lived hysterical laughter and smells like an explosion in a dry cleaners. Under the influence of this highly toxic substance, we did briefly invent overarm ten-pin bowling, much to the delight of the staff at the alley.

I only met Morrissey once after those sessions, backstage at a show in London a year or two later. He was monosyllabic and cold. I enjoyed working on his music, but his contrary (and frankly nutty) views on all sorts of contentious issues have made him a vainglorious and eccentric figure, and maybe a bit tragicomic. His recent weird racist outbursts and support for various fringe right-wing loonies may have alienated him from many of his early fans. Like many great artists, Morrissey doesn't share the world with the rest of us, he creates his own. And it's not always pretty. Can we separate the art from the man? The jury's out.

Bona Drag was never destined to become a fully realised Morrissey solo album but a part rehash of earlier solo tunes, with the addition of the newer originals we recorded. The album reached number nine in the UK chart.

Clive Langer and Alan Winstanley sold Hook End Manor and the studio to whizz-kid 80s producer Trevor Horn. This was the place where the terrible tragedy occurred that resulted in Trevor's wife Jill Sinclair (head of the ZTT label) being accidentally shot by their son while out hunting. Jill was in a coma for many years until she died. It's impossible to imagine the devastation on that family.*

I only met Mr Horn a couple of times and he seemed such a modest character. I was doing a session of my own songs once at Sarm West Studios in Ladbroke Grove in 1984. Trevor had just bought the studio and renamed it. The former Basing Street studios was where Bob Marley recorded, and where Led Zeppelin made 'Stairway to Heaven'. I was having a coffee outside the control room when a bespectacled, softly spoken guy approached me.

'Would you mind me sticking my head round the door of the control room to listen to the monitors?' he asked. He was so polite and mild-mannered that I assumed he was a maintenance man or technician. But it was Trevor, of course. He'd just installed some new speakers and wanted to check them out.

The chef at Sarm West in the 90s was one Lucky Gordon. A West Indian immigrant, he had been there all through the Basing Street era in the 70s, when Island Records supremo Chris Blackwell had owned the place. Apart from being a fantastic cook, Lucky was also well known for being Christine Keeler's regular boyfriend at the time of the Profumo scandal. He did jail time for beating her and was forever telling me about the 'tell-all' book that he was writing from his perspective (but never did).

Lucky had stowed away on a ship from Jamaica in the 1950s and was a fixture at Sarm for many years after Trevor Horn acquired it. He was always in the kitchen, playing King Pleasure records and surrounded by delicious cooking smells. The studio also became well known as the place where the Band Aid single 'Feed The World' was made.

---

* Trevor sold the house in 2007. Hook End Manor fell into the hands of absentee foreign owners and is now abandoned in a state of severe dereliction, which is a shame for such a magnificent building.

CHAPTER SEVENTEEN

LOST IN
A DREAM

§

EARLY IN '92, ONE OF MY FRIENDS IN PORTOBELLO INTRODUCED ME TO AN OLD SCHOOLMATE OF HIS. David Vatchnadze (or Dave Vatch) was a posh ex-public-schoolboy from a Georgian family. He spoke with a cut-glass, military-grade English accent. At first, I didn't like the condescending and haughty way he spoke, but he was one of those people who, once properly decoded, turn out to have a heart of gold. And he had taken it upon himself to try and resurrect the career of wayward 70s rock star and seminal English troubadour Kevin Ayers.

Dave Vatch had a background in music himself, with a brief career in an electronic band called Spy in the 80s. He had enough knowledge of the business and the sheer balls to impress the A&R department of the French label FNAC, from whom he secured a budget to record and produce Ayers' first album in many years.

Kevin Ayers had started out as part of the late-60s Canterbury scene that spawned Soft Machine, Henry Cow, and Mike Oldfield. His early work was, and is, oft-quoted and highly regarded. But he had made the cardinal career-killing error of running off with Richard Branson's wife whilst being a Virgin recording artiste in the mid-70s. What success he did have funded a move to the sleepy town of Deià in the north of Majorca. He lived in a rundown Roman villa with an artesian well in the living room and almost no furniture.

My first meeting with this louche, laid-back, and dissolute

gentleman was at John Foxx's Garden Studio in Dalston in London's East End. I recorded guitars on a song called 'Feeling This Way', which was a sort of breezy Velvet Underground 'Sweet Jane' affair, with Kevin's laconic and world-weary voice floating over a blend of acoustic guitars and drums and my freewheeling Strat stylings. This became the opening track on the excellent album *Still Life With Guitar*. My performance on the record pleased Kevin, and he asked me to go on a trip to Japan with him as a duo.

I didn't notice it at first, but it soon became clear that Kevin Ayers had a number of quite self-destructive habits that he wasn't going to give up easily. A constant thirst for alcohol and a hunger for drugs had rendered him something of a broken figure. He still had charm and talent, but his best years were very much behind him. He was a perennial wearer of sunglasses indoors, even at night. The blonde mane of hair that had attracted so many women in his life was now wispy with age and hung in matted curtains half covering his face. The lines on his once very handsome visage spoke of too much exposure to the Mediterranean sun. His life in Deià consisted of accepting food parcels from friends and dodging the unwanted attentions of various clingy women and irate husbands. His existence was somewhat chaotic, to say the least, and it was into this twilight-charmed world that I wandered.

A few days before our Japanese tour, I had gone through the worst break-up in my life and, though this book will not dwell on my major relationships, it had left me shattered. It was an utterly life-changing moment. In my passport picture taken at this time, I look absolutely haunted and sunken-cheeked. The two Kevins, Ayers and me, were in a similarly sad condition when we set out to Tokyo for our duo tour. We took the Shinkansen bullet train between gigs in Osaka and Matsuyama, with our patient and charming minder, Hiro, showing us sleight-of-hand magic tricks as we barrelled across the landscape at three hundred miles per hour. I spent the time on days off exploring the Tokyo underground while Ayers was asleep or nursing a giant hangover. This was no mean feat as I had to find someone who spoke a little English to help me decipher the maps and ask my way around. It was like landing alone on a different planet with my exploded life.

The Japanese promoter had organised a signing at Tower Records in the Ginza district, and it fell to me to persuade Kevin to do it. It was only then, that I had to engage fully with his Eeyore-like nature. He had a seriously depressive side, and sometimes his negative energy could suck the air from a room. He gloomily predicted that 'no one will come' and, for that reason, he 'didn't want to do it'. On the morning of the signing, an hour after we were supposed to leave, I was banging on his hotel room door trying to get him out of bed. Eventually, the extremely hung-over artist cracked the door, stuck a dishevelled head out of the room, and blinked at us. His rheumy eyes peeped out through his lank and crispy hair, a bent pair of shades perched low on his nose. He stank of booze. We spooned him into a taxi and had to listen to him complaining all the way there.

When we got outside Tower Records, to our absolute amazement there was a long queue of fans, some with albums going back thirty years and even old guitars he had owned, all waiting to meet the great man. He entered the store and, as was his habit when he could get away with it, insisted on the lights being lowered as it was 'too bright' for him. Tower Records, being a retail space, had many overhead neon strip lights but no dimmers. A small army of willing staff mounted stepladders until enough neon tubes had been removed to render the resultant gloaming satisfactory to Mr Ayers. He peered out from his jet-black shades and finally gave his approval.

Sitting down behind a table piled with CDs, Ayers spent the next two hours happily signing albums and talking to fans, many of whom were very knowledgeable about his records and history. We played a couple of songs to an ecstatic response. It seemed like a very successful affair to me, against all odds. I think it pleased him, too, but it was hard to tell. One thing I learned was that the Japanese really know how to show love to musicians and will do their homework like no other fans on Earth.

* * *

Later that year, my new girlfriend Angelica—now my wife of twenty-eight years—and I spent some time at the house in Deià with Kevin, Dave Vatch, and Kevin's daughter Rachel. Kevin wrote the song 'Lady Rachel' for her. Angelica and I were asked to perform some of her songs at a local festival organised by Robert Graves's son, Tomás, after Ayers pulled out. We urged Kevin to reconsider, but he was adamant that he wouldn't play. At the last minute, he changed his mind and turned up.

Backstage after Angelica and I had played, Kevin appeared wearing his customary black shades and a hoodie. We were glad that he had come and decided to sing after all, but once he caught sight of the crowd, or maybe someone in the crowd, it wasn't to be. *Whoosh*, he was gone. He probably spotted the cuckolded husband of one of his secret lady friends.

When we returned to London, Kevin decided to ask his old bass player, Archibald Leggett, to play some dates in Europe. Archie was a larger-than-life Glaswegian fellow in an almost more decrepit condition than Kevin but an entirely contrasting character in being a loud extrovert. He had played on loads of Kevin's old records as well as being John Cale's bassist, and he'd even done sessions with Jerry Lee Lewis.

Although he was now in his mid-sixties, Archie still wore black leather trousers and giant Elvis shades, and he was continually steaming drunk. There would have been something vaguely heroic about this if he was still a great player, but Archie was a long way past his golden years. He couldn't really remember songs very well, and he just winged his way through stuff. He could be very direct too. He once enquired of Kevin, who was devouring a jar of pickled herrings in the back of the van, 'Whit's that fuckin' genkin' smell, man? Are yous eat'n they kangarews' cunts again?'

I often sat between the two men on long drives. I would have Kevin's lugubrious tones in one ear, whispering to me, 'Please make sure Archie doesn't get drunk tonight and forget the chords to the songs.' Once Kevin had started snoring, Archie would slobber into my other ear, 'Please dinnae let that bastad drink tha'neet, cuz he fergayts the feckin' words.' The pair of them were like a couple of broken-down old tramps, but some of the music we made was rather fabulous, and I don't regret the experience one tiny bit.

I later spent a few days with Kevin after he had sold his place in Deià and moved to a tiny fishing chalet on Menorca. He would get up and go diving to catch a fish for dinner and spend the days drinking and sunbathing. We were supposed to be writing songs, but I could only get him interested in music for about an hour, once he had visited his 'friend' Juan in the local taverna and scored some cocaine.

After a few days of half-hearted attempts to write, Kevin disappeared, and I was left alone, stranded on Menorca with three days to kill. I flew back to London via Barcelona, spending two days wandering around Gaudi's Parc Guell and the Sagrada Familia.

Soon after this, I heard through friends that Kevin had moved into a mobile home with his stepdaughter somewhere in the Pyrenees. He would spend his remaining years there in the tiny village of Montolieu.

Dave Vatch and Kevin Ayers died within six months of each other, both from pancreatic cancer. Kevin was a bit all over the place, to say the least, but he had a beautiful, poetic soul and left many hidden treasures for us all to enjoy. His deeply British distrust of ambitiousness and deep-seated lack of self-confidence would be his downfall. My time with him was a window on a bygone age of innocent, dreamy hedonism that could hurl its noble casualties toward untimely ends. Lonely, often poverty-stricken obscurity awaited those who failed to attain their rightful royal status. John Martyn, Nick Drake, and Kevin Coyne all belong to this tragic pantheon of lost geniuses.

CHAPTER EIGHTEEN

OUTSIDE, NOW

§

ONE DAY IN 1994, MY STUDIO ASSISTANT, KEVIN GREEN, TOOK A CALL AT LAYLOW.

'David Bowie for you, Kev.'

'Hello, Kevin,' Bowie began. 'Listen. Do you remember that tune of yours we worked out with Tin Machine?' We called it 'Now'.'

'Yes.'

'Well, now it's called 'Outside', and it's the title track of the new album I'm making. Would you like to pop round and play a few things on it for us?'

'Us?' I asked.

'Yeah, me and Brian Eno. We're just around the corner at Westside again—you know, where we did *Beginners*.'

'I'll be right over.'

Kevin Green and I hopped into a taxi and pitched up at Westside, which was only five minutes from Laylow. David introduced me to Eno, who encouraged me to stand next to him at the mixing desk with my Telecaster plugged straight into a multi-effect processor called an H3000 Ultra-Harmonizer, which was all the rage at that time. As Tony Visconti reportedly said, 'It fucks with the fabric of time.'

Eno wanted me to add guitar to a song called 'Thru These Architects Eyes', so I just reacted and played the first thing I could come up with. I didn't get a chance to learn the song, and I only got to go through it once. While I improvised, Eno tweaked the controls of the machine, turning my guitar sound inside out and backwards.

Behind me, David smoked a Marlboro. He was sat next to one of the most beautiful women I had ever seen, his new fiancée, Iman. Sabrina Guinness, an old friend of David and Brian's, was also there, and had come with a camera crew made up of local kids she was training to make films. They shot stuff all day and asked Eno if he wanted to be interviewed about being a producer.

'Only if you all sing on one of our tracks,' Eno replied.

The children you hear on 'The Heart's Filthy Lesson' are these same West London street kids who had come with Sabrina to shoot footage of the strange men in the music studio of whom they knew nothing. They ended up gathered around a microphone, being conducted by the godfather of ambient music.

When it was time to fulfil his part of the bargain and do the interview, Eno generously included me as a 'fellow producer', after ascertaining that I was responsible for Keziah Jones's debut album. 'I love that record,' he said. Some years later, Brian and I became friends and developed a bond at his singing group.

The album *1. Outside* was seen as a return to form for Bowie after the patchy output of the late 80s. It's even more highly regarded now than it was then. He had spent weeks at Mountain Studios with some of his favourite musicians, just jamming and experimenting as the songs evolved. That was Reeves Gabrels' artful way of getting David back in touch with his more experimental self.

I wish I had been included in the early part of the making of *Outside*, but as it was, I got to make a small contribution to a few tracks that were almost finished before I ever heard them. 'Thru These Architect's Eyes' is one, the aforementioned 'Heart's Filthy Lesson' another, and of course 'Outside' itself. I am very pleased to have co-written that piece. My original chord sequence is the same one I wrote in 1981 for my own song, 'Love Is Essential'. I wrote that song over a period of intense hours on my feet, pacing with a guitar in my tiny room in Brixton, and it's fitting that it found a good home on such a cool, late-period Bowie record. And as the title track, to boot!

* * *

In 1995, Angelica and her friend Gina Langton were asked to take over a local poetry and open-mic night in a small underground dive in Notting Hill's All Saint's Road. The place had once been the famous Mangrove Club, run by legendary Jamaican community leader Frank Critchlow, and it was still the regular haunt of some of the original Windrush immigrants and their children. Now it was called the Mas Café, and its cosy downstairs bar provided a venue for Angelica and Gina's cabaret evening, the appallingly named Pinkypoos.

The club attracted many colourful locals and soon built a regular crowd. One such Notting Hill turn was the unique oddball singer and comedian Earl Okin. Picture this, a bespectacled, portly man with large glasses takes to the stage dressed like the opera singer Caruso in 1901, complete with spats and a cape, a waistcoat with a watch chain, and a suspicious-looking mat of 'black hair'. He climbs onto a stool in the darkened smoke-filled gloom, plucks a chord on his Spanish guitar, and asks, 'Can you hear the guitar?'

'Yes,' someone says.

'Pity,' he replies gloomily, and then quietly starts to play and sing a João Gilberto bossa nova, expertly and sweetly, in syllable-perfect Portuguese. This eccentric figure, whom the audience had expected to be just another deluded local saddo, is in fact, a world-class jazz artist. He's bloody funny, too. He would also do ironic, Latin-style versions of pop hits, a favourite of ours being 'Teenage Dirtbag'. You seldom get to see such great comic timing and musicality on a Tuesday night in a small urban basement club.

Pinkypoos started to attract a few stray celebrities, both on the mic and propping up the bar. One night, I sidled up to INXS singer

Michael Hutchence, who I'd spotted lurking in the shadows, and asked if he would sing. He said he was terrified of small crowds and politely declined. On another occasion, Kevin Ayers agreed to play at the club. He came, scored some crack, played at the club, slept on our sofa, then slid away in the morning.

Hands down the funniest regular turn we hosted was Geordie Günter The German Porn Star (actually a graphic designer called Dave). His frantic sixty-second act reduced people to helpless tears of mirth. To the accompaniment of either house music or a Bavarian oompah band, Geordie would rush into the room sporting an unfeasibly large handlebar moustache and a leather cap but other than that clad only in a tiny pair of leopard-skin trunks with a hooter stuffed down the front. He would start humping a chair or someone's face, all the while feigning sexual ecstasy, hooting on his pants, and declaiming, in a broad Newcastle/German accent, things like 'Aaaaww, ja, lickenzieschaft' and 'Shlurpetyfumpfennacht!' It's making me laugh just writing about it.

Pinkypoos played host to Sandie Shaw, my old friend writer Will Self, and international outlaw drug smuggler Howard Marks, who gave preview readings from his forthcoming book *Mr Nice*. We threw out film director Alan Parker once for being drunk and Robbie Williams would come down with his mum.

Angelica and Gina built the night into something that pulled in a full house every time and soon took advantage of the offer to relocate from the basement at the Mas Café to the much larger Tabernacle Theatre in nearby Powis Square, the location for the moody, semi-derelict interiors of Nic Roeg's amazing film *Performance*. Pinkypoos now became the Pinkypoos Experience.

The monthly shows continued for another five years and drew a loyal cult following. Pinkypoos generated so many connections between creative musicians, comics, filmmakers, and writers, as well as the twenty-strong crew who worked hard to make it happen, and I ended up producing records for a few of the artists that played there. Notable among these was Anton Walgrave, a great young troubadour from Leuven in Belgium.*

I also got involved with an improvised funk band called Sacred People that played every week somewhere around West London. I still play gigs with this band today, just for fun and beer money. The frontman was (and still is) a remarkably talented singer/songwriter called Blair Mackichan, whose sister is well-known comedy actress Doon. Blair is one of those naturally extroverted performers who can make a party out of a toothpick and a frying pan. He has a knack for controlling a band, making it turn on a sixpence with just a few hand signals or vocal cues. He has a wicked sense of humour, too, with a great line in off-the-cuff gags. He's also a funky piano player and a guy whose prodigious talent has seen him co-write songs with Amy Winehouse, Will Young, and loads of other top popsters.

Sacred People had Soul (from Keziah Jones's band) on bass and a series of amazing funk drummers, including Richie Stevens, Quillon Larratt, and Euston Lyburd. We never rehearsed anything, but it remains one of the best groups of musicians I have ever heard in my life. We used to play regular nights at the Cobden working men's club off Ladbroke Grove. Soul diva Mica Paris would sometimes jump up and sing with us, as would various local rappers and visiting rock stars. There was a reliably great vibe every time on those smoky nights beneath the low ceiling of the Cobden. Despite being a bog-standard old club with cheap drink and sticky carpets, it had a history as an off-grid speakeasy and a crucible of much musical talent going back decades. It was one of London's best-kept secrets.

One night, a young, blonde-haired Australian girl got up and sang with the band. We were absolutely stunned by her talent. She came from nowhere but was definitely going somewhere. Her name was Sia Furler. Blair and I would go on to co-write 'Blow It All Away' for her

* Check out his album *The Hum* on EMI Belgium.

album *Healing Is Difficult*. And Sia would go on to be the highest-paid songwriter on the planet.

* * *

Although a good amount of studio work still flowed in the late 90s, it had to be admitted that, as the professionals started to build their own project studios and everyone else started to make music on home computers, the quality of the clientele in the basement of 307 was slipping. In those years at the coalface in Laylow, under the antique shop on Portobello Road, I worked on so many different styles of music, and in such an intense way, that I found myself losing perspective. I wasn't sure where my will to continue making music was. After eleven good years, Laylow had to move on.

A house move further out into northwest London in 2001 gave me the opportunity to bring the studio (rent-free!) to an outbuilding in my garden and quit the crazy world of Notting Hill, with its neurotic DJs, wannabees, junkies, and hustlers. We had made a mark on the neighbourhood for sure, and I had learned a lot about recording technology and production in the years we were there. But running a recording studio as a business is a full-time commitment, and I was tired of working around the clock for little reward. The early 2000s, for me, were spent almost exclusively in the home studio, recording artists ranging from Will Young to Des O'Connor and producing projects at a far more relaxed pace.

Being a musician has its lifelong challenges. You have chosen to be on a tightrope. For many people, the idea that you can never be sure of where your next dollar is coming from may be just too scary to consider. Yet this has been my reality for almost fifty years.

Money isn't the only worry. There is the constant niggling feeling that you are never going to be good enough. The inner critic who never shuts up is a continuous presence for many of us. The black dog of depression has also visited me many times.

The most difficult thing about walking this precarious path is allowing yourself to let go of the voice of doom that rattles away in your ears. I have learned that negativity takes place in your own head ninety-nine percent of the time. Most people who see and hear your work are almost always extremely supportive and complimentary. They love what you do and will tell you so, even as the self-sabotaging demon in your mind tries to argue with them. You have to cling onto first principles; to remember that what brought you here was precisely the wish to avoid the strictures of a conventional working life. And, just when you've convinced yourself that you'll never work again, that nobody loves you and you're going nowhere, the phone will ring, and you're on the merry-go-round once more.

West London life revolved around the studio and playing in local clubs. My more adventurous exploits of the 80s and early 90s seemed to be receding into the past. I never expected to return to life as a high-profile touring musician, but, like many others, I also hadn't foreseen the steep decline in revenue from sales of recorded music. This would mean that live concerts became the principal source of income for most artists, and that experience like mine would be in high demand again (at least until COVID stopped the world from turning).

* * *

Since lending her majestic voice to The Communards' 1986 hit 'Don't Leave Me This Way', Sarah Jane Morris had carved out a loyal following for her solo work, especially in Italy, where she still gigs regularly. After she came to record with my partner Rod Beale in our studio in Portobello, he recommended me for a role in Sarah's band as a replacement for Dominic Miller, who had to return to Sting's employ. I joined and began a few years of regular early morning Ryanair flights from Stansted airport to Rome or Milan or Naples to enjoy relaxed summer concerts in medieval town squares and castles all over Italy.

My guitar partner was often Neil MacColl, brother of Kirsty

and son of Peggy Seeger and Ewan MacColl. Neil is one of the only guitarists with whom I have really bonded onstage. I love his playing, and we were a powerful team in that band, which also had the excellent Henry Thomas on bass and Shriekback man Martyn Barker on drums.

I continued to travel back and forth to Italy with Sarah Jane for a number of years in the late 90s and early 2000s, and, in the process, I expanded my guitar technique into new areas. I can now confidently carry a gig with just my hands and a nylon guitar, which is something I never imagined I could learn to do. Until now, I'd always been an electric guitarist, but it was a massive boon to my personal songwriting efforts to acquire solid acoustic skills quite late on. Playing with Sarah Jane really helped me to develop my musicianship and rekindle my creativity with the guitar.

Sarah Jane is a remarkable and kind person who looks after her band members with great care and continues to work harder than anyone I know to put a quality line-up in front of happy crowds. Possessed of a keen campaigning nature and never one to hold back, she speaks out in her songs against injustice and political corruption in a way that is brave but can sometimes be less than helpful to her professional advancement. I have seen her pontificate about the shortcomings of pound-shop Mussolini Silvio Berlusconi at swanky jazz clubs where his friends and relatives are likely sitting there in the first row. She has played gigs in Sicily in front of mafia bosses and railed against local sleaze, right to their faces.

Maybe it's the fact that she's speaking to them in English that lets her get away with it. Sometimes she is really funny, too.

On more than one occasion, Neil MacColl and I have nearly wet ourselves at some of Sarah's unintentionally comedic remarks. At a gig in Rome, she introduced the song 'Never Ever Gonna Give You Up' with the words, 'This one's by the late, the great, the oh so very dead Barry White.'

Another classic was when we were doing a retrospective concert, looking back over her entire career. A large ensemble of the many illustrious musicians she had helped over the years was rehearsing onstage at the Bloomsbury Theatre. I got a call from Sarah Jane explaining that she had been in an accident with her ex-husband, David Coulter, which had involved her pinning him between her old Mercedes and a brick wall. When we went onstage half an hour late, she earnestly addressed the audience.

'I apologise for the late start, but this afternoon I reversed my car over my ex-husband in the car park of Sainsbury's.'

Cue gales of laughter. Thankfully, apart from some bruised ribs, David was spared serious injury.

Sarah is a one-woman whirlwind who never fails to spot a promotional opportunity when it presents itself. Once, we were on an airbridge waiting to board a flight when she noticed actors Dame Judi Dench and Charles Dance standing right behind us in the queue. She went into professional overdrive.

'Judi, hi, Sarah Jane here, we used to live near each other years ago and I used to walk your dogs, do you recall?'

The cornered national treasure and her companion looked slightly alarmed at the charismatic red-haired apparition before them. Bassman Henry Thomas whispered to me, 'Oh, God, she's going in.'

Sarah Jane continued blithely on as the embattled thespians shuffled from foot to foot, smiling wanly. Finally, she reached into her bag and proffered her latest CD. Charles Dance shifted his glasses down his nose imperiously and peered at it.

'Oh, we are in luck,' was all he could manage.

Sarah's indefatigable energy still sees her working with everything from classical duos to big bands, string quartets to full orchestras, and of course her regular group. She has also written a musical theatre piece as a tribute to ten of the most iconic female singers, *The Sisterhood*. She is a truly original performer, constantly firing on all cylinders.

CHAPTER NINETEEN

SINÉAD &
THE ELGINS

§

IN 2006, A FRIEND ASKED ME IF I KNEW THAT BRIAN ENO RAN AN INFORMAL SINGING GROUP AT HIS STUDIO IN NOTTING HILL GATE. I didn't, but I had an email address for Eno, so I sent him a message.

'Hi Brian, do you remember when I came and played on *Outside* with you twelve years ago? I am interested in coming to your singing group.'

Brian replied to say that of course he remembered me and I was welcome to come along, but there were a few rules that he asked people to follow. The regular singers in the group were mostly locals, but on occasion there would be special visitors, so you never knew who you might find yourself standing next to. He didn't want these guests to feel hassled during what was supposed to be their downtime, he said, so he discouraged other members from asking them what they were working on or telling them that they admired their work.

'Fine,' I said. 'You know I've worked with a few well-known types. I'll just shut up and sing.'

From then until I left London in 2013, seven years later, I became a regular at Eno's singing group, known informally as The Elgins. Brian's idea was that singing often in a small group of people makes you fitter, smarter, and sexier, quite apart from turning you into a better singer. The Elgins, therefore, only exist to sing together. They exist not for recording or public performance or to exploit in any other way, but purely as an end in itself. It has remained that way until this day, and it seems to be the thing that gives Brian the most joy in his busy, mercurial life. His commitment to the group is tenacious: despite his packed diary, he always makes time for it.

The gatherings are usually held on a Tuesday evening in his studio, starting at around 6pm and running until 9pm or sometimes later. Eno's place is at the end of a mews and a small door leads to a long corridor that widens onto an open-plan workspace. Floor-to-ceiling Dexion shelving houses thousands of records and hundreds of books. Around the walls or on the floor lie various of the installation pieces that he has made for exhibitions and recording projects past and present. I first saw his *Seventy-Seven Million Paintings* generative art software there. He later displayed it at the Venice Biennale, and it was also projected onto the Sydney Opera House. Sometimes, you could see his computer music setup left with work in progress displayed on the screens. Brian would share this with us on occasion and also play records to inspire his singers.

It may come as a surprise, but Eno's very favourite music is old Gospel stuff like The Golden Gate Quartet or The Mills Brothers from the 1930s. He once told me that, while living in Brooklyn, he had become 'the only atheist member of a church choir'. Much of the singing we did was from an ever-changing list of classic pop songs, mostly gospel and country tunes. Nothing much from after about 1973 really cuts the mustard for him. He would choose simple songs that had a I–IV–V chord structure—and there are hundreds. We would do Bill Withers' 'Lean On Me' or traditional folk tunes such as 'Will The Circle Be Unbroken?'; Leadbelly's 'Tell Him I'm Gone' or Gillian Welch's 'Orphan Girl'. These are the kind of songs that can be picked up by group regulars or one-time-only visitors alike.

My fellow Elgin members during my time at Brian's were a diverse bunch, from peers of the realm to heads of think tanks, politicians, writers, artists, actors, models, filmmakers, and musicians: the sculptor

Emily Young (Syd Barrett's girlfriend and inspiration for the Pink Floyd song 'See Emily Play'), *Viz* publisher John Brown, Jason Donovan, Chris Martin's mum Ali, Coldplay drummer Will Champion and his wife Marianna, Annie Lennox, Paul Simon. David Byrne, Sabrina Guinness, and Jerry Hall all came and went, as did producer and 60s tastemaker Joe Boyd and his wife Davia. I wouldn't want to give the impression that the group is made up of professional singers, though. The majority of regulars qualify more as 'gifted amateurs'.

Eno's rule about 'not gossiping or asking impertinent questions' often breaks down completely after the first few glasses of expensive vino disappear and loosen up the atmosphere. In fact, I have seldom laughed as much as at these very flirtatious and fun evenings. One time, a discussion about pop lyrics started up with Brian saying he didn't much care about lyrics as long as they sounded good phonetically and went with the music, but others disagreed strongly, saying how important they thought they were to songs. (Ali Martin stayed out of that one.)

We were usually between six and twenty people, depending on who bothered to turn up so early on a weekday evening. Smaller groups are usually better when a core of half a dozen really good singers can carry the rest. Sometimes it would be just those six and a couple of others, and, on those nights, the sound we made could be sublime. At other times, there were too many part-timers and hangers-on who didn't contribute except to chatter too much or over-sing. On these nights, Eno could get quite shirty and let his frustration show. Every so often, when the group got too big or unruly, he would send around a message asking them not to come again. These purges would occur about every six months, in an attempt to preserve the quality of the singing and deter the more persistent liggers.

On my birthday, which fell on a Tuesday in 2011, I went along with Angelica. As we came down the corridor, the company all sang 'Happy Birthday'. I looked around and noticed that Paul McCartney was enthusiastically joining in. His son James was sat in glum silence at the round table in the centre of the room. Everyone else was standing.

'Have you met Paul, Kevin?' Brian asked.

'Well, yes, actually, we worked together once, didn't we, back in '88?' I said as I shook his hand.

The room fell silent and all turned toward us.

'Did we?' he deadpanned. 'What happened?'

'You sacked me,' I said.

Brian's jaw dropped. Tumbleweeds. McCartney simply turned to Angelica sticking out his hand and saying, 'Hi, I'm Paul.'

Thankfully, the awkwardness didn't last long, as McCartney soon departed. After he left, Eno said to me, 'What did you say that for!?' My sense of unfinished business with the ex-Beatle remains just that.

It was permissible to take guests to Elgins evenings but very important that they properly contribute to the sound. I introduced a couple of good regulars to the group, namely my talented daughter Olivia and my friend Marc Fox, the ex-Haircut 100 percussionist, A&R man, and very useful baritone. The guests that were always welcome—apart from good singers—were young women. The more attractive they were, the more welcome. As the urbane and splendid John Brown once observed to me, tongue firmly in his cheek, 'Let's face it, Kevin, this group is basically us five blokes and fifteen women who want to fuck Brian.'

* * *

At one of Eno's singing nights in 2007, I caught up with Sinéad O'Connor's long-time bassist and friend, Clare Kenny. I had known Clare for ages as she had once been Matthew Seligman's girlfriend. She asked me if I would like to play with Sinéad's band on a tour of the States. This was an unexpected but very welcome invitation after such a long break from high-level live work.

Much has been said about Sinéad since her very public Popeportrait-ripping gesture on American television in 1992—an act so shocking to the watching TV audience that it virtually killed her popularity in the US overnight. She was making a sincere protest born of righteous indignation at the behaviour of the Catholic Church and its denial and cover-up of widespread child sexual abuse by priests, but it was mostly seen at the time as the act of a mad person and precipitated a dismissive and hostile attitude toward her.

The furore was probably a mixture of old-fashioned misogyny and a knee-jerk reaction to her mental health problems, as much as it was a rejection of her protest, but various revelations over the years have vindicated her stance on the culpability of the Catholic Church in systemic child abuse. Eventually, instead of being dismissed, Sinéad became more likely to show up as a commentator on serious news shows or be touted as an authority on the Vatican Council and the scandals surrounding the church. She was proved right all along about the priests, the paedophilia, and the cover-ups. A messed-up Irish pop singer, trying to expose a deep evil that had been a shameful secret for decades, had sabotaged her own career with an angry cry for justice. In truth, she blazed a lonely trail for many outspoken female artists of today.

Playing for Sinéad seemed like a more than interesting gig, so I said yes. I knew that John Reynolds would be along to lead the band, and that was a plus for me too, as I liked John. John was the father of Sinéad's first-born son, as well as being her ex-husband, producer, and drummer, and was one of the very few people she trusted completely. Her childhood had involved terrible neglect and suffering, and she had obviously been damaged by those experiences.

Though I'd never met her properly, I was aware of Sinéad's reputation for instability, and John warned me about what may be in store. 'Expect the unexpected. She might not show up, she might do a week and then fire the whole band. It might happen, it might not.' I tried to keep an open mind when we started rehearsals. When she did arrive on the last day, Sinéad was polite but emotionally distant, to the point of almost not being there. She was smoking a fat spliff and wearing a hoodie that covered her face. She went through the songs in a whisper, and I had no idea if she even registered my presence as a new member of her band.

Sinéad's album *Theology* had just been released, and we played a few songs from it in the set. I struggled at first with the restrictions she imposed on the music. The songs were made up of two or possibly three chords, alternating every two bars at about sixty beats per minute, with absolutely no other harmony other than root, fifth, and third. Grade-one piano triads plodding along for six minutes at a time, at a funereal tempo, under semi-whispered lyrics from the Old Testament. Not a huge amount of fun for the band. After being in Sarah Jane Morris's lively combo, where improvisation and harmonic colouring were positively encouraged, it felt like playing with gloves on after someone had hit you over the head with a baseball bat.

It took a few shows for me to understand why the tonal and rhythmic palate was so tightly restricted. When Sinéad was on form, she could weave a spell over an audience and perform with a rare honesty and emotional commitment that put other singers to shame. The band was there merely to provide as blank and opaque a canvas as possible on which she could paint. Our job was, in effect, to be largely unnoticeable. Much of the music was rooted in Irish tradition and her religious beliefs, so a certain reverential atmosphere is her comfort zone.

The first gig we played was at Dublin Castle—no, not the well-known rock pub in Camden Town but the actual castle in Dublin, Ireland. Sinéad's voice had changed over the years (her speaking voice is surprisingly deep), partly due to smoking and maybe her age, so many of the older songs had to be played in dropped keys and some with a capo on the guitar.* I had an array of guitars tuned in various

---

* A capo is a device that clamps on to the fretboard and changes the default tuning of the guitar, making it easy to play 'first position' chords in any key.

ways for different songs, so it was quite a complex task for me and my tech to navigate the changes during a set. Our first gig would have gone brilliantly if only I hadn't started the opening song with my strident, unaccompanied chords ringing out over the crowd in the wrong bloody key! Sinéad began singing over my guitar and the band came crashing in on verse two in the correct key—a semitone lower—making the whole thing sound, for a split second, like a sonic train wreck. I corrected the key and Sinéad recovered, but it wasn't the most auspicious start.

Being around Sinéad and John Reynolds can be a real laugh, as both of them suffer from a kind of Tourette's syndrome, or pretend they do. There is a refusal to obey social convention that in John's case, at least, belies a warm and generous character, and makes him impossible not to love.

Once, on a transatlantic flight, Sinéad stood up, several rows in front of me, and loudly asked, 'Kevin, have ye got any o' that there deodorant? Me minge is kicking awf like a box of owld fish.' I mean, what do you say to that? I was so embarrassed I wanted the ground to swallow *her* up.

On the London date at the Royal Festival Hall, my mother came to see us. After a particularly slow and spiritual number, Sinéad addressed the audience.

I have been to see my doctor and he told me in no uncertain terms that I should stop masturbating.

    'Why?' I asked him.

    'Because I'm trying to examine you,' he said.

Another time, John asked Sinéad, 'Hey, Ted, what's the collective noun for cocksucker?' She replied, without missing a beat, 'A Westlife, Ted. A Westlife of cocksuckers.'

In the late noughties, I was a frequent visitor to John Reynolds' studio in his giant attic in North London, and I played on many records by Irish artists in that room: Sinéad, Damien Dempsey, Maire Brennan, Andrea Corr, Shane MacGowan, Paul Brady, and others.

At one session, John got an email and read it out.

'Oh look, it's from Mary,' he said.

'Dear friends,' it began, 'I have booked seats for the English National Opera tonight to see *La bohème*. I can't go, but if any of you darlings would like a pair of free tickets please don't hesitate to get in touch.'

'How lovely,' said John, before replying to the email with the words, 'Dear Mary, stick them up your arse. John.'*

At the start of Sinéad's tour, we had a gig in Poland to play for seventy thousand people on the campus of Poznan University. Sinéad had never gigged in Poland before, so it was a pretty big deal. Her tour manager, larger-than-life Dubliner Paddy McPoland, had a trick up his sleeve to get us through airports.† First, he would discreetly inform the fan club what airport Sinéad was flying from and when. Then, when fans turned up in some numbers, he could say to security staff, 'Hey look at all this hassle we're getting from people.' And then— bingo!—we were more often than not ushered smoothly past every queue straight onto the tarmac.

On our arrival in Poland, we experienced no passport control or immigration checks. We came off a commercial flight and were whisked off in black vans, first to the local TV station and then to a restaurant in the middle of the town. A reception dinner, hosted by the mayor and his wife and other dignitaries, had been laid on in an upstairs room of a restaurant overlooking the town square. A huge image of Sinéad's

---

* Clearly, they've passed on their penchant for withering sarcasm to the next generation, too. John told me that if Sinéad ever had occasion to ask their son Jake for help with something around the house, he would reply drily, 'Why don't you get Prince to do it for you?' Her biggest hit, 'Nothing Compares 2 U', is, of course, a Prince song.

† I shit you not. We went to Poland … with Paddy McPoland.

face, thirty feet high, had been mounted on a building opposite and was clearly visible through the windows. She hated that. It dominated the town centre, but she was just embarrassed by it.

The tables were arranged in a big rectangle so that twenty people could be seated facing in toward each other. We were served extremely strong aperitifs called Mad Dogs, which slipped down a treat. It was after we had downed six or seven of these fruit-based but highly alcoholic beverages that the dinner, somewhat unsurprisingly, degenerated into pissed-up mayhem. The guitar tech Warren Kennedy ended up with his tongue down the mayoress's throat in between lugs on a giant Cuban cigar, while the mayor danced on the table, trousers round his ankles, singing Polish folk songs at the top of his lungs. Sinéad herself had long since made a run for it, but not before meticulously removing all the heads from a plate of whitebait with her knife and fork and leaving them in a neat pile.

Sinéad's gigs could range from transcendent to downright boring, entirely depending on her mental state. On the day of the gig in Poznan, her mood was dark. She locked the dressing room door and smoked hash for hours. The gig itself was a rolling disaster, as she was stoned, depressed, and attired in a shapeless tracksuit. She shuffled around the stage looking at the floor, barely singing above a whisper. Luckily, the audience remained docile, but if I were them I would have asked for my money back. As cellist Caroline Dale bleakly observed after the show, 'Well, nobody died!'

The aforementioned 'snogger of the mayoress', Warren Kennedy, had started his working life as a roadie for Dr Feelgood and is a Canvey Island boy through and through. He had played guitar in Eddie & The Hot Rods, too, and he was a real pleasure to work with. He is another of those solid blokes whose seemingly brusque and even rude manner belies a kind heart. He's very funny, too. One of the tunes in Sinéad's set was a reggae song called 'Lamb's Book Of Life', in which I played kind of backward wah-wah chops and dub-inspired echo effects. I would often forget to turn off the wah-wah pedal. This meant that when I played a big creamy power chord on the next song, 'Thief Of Your Heart', it would be harsh, brittle, and nasty. When the Sinéad tour played its first German date in Munich, I asked Warren to put a reminder near my pedalboard about turning it off and, true to form, I got onstage and looked down to see a sign that read, 'DON'T MENTION THE WAH!'

We also played a gig in Moscow. It was my first visit there, and I had always been curious about Russia. Some of the rumours about it were well-founded. On our way from the airport into the city, we were 'randomly' pulled over by uniformed police of some sort. A curt exchange with the driver resulted in a fat wad of cash changing hands, and, with that, we were allowed on our way again. The gig was in a medium-sized theatre in front of a rabid crowd, and it was great. We stayed in the Ambassador Hotel on the Moskva and spent a fun evening observing the comings and goings of various wrinkly oligarchs and their beautiful young whores, while Caroline Dale poured vodka from her bag under the table into our glasses of tonic water.

Moscow felt a bit edgy, though, and it was one of the only places I have ever been where I didn't feel entirely safe walking around. Crossing a main intersection via underground tunnels, I had the urge to look back over my shoulder in case someone was following me. I also noticed quite quickly that most Russians don't smile. It's such a contrast to the grinning Americans. Waiters in restaurants, hotel staff, people in the street—they all just look at you with a deadpan stare. Perhaps there's never been much to smile about in Russia, I don't know.

On the way out of the country, we were subjected to the 'official hijack' once again. Paddy McPoland was summoned to a small office in the airport. He sat opposite a uniformed boss man in an interrogation room and literally had to keep shovelling cash under the table until the guy was happy to release our equipment and allow us to board the aircraft.

By the end of the American leg of the tour, Sinéad's mood had lifted. She had taken to wearing a man's suit and Dr Marten boots, which looked really good on her. She sang wonderfully, too and, on occasion, she could take the roof off a place. We finished with some dates in Australia and parted on good terms.

I later played on Sinéad's 2012 album *How About I Be Me (And You Be You)?*, which she had wanted to call *How About I Be Me And You Fuck Off*. Since then, there have been other tours with different line-ups that have hit the buffers. There are stories of all kinds of problems, from financial and sexual shenanigans to the summary sacking of managers and bands. I think I got off lightly as a sideman for one of the most volatile artists I have ever played for.

CHAPTER TWENTY

TV HELL

EARLY IN 2008, MY WIFE NOTICED THAT AN INORDINATE NUMBER OF TV COMMERCIALS WERE ACCOMPANIED BY SIMPLISTIC UKULELE TUNES AND URGED ME TO JUMP ON THE BANDWAGON. 'It's all twats strumming ukuleles and whistling Kev. You could be one,' she suggested helpfully.

Returning to my garden studio from a music shop in North London on a rainy day in February, I thought I'd give it a go. I went out and bought a soprano ukulele for the princely sum of £17. I pumped it vigorously into a microphone for a couple of hours and created my biggest-selling original piece of music to date: a laughably simple twelve-bar ditty with a few handclaps that found its way around the world on commercials for everything from toilet hygiene products to insurance.

After this initial stroke of good luck, blind optimism and over-confidence drew me inexorably into working on numerous TV ads, and I found myself dragged into the seedy and frightening world of 'production music'. A friend had introduced me to an agent in Soho who specialised in library and bespoke commercial soundtracks, and I began to be asked to pitch for jobs. This slowly led me to the understanding of a world so steeped in bullshit and doublethink that it beggars belief. A tawdry realm of shifting, insecure employment and fleeting glimpses of high reward for supposedly little effort. A world where the strings are pulled by complete cretins while those who work hard at the creative coalface are at the bottom of a steaming dunghill of vacuity, broken dreams, and empty promises.

The narrative works something like this: on Friday at about 4pm, the breathless call comes.

'Kev we need you to work on a piece for a multi-million-dollar TV ad that will run for at least a year and involves recreating an orchestra doing *Peer Gynt* crossed with a band that sounds like Slayer—but make it light and fun, yeah?'

'Er, okay. When do you want it and how much?'

'Well, they need to hear something urgently by 8pm tonight, and the director loves that thing you did last year, and he's a really big name . . . so it could lead on to loads of great work but . . . there's no budget for the music.'

'What? None?'

'Not for the pitch, no . . . but you're the only one doing it, so it's virtually in the bag.'

'So what you're saying is, the ad will cost millions, but they've no money for this at all?'

'Sorry, no.'

'Who's the client?'

Agent names one of the biggest insurance companies on the planet.

It can't be overstated how utterly fucked-up this is, of course.

The bank (the Client) will have spent three million pounds on an ad agency (the Creatives) like Saatchi & Saatchi or Bartle Bogle Hegarty to create a lush visual masterpiece with helicopter drone shots of stunning locations and hordes of extras. The music is, too often, an afterthought. Advertising agencies have a high turnover of young professionals trying desperately to make their mark, and all of them will be vying to get their two cents in during the process, whether they know what they're talking about or not.

The hierarchy is thus. The Composer never gets to speak with anyone except the Agent, who never gets to speak to anyone except the Creatives, who then pass up the work to the Client (who has the money) for final approval. When there are at least two layers of people between the Composer and the Client, proper communication about such a subjective thing as music is pretty difficult. The chances of making anything remotely good are vanishingly small in such a world of Chinese whispers.

So, I cobble my pitch together at breakneck speed and send the audio file to the Agent, who passes it on as far as the Creatives, then calls back on Saturday morning.

'It's really good, Kev, but could you just redo the ending and tweak that guitar sound?'

I redo the ending and tweak the guitar sound.

I hear nothing for two days.

On Tuesday morning, I get another call from the Agent.

'Kev, the Creatives love it! They just need you to redo the ending again and do a version without the Tibetan nose flute.'

'Still no money?'

'Er, no.'

I keep going and submit the suggested changed version, which then gets approval from the Creatives. Then, this time, it goes over to the Client for approval.

Thursday.

'Kev, The Client loves it too! But they just need a rethink on the whole idea and want you to resubmit something based on the score from *Psycho* but with shades of mid-period Elton John. Okay?'

'Still for no money?'

'Well, I'll ask. I think I can get them to part with a hundred and fifty quid.'

I plough on for a third day and submit something that is now a million miles away from what we started with. I hear nothing for another two days.

Eventually, I call the Agent.

'Er, what happened to that job?'

'Oh, they ended up licensing an old Duran Duran track.'

'How much did that cost them?'

'Five hundred grand, but they liked your thing, and I've had something else come in if you're interested. It'll be good for your profile.'

'Tell you what, I'm busy nailing my scrotum to the skirting board while having root canal treatment without anaesthetic, but I'll give it some thought.'

* * *

Another time I was asked to make a copy of the music for a successful ad by a major high-street bank to launch a follow-up campaign that would cash in on the familiarity of the first one involving a disco-dancing plastic flower. (I know, shit, right?) The idea was to make a piece close enough to remind everyone of the previous ad but not close enough to infringe the copyright of the previous composer.

When you do this kind of 'soundalike' work, there is a process involving a 'musicologist' who is hired to judge exactly how to copy something, technically, without incurring a lawsuit for plagiarism. Musicologists are required as expert witnesses in court battles involving huge royalty claims when the similarity between certain songs is a matter of dispute. Their word is often the deciding factor in such cases.

In commercial work, you start by copying the reference piece exactly. Then the musicologist will tell you which notes or elements to change until they are satisfied that you're close enough to (but far enough away from) the original. You must fulfil the brief but not be accused of stealing. So far, so boring. I did the job, went through the changes, it went to TV, and everybody was happy.

A few months later, the Agent called me again and said, 'Kev, we are doing a new campaign for a different bank where you copy the track but make it legal, just like we did before. The same musicologist is on board, but we have to be in Cannes for Midem,* so I'll leave you in the capable hands of the Creatives at the ad agency, okay?'

'Okay.'

But they weren't capable hands at all, and it wasn't okay.

I started the job as usual by copying the 'reference track'. I sent it to the ad agency, did a few tweaks for the musicologist, then never heard anything back for weeks. I got paid and forgot all about it until I got a panicky call from the Agent saying they were being served with a writ for tens of thousands of pounds in damages by the previous agency, whose campaign we had apparently ripped off the music from. Oops!

The dickhead Creative at the ad agency had put my first draft out for broadcast, not the one approved by the musicologist. The ad was pulled, money was returned, and the requisite amount of shit pie had to be eaten by my agent. This sort of cock-up is so completely typical of the production music industry. At least now I can see the funny side.

The one good thing about doing ad pitches is that you can use the rejected work as library music, so it's never entirely wasted. You just repackage it and do a few edits at different lengths, and it can sit on a digital library for sale as generic background stuff forever. Quite often, I will have a failed pitch for a commercial go on to have a new life when it's plucked from a library, months or even years later, for another use. Everything you make might eventually create some income.

People who compose library stuff like this every day, all year round, can do very well indeed out of it. I could probably sit in my studio and just churn out library music forever but, frankly, that would drive me up the friggin' wall. I need to get out and play with people—to make music for other reasons than just to get paid.

* A big annual music industry event.

CHAPTER TWENTY-ONE

THE TIME
CAPSULE

I HADN'T SEEN OR HEARD FROM THOMAS DOLBY IN TWENTY YEARS WHEN HE ASKED ME TO JOIN HIM AT PETER GABRIEL'S REAL WORLD STUDIO IN THE VILLAGE OF BOX IN DEEPEST WILTSHIRE. It was great to play with him again on some original new material. His 2011 album *A Map Of The Floating City* was the usual perfectly crafted vehicle for his songs. Everything sounded as shiny and sophisticated as Dolby ever did. The song 'Simone', about Thomas and Kathleen's trans son Harper's journey through adolescence, is a Dolby masterpiece.

After the record was finished, we assembled to make a video for the country hoedown pastiche 'Toadlickers'. The shoot took place in a hay barn on the farm that hosts the western-inspired Maverick Festival in Norfolk. After we finished filming, we did a quick set for the festivalgoers, still wearing our cowboy clobber and accompanied by the burlesque dancers from the video. Pedal-steel guitar genius B.J. Cole sat in with us.

Thomas wanted to do something more ambitious to accompany his new album. He designed the *Floating City* internet game, which caught the attention of several thousand people around the world who formed what amounted to an online cult just to play it. Dolby's time as an early mover and shaker in Silicon Valley had given him the wherewithal to conceive and build stuff like this.

For the accompanying Time Capsule Tour, Thomas commissioned

and customised a chrome, two-wheeled, teardrop-shaped trailer and kitted it out in steam-punk style with old pipework, gauges from submarines, and bits of military aircraft. We would tow it around America behind the tour bus and park it outside every venue we played. It was equipped as a video booth, where people could sit inside and record a message for future generations. The resulting content would be posted online and then, at the end of the tour, the physical media containing the messages would be buried in the Arizona desert.

We rehearsed for about a hundred hours for that tour. Thomas had recruited drummer Mat Hector, and we would go out just as a trio: Dolby, Mat, and me. Musically, the shows relied on Thomas's laptop as the central brain. He would programme bass sequences and other stuff 'live' at the beginning of the songs, and then we would play on top. The audience could see him inputting the data during the intros, demonstrating that it wasn't just a playback. It was quite a feat of dexterity, controlling all that hardware, playing keyboards, and singing too!

Mat had click tracks in his ears, so he was hooked into the computer's timing. He played electronic rubber drum-pads as part of his kit, with all kinds of triggers and samples going on. It was very hi-tech and reliant on everything working properly—which, for the most part, it did. I had the easier job of playing the guitar and singing background vocals.

We started our North American journey at the festival in Austin, Texas, known as SXSW (South By South-West). For one week each year, a million people are out on the streets of Austin, and every bar and restaurant is host to live music. After that, we managed to crisscross America in twenty days, playing mid-sized theatres and clubs from New York to Los Angeles, with a couple of dips into Canada for good measure.

The venues were places like the Iron Horse in Northampton, the Birchmere in Alexandria, the Bluebird in Denver, and Tipitina's in New Orleans. These are the most atmospheric of small American venues, with loads of cool history.

We also stopped off at various local FM stations to do live sessions and met great DJs like Jake Rudh, host of *The Current* in Minneapolis. These guys are still the beating heart of American radio. After the long haul across the featureless plains of Idaho and Montana, where we didn't see a car or a building for half an hour at a stretch, we stopped in a little town called Glendive. The place boasts a creationist dinosaur museum, which is something you don't see every day, with exhibits that juxtapose dinosaur skeletons with figures of early humans carrying spears.

The ability of museum founder Otis Kline to regard *The Flintstones* as historically accurate seems like quite a harmless delusion compared to some of the other widely held beliefs that have since taken root in modern America. The heady mixture of fundamentalist religion and ultra-nationalism is the sort of weirdness that burst from the boondocks of Montana and stormed the Capitol in Washington DC on January 6, 2021, in an inchoate bid for glory. God, guns, Q-Anon, Trump, and fucking dinosaurs. Yeeehaw! I blame the diet.

Dolby's tour gave me renewed confidence and an impetus to keep improving my skills in the face of a very favourable reaction from audiences across the USA. One reviewer from San Diego said, 'Armstrong really nails that Bakersfield sound.' I still don't know what that is, but I bet it's good.

* * *

In 2013, my family and I relocated to the south coast of England, near Hastings. I built a new studio, and for a while I continued to work on TV projects and even started to think about releasing some original recordings of my own again. Pretty soon, I was diverted from this course when Keziah Jones asked me to join his band for some European dates.

This was a challenge for a number of reasons. Keziah had never had another guitarist in the band. His own guitar style had evolved into a sort of slapping technique, still on nylon strings. I would have to be quite careful not to overplay and drown that out. He wanted me to play some keyboards, too, which meant brushing up my very basic piano and organ skills. I hadn't handled guitar and keyboard duties in a band since the mid-80s with Thomas Dolby.

Keziah's band was great, though, with Amy Winehouse's drummer Nathan Allen, funky bass genius Otto Williams, and a horn section made up of a rotating line-up of some of the very finest British jazzers: Jason Yarde, Byron Wallen, Denys Baptiste, Harry Brown, Shabaka Hutchings, and Julian Siegel. On occasions when Julian wasn't there, I was left as the only white guy in the band. Horn sections always have the best sense of humour and there was much laughter. They also never stop making a bloody noise, farting sounds as they warm up their mouthpieces and practising endless scales in dressing rooms.

Touring with Keziah after all these years was great, apart from an encounter with one of the very few genuine idiots I have had the displeasure to work alongside in many years. This guy had been hired to do two jobs by cash-strapped management trying to save money and was supposed to be both tour manager and guitar tech. I thought it was somewhat optimistic to expect one person to fill both roles, and it soon became apparent this bloke couldn't have covered even one of them adequately. For the sake of discretion, let's call him Paul Dimsey.

From the very first meeting with Paul, it all went tits-up very quickly. Otto and I were driven on a two-hour detour around rural France, and when we finally got to the right place, Dimsey was casually leaning on the bonnet of a car, rolling a spliff.

'Oh, hi guys,' he giggled. 'Sorry about the detour, my fault entirely. Anyway, I've got this great hash we can smoke, but we have to watch out for the police as we go yeah?'

Dimsey was gradually relieved of his duties, bit by bit, until the reality slowly permeated even his thick skull that he was being frozen out. He left the tour and wrote an embarrassingly long, self-pitying tract complaining about his treatment, which he sent to everyone, including the bus driver.

For every one of those rare times when one meets someone so remarkably disagreeable and stupid as that guy, there are a thousand times I'm truly grateful for crew members. They're usually skilled, kind, helpful, and generous. They look after you, fix your shit, and, more often than not, they're excellent company. I would trust a roadie in an emergency, or a fight, anytime. Without them, your favourite band wouldn't be able to tie their own shoelaces.

CHAPTER TWENTY-TWO

SKULL RING

§

SELDOM DO YOU GET A SECOND CHANCE IN LIFE TO DO SOMETHING AS COOL AS PLAYING GUITAR FOR IGGY POP. Especially when you've spent half a lifetime beating yourself up about how you could have done it better the first time around, if only you'd done X, Y, or Z.

Sitting in bed one afternoon in late November 2014, suffering from mild flu-like symptoms, I was trawling through some old YouTube clips, like one of those old Hollywood actresses who shut themselves in a darkened room, drink gin, and watch their old movies, dreaming of their glory days. I'm in touch with my inner Norma Desmond as much as the next man.

Browsing for 'Iggy live 86', I came across a newly posted, high-quality version of a gig we played at the Ritz theatre in New York, featuring a close-up of my left boot stamping out a rhythm and Iggy crawling around the stage like a caged animal, psyching out the crowd. Taken from the first leg of the hundred or so gigs we did after the *Blah Blah Blah* LP was released, it was the performance from which cuts were thrown together for the 'Real Wild Child' video. Gavin Harrison on drums, my old school buddy Philip Butcher on bass, Seamus Beaghen on keys and second guitar—there we were, twenty-eight years ago, in living black-and-white.

I remembered the buzz of that gig, the crowd, David Bowie and Carlos Alomar showing up in the dressing room afterwards. I barely recognized myself in those clips though. A leaner, meaner me, so full of himself and so snottily over-confident. There's a telling moment during the gig, where I attempt to walk on the crowd, as Iggy used to do. I had tried this semi-successfully before at other shows, though I'm incredulous as to why.

At the Ritz, I had been suffering a stomach upset all day and was feeling quite unwell. It didn't stop me from attempting the audience walk anyway, but I missed my footing and fell. My old mate Jos Grain had to haul me out of the pit and save me from drowning in the throng. What a chump I was, trying to upstage the star turn.*

At that precise second, a Facebook message popped up on my screen from Henry McGroggan, Iggy's manager. It just said, 'Kevin, are you around for a call?' Henry had been the tour manager on *Blah Blah Blah*. He stuck around long enough and proved himself so capable that he became Iggy's permanent business manager. I had spoken to him only once since then, but some months ago, in 2013, I'd met a guy called Tom Wilcox who asked me to take part in an Iggy tribute event at the ICA in London. I was to play with Erdal Kizilcay and Andy Anderson (both ex-Iggy musicians from the *Blah Blah Blah* period), as well as Steve Norman from Spandau Ballet.

The show had marked the twenty-fifth anniversary of the release of *Blah Blah Blah*, and, during the run-up to the gig, I'd sought Henry out and asked him if Iggy might give his blessing to the event, or maybe even show up. Henry said there would be a message of support from Iggy, and I ended the call by thanking him and saying, half-jokingly, 'Well, if he ever needs a guitarist again . . .'

It was a throwaway comment to which I never gave another thought. Until now.

All Henry would tell me was that there were two gigs in London

---

* Check out the end of the 'Real Wild Child' video and you can briefly see my predicament exactly as it happened. If only I had that time again, I wouldn't be such a wanker.

planned for June 2014, that were going to be big, and would I care to provide a band for Iggy Pop again?

'Yes, I bloody would.'

A week later, mid-morning, the phone rang. That familiar, slightly self-effacing but sonorous baritone chuckle.

'Hi, Kevin . . . this is Jim.' It was Iggy on the line from Miami.

I knew the call was coming, but I was caught quite unawares by how easily our conversation flowed after so many years. We talked a little about where we'd ended up living, some old friends in common. Water under bridges, our children becoming young adults. I offered sympathy for the loss of the Stooges brothers, Ron and Scott Asheton. I knew that they too had left Iggy's orbit and re-entered decades later as long-lost compadres, probably just as unexpectedly.

When we started to talk about music, I was tentative at first about offering an opinion. I'd been watching clips of the late-period Stooges and other, later Iggy bands, and I thought I had a pretty good idea about what was needed from a new line-up. The savage beauty I can hear in the early Stooges records is partly due to the passage of time and the place they have found in the wider story of popular music. The way we hear music has a great deal to do with when it was made and what has happened since to contextualise it. Our appreciation can evolve over time. Some music never ages, some of it dates weirdly and some music just keeps getting better years after you first hear it.

I have grown as a musician in forty-odd years, and my ears are more open than they were, so I make very different judgements. I loved the music from first hearing The Stooges, but there are things I hear now that I didn't understand back then. Some of the later bands that played with Iggy were, it seemed to me, lacking in sensitivity when it came to Iggy's oeuvre and instead settled for a kind of 'cock-rock at maximum volume' approach, which led to the songs being played at double speed and seemingly without much of the style and swagger of the original records.

My feeling was that, at this point in Iggy's history, a more reliable reading of the songs with a nod toward those amazing early records would work. Nobody needs to hear a new Iggy band tearing through his stuff in a slapdash way, trying to outgun each other with volume and speed. If I was going to see Iggy now, as a ticket-buyer, I would want to be reminded of why he was so great in the first place and hear those songs done right, with all the fire and fury, but keeping the tunes intact. Especially as all the evidence suggested his singing voice was as strong as ever.

I was reticent to bring this up with Iggy, as I wasn't sure how much he'd controlled those bands or just let them go their own way. It was certainly the case that he almost never commented on what we played in the *Blah Blah Blah* band all that time ago. Occasionally he would say when he liked something, but mostly we just played what we wanted to, and he left us alone.

I've always had good memories of that band and the way it evolved over eighteen months, but I had many reservations about my own part in it. Back then, I made the typical English error of overplaying, and my guitar sound was too often a thin, scratchy disaster, partly down to lack of experience and partly because it was sort of fashionable at the time.

We started to talk about a musical approach for the upcoming gigs, and I told him I could hear the Motown—or, as he pointed out, Stax-Volt—influence in The Stooges records. I thought it might be important to respect that. I also noted how, on Iggy's so-called 'Berlin period' albums, *The Idiot* and *Lust For Life*, drummer Hunt Sales' style had a huge influence. Having toured and recorded with Hunt and his brother Tony on Bowie's first Tin Machine album, I knew what a powerhouse they were and how much brilliance they brought to Iggy's sound. I wanted to summon that feeling again. Iggy agreed and said he was more than happy to approach it that way. The first gigs would be opening for the Foo Fighters at Wembley Stadium for two dates in June 2015. No pressure there, then.

It occurred to me that not many musicians would be able to say that they played both the old and new incarnations of Wembley Stadium.

In discussions with Henry McGroggan, it was clear they preferred enthusiasm over experience when it came to picking people for the band. I started to make lists of rockin' bass players. One name on my list stayed there, and it wasn't a hard call: Scotsman and ex-Seraphim member Ben Ellis was to be our guy.

I'd done one gig with Ben, two years previously. It was for a show with West London art-rock terrorist Alex Zapak in a hastily assembled band called The Cun$t Rock Revolution.

It was Alex who had fronted the event at the ICA to commemorate Iggy's *Blah Blah Blah* album. She had screamed her way through the set list while divesting herself of clothing and ending up topless, wearing only a supermarket plastic bag as a pair of makeshift panties. Iggy had seen clips on the internet and quite liked the performance.

Ben had impressed me with his no-nonsense Fender Precision/ Ampeg-driven sound. I have worked with a lot of technically amazing bass players in recent years, but none of them had the solid, old-fashioned, huge rock feel that Ben has. As well as being a great player, he's an aficionado of Iggy Pop's records, from The Stooges through the Berlin period and onward.

Drummer Mat Hector and I played the Time Capsule US tour with Thomas Dolby in 2012, and he'd remained a close friend, but I admit to having initial reservations about offering him the gig. His playing with Thomas had been flawless, but this was going to be a challenge of a different kind for Mat. I didn't think of him as a natural rock player, even though I knew he would work harder than anybody to learn new skills and nail them down. We talked for a long time and looked at lots of video together, mostly of the incredible force of nature that is Hunt Sales. Mat impressed me with his willingness to take it on, even though he would likely have to reinvent his whole technical and aesthetic approach for Iggy. He's never let me down.

Lastly, I needed someone who could play some keyboards and second guitar. the only name that made any sense was my fellow veteran of the first *Blah Blah Blah* tour, Seamus Beaghen. A ninja-level Hammond organ master and someone who had already done an album and two tours with the man, he seemed like the only choice. From Death In Vegas through Madness, from Paul Weller to The Blockheads, Seamus's reputation among musicians is that of someone who can bring the right thing every time. He also has a pretty mean and rootsy rhythm-guitar style and a razor-like way with funny punch lines. I looked forward to patching things up with him on a personal level, too, now that we were older and wiser.

The goal was to have a band ready to go by mid-2015, so we started to meet and have a few preliminary rehearsals on our own, at least six months before we would be required to do it for real. There was a fair bit of interest in us being Iggy's new band, and I did a number of radio and local press interviews.

I filmed and recorded some of our early progress and emailed the clips to Iggy. He responded thusly:

Kevin,
I really, really liked the music. Wow, you guys made my day. It was so much fun to listen to. The groove, the balance, the beat, the vibe, the sense of intelligence and fun, as well as respect for and understanding of the material. It made me feel really good.
Thanks,
Jim.

It made me feel really good to get that email. For the first time in my working life, I almost felt qualified for the gig.

The date of the Foo Fighters gig at Wembley was approaching, so we set up in a large room at John Henry's rehearsal complex in North London. I had spent so many days in that building in the 1980s, and it hasn't changed much. It's a great place to meet other musicians in the café (the same one in which I'd heard, second-hand, about being dropped from Iggy's band in the 80s).

That session in the larger space of John Henry's gave us an opportunity to scale the band up to performance level. Professional crew and sound engineers appeared, and we were ready for Iggy's arrival. Seamus and I, having played on the *Blah Blah Blah* tour together, were naturally looking forward to seeing Jim again, but Mat and Ben were a trifle nervous to meet Iggy Pop in the flesh, especially after so long spent routining the songs in our cramped rehearsal room in the Kent countryside. As it turned out, the moment could not have been sweeter.

We were playing a song called 'Skull Ring', which is basically Henry Mancini's 'Peter Gunn Theme', only louder and with more attitude. We had just begun to get it really smoking, shaking the walls with the monstrous riff and pounding backbeat. The band had started to impress the crew, too. They were standing around, getting off on the storm of guitars and drums, when, almost unnoticed, a slim figure dressed in skinny black jeans and a Lewis Leathers bomber jacket strode across the room. His rugged face was slightly obscured by shoulder-length blonde hair. He grabbed the mic and the familiar baritone boomed from the PA speakers.

'SKULL RING! FAST CARS! HOT CHICKS! MONEY!'

Within five minutes, he was shirtless, straddling a chair in the centre of the room, and having us rip through the whole set. This was our reintroduction to the phenomenon known as Iggy Pop—decades on, still a force of nature.

All went swimmingly at John Henry's for the next few days, until drummer Mat's phone buzzed as we left an Islington cinema after watching the excellent *Mad Max: Fury Road*. Foo Fighters frontman Dave Grohl had broken his leg tumbling off a stage, two numbers into the band's set in Gothenburg. After his fall, Grohl had gone to the emergency room and had a cast fitted, before bravely re-joining his band onstage. It would be the last Foo Fighters gig for a good while, though, so our long-anticipated Wembley gig was a write-off.

At the time, this felt like a tremendous let-down, but it turned out to be more of a blessing. Instead of debuting at Wembley Stadium, with all that pressure to be great on our first gig, we got to start our Iggy journey at a relatively obscure festival in Utrecht called Down The Rabbit Hole. We'd get a few more low-key festival dates under our belt before playing in front of our home crowd.

Although it seemed amazing at the time, looking back at this first gig in Utrecht, it's obvious that we had a long way to go before we could really call ourselves a great Iggy band. I can't really define it in a technical way, but there's a subtle combination of factors that a band has to get right before it really takes off. It's to do with playing style, awareness of each other, and a restlessness to improve. And, with Iggy, it's all about a physical commitment—a connection with his energy that makes you push yourself into places you wouldn't normally go. The music is simple to play but not easy to play with the ferocity that really sets it on fire.

Luckily, this group of people all shared a similar characteristic: a desire to get better at what we're doing and never let it rest until we've taken it to a new level. What was good enough last year can be improved upon this year. Iggy had that same ethos with his own performance too, even after nearly fifty years as a showman.

What may be surprising to some is that a guy who is known for being one of the wildest most spontaneous frontmen in the history of rock'n'roll is such a calculating and well-prepared performer. This only really became apparent to me once I started looking at the myriad of phone clips that would appear on YouTube over 2015–16. In certain songs, he would be in the same area of the stage, doing the same kind of moves, at every gig. Even the seemingly random action of swigging water, pouring it down his torso, and then flinging the half-empty bottle out into the audience, would occur with meticulous planning and execution. Often, it would happen in the same bar in the same song, in different shows.

I realised then that, on some level, Iggy thinks about the performance as a choreographer might. His high kicks, twirls, and pony-stamping are thought out well in advance. I was glad he seemed to have abandoned the habit of inviting the entire audience onstage, although at the second gig he alarmed the roadies by reverting to an old favourite move: chucking himself into the crowd. I asked him about it afterwards, and he said, 'Oh, sometimes I still like to do a little divey-poo.' He confided that he always picked the biggest, strongest men in the crowd to launch himself onto, to try to avoid injury.

Most of the gigs we played that summer were at open-air festivals, where usually you'd find a crowd barrier ten feet or more from the stage and about four feet high. The stage itself might be up to eight or nine feet high, and thus the opportunity for a 'little divey-poo' would only arise on stages with a so-called 'ego ramp' jutting out in front (as far as sixty or even a hundred feet in a big arena).

Iggy might say he hates these ramps but, of course, whenever there is one, he'll feel compelled to use it. This would present a particular musical challenge for the rest of us. Out on a walkway that far away from the stage, Iggy would be hearing the band from the main PA speakers, not the floor-mounted stage monitors. The physical distance the sound had to travel to reach his ears created an actual time lag, so he would typically start to sing later than we were playing as he was hearing his own voice travel across the huge space between him and the PA. If we were to try to keep time with his singing, we would end up slowing down to try to compensate, so we learned to plough on with our tempo regardless, with his singing sometimes half a beat behind the band, thus avoiding a vicious circle of sonic entropy. This is a tricky thing to master, but it's absolutely necessary with a singer who is not interested in wearing in-ear monitors, as so many artists do now.

The great thing about playing to huge crowds is that you learn to scale up the sound to be effective for the space. It can be intimidating at first to play so far away from each other on a huge stage and at such earth-quaking volume as to satisfy Iggy's need to feel right. Once you get it running like clockwork on a festival stage, though, it's all the more wonderful to go back and play a theatre show and realise that you can almost blow the walls out with the power of it.

After a year of only open-air gigs, we had an invite to play at the Palais De Tokyo in Paris for the writer Michel Houellebecq's birthday party. I think we even surprised ourselves at the rolling dynamite we could now produce in a confined space. I can't begin to describe how great it feels to dig into 'Repo Man' or 'Search And Destroy' at maximum volume—how fantastic it is when the band becomes a unified instrument working together, and how Iggy rides that wave, his voice effortlessly cutting through anything we throw at him.

* * *

Typically, the shows go like this:

Iggy will arrive three hours before a gig and ensconce himself alone in his trailer or a dressing room. He will often call me or the whole band in for a few minutes to discuss a change to the running order, or to let us know exactly when he intends to speak to the crowd. He might flag up the moment when he plans to go down the steps to crowd level and climb the barrier, meaning we should extend an outro until he can climb back up the stairway to the stage.

After giving us these instructions, he will stay in his room, often doing Qi Gong exercises. He will spend time sitting in a chair, which he makes sure is oriented toward the audience—even if the stage is a quarter of a mile away, he will want to know the exact direction the crowd is in, as if he is sending energy toward them in readiness for the moment he appears.

Gradually, over the next three hours, he undergoes a personal transformation and morphs from James Osterberg—the laid-back, polite, erudite Midwestern gentleman who you could happily introduce to your mother—into Iggy Pop—the foul-mouthed, wild motherfucker who might rip your head off and shit down your neck if you get too close.

An hour before the show, you can't even talk to him. Once we are all onboard the minibus shuttling us from the dressing room compound to the stage, he climbs on last, shirtless, up front next to the driver. The five-minute drive might be punctuated by nothing but Neanderthal grunts and animal yelping from the front seat. We remain silent in the back, if we know what's good for us, as we are now in the presence of the monster.

The moment we arrive at the ramp to the stage, the noise of the crowd increases to a roar as they notice a roadie do a final 'walk on' and torch-check the gear. We climb the scaffolding steps together and are ushered to the entry point from where we can see the techs holding our guitars with straps aloft to make it easy to step into them quickly.

Iggy gathers us in a huddle around him, arms linked. He shouts into each of our faces in turn.

Are you ready? Are you ready? Are you ready? Are you ready? Then GO, MOTHERFUCKERS!

We belt onto the stage and the noise of the crowd becomes deafening. Mat counts off 'I Wanna Be Your Dog' and Iggy bounces across the stage, arms flailing as he whips up the audience of sixty thousand into a foaming frenzy. Typically, we power through songs with almost no gaps in between. As one song's final chord is dying away, Iggy screams for the next one, sometimes in highly insulting terms.

C'mon, beat that drum, cocksucker! or *'Skull Ring' now, now, now! Or I'll fuckin' kill somebody!*

As the energy gets fiercer, Iggy starts throwing stuff around. He can accurately hurl a mic stand right across a big stage and it will land at the feet of the drum tech and noiselessly fly apart but never once hit anybody. He's like a javelin thrower. It looks like dangerous chaos, but he knows exactly what he's doing.

The set rollicks by, front-loaded with the hits and his most famous songs: 'The Passenger', 'Lust For Life', 'Five Foot One', 'Nightclubbing'. Toward the end, we start ripping into Stooges songs: 'Search And Destroy', 'No Fun', 'Down On The Street'. Part of my brain is still that eleven-year-old kid, hearing these songs for the first time, as I grind out the riffs and hear my guitar howling across a fifteen-acre field.

The set ends with the doom-laden industrial ballad 'Mass Production', complete with ship horns and drones that continue as we quit the stage. Sometimes we look back, and there's Iggy beating his chest and stomping around the stage for a full five minutes, like an alpha gorilla fending off a rival as the crowd bay for more.

Despite his age, there are always a huge number of young and beautiful fans in the front. Some performers of his vintage only attract their older fans who are often (like us) middle-aged, balding, and a little overweight. Not this lot. Iggy's crowd are all ages, and there are still girls riding on their boyfriend's shoulders, pulling up their shirts and waggling their mammaries at us. There are the crowd surfers, divers, and moshers, too, raising clouds of dust and whirling around in human eddies of joyful aggression. It's always like that when he plays, and the spectacle that unfolds at an Iggy Pop show never loses its thrill for me.

At the end of the gig, when he comes offstage, Iggy is, for a moment at least, exhausted. He is escorted through the darkened backstage area by his manager and tour manager (or sometimes me). Ushered to a waiting car, he either shoots away to recuperate in some sumptuous suite somewhere or heads back to the dressing room for a glass of something red and French. Occasionally, after a gig where he was particularly happy with everything, he will shout out from his lair, 'Hey, Kev, come in and have a glass with me.'

Whereupon I and maybe one other band member will go into

his room and find him completely naked on a sofa, legs spread, wine goblet in hand. He will grin broadly and say, 'Pull up a chair and sit!' We share a few laughs, maybe a bottle of champagne, and chat about what went well in the gig, all the while trying to avoid making eye contact with his enormous penis.

* * *

We did finally get to open for the Foo Fighters in England. The concert was rescheduled nearly six months later, but not at Wembley, so my dream of playing both incarnations of the stadium remains as yet unfulfilled.

The gig was now to be held at Milton Keynes Bowl, before an audience of sixty-five thousand. At huge events such as these, it is possible to bring some friends and family, so I took the opportunity to invite Tom Wilcox backstage to meet Iggy. I almost never do this, but I felt gratitude to Tom for creating the ICA Iggyfest event that put me back in the man's orbit. Tom had come to the gig with Mick Ronson's daughter, Lisa, so I thought that Iggy would enjoy meeting her too.

These giant gigs have something akin to a small village erected behind the stage, with groups of well-appointed Portakabins and tents containing industrial-sized catering facilities. There is space enough for the hundreds of people working at the festival to eat together. We would often meet old friends in these situations and make new ones. We had other visitors to our compound during the day, including Dave Grohl, who was still on crutches, and the Foos' drummer, the late Taylor Hawkins, who had portrayed a young Iggy in the film *CBGB*.

The gig itself was a bit perfunctory in the end. Being the opener for a huge stadium act like Foo Fighters often means you play in daylight and to an audience that's only there to see the headliner. It wasn't a bad show but it was harder work than many. We were still in our first year with Iggy, and there would be much better gigs to come. That night, though, we celebrated in a nearby hotel. I was introduced to something called Jägermeister, and it didn't end well. The next morning, the band had all left and I was alone. I woke ten minutes before checkout time with probably the third worst hangover I've had since the one with Dolby in Belgium thirty years before. I somehow managed to pull on some clothes and locate my car. After a very shaky seventy-mile journey, I crept into bed to waste the rest of the day recovering from my wretchedness and thanking heaven that my idiocy hadn't resulted in anything worse than a banging headache.

I mostly behave myself these days and try and avoid the excesses of yesteryear. I've never been arrested or missed a flight or been drunk at a show. The worst thing I've done this second time around with Iggy is to recklessly add my fourteen-year-old son Fox to the roadcrew without asking. I'd pre-prepared a moment with the help of my amazing tech, Alaric Lewis, where Fox would do the quick guitar change-over for me in front of twenty-five thousand people at a huge show in Finsbury Park with Queens Of The Stone Age. I don't know what Iggy must have thought when he turned around between numbers and saw my son striding onstage toward me with a Telecaster at the ready, but manager Henry McGroggan let me know with a raised eyebrow that it was a surprise to him.

In October 2015, Iggy was invited to play at the premiere party for the TV series *Ash Vs. Evil Dead*, Sam Raimi's comedy horror tale starring a somewhat older but still ruggedly handsome Bruce Campbell. So it was off to Los Angeles, just for this event. We were booked into the Roosevelt Hotel on Hollywood Boulevard, right opposite Grauman's Chinese Theatre, where the show would be aired.

Upon check-in, the receptionist said, with her best Tinseltown smile, 'I put you all in rooms next to the pool, okay?' I knew from experience that the pool area in a Hollywood hotel becomes a party zone late into the night, full of loud drunken arseholes trying to impress teenage girls.

'Could you possibly put me somewhere else?' I asked.

She looked at her screen for a moment and said, 'Well, I could give you suite 1001 on the top floor. It's normally $5,000 a night, but as it's you guys, if you share it with someone in your group, I guess there's no extra charge.' Thus, it was that drummer Mat and I found ourselves in the three thousand two hundred square foot, multi-level penthouse that Clark Gable and Carole Lombard had once called home in the 1950s. It had two floors, three bedrooms, a bar, a roof terrace on which stood the giant, twenty-foot high, neon Roosevelt Hotel sign and a living room that overlooked the Boulevard and the Hollywood sign in the hills to the north. Every surface was made of either crocodile skin or mirrors. We just fell about laughing at the ridiculousness of it all as we went in the door. That night, we watched out of the huge picture windows as riggers erected a stage some two hundred metres below us that blocked off Hollywood Boulevard. They were building the platform for our gig.

The next morning, I had breakfast with Tin Machine and ex-Iggy bassist Tony Sales and his wife Cindi at the Roosevelt's excellent diner. Tony and I hadn't seen each other since the Tin Machine tour twenty-seven years earlier. It was great to catch up with him, and I was really pleased that he would see me play with Iggy. I got to meet Josh Homme for the first time that day, too, as he had come to watch from the side of the stage. Iggy conducted his usual earnest briefing before the gig in the Winnebago backstage. He instructed us to wait for Bruce Campbell to finish his speech, and then we would go straight into 'No Fun' with no introduction. When it came to it, though, Iggy pulled a very rock'n'roll move on poor Bruce.

We were in position onstage, with our instruments, and the venerable Mr Campbell had just started to speak about the new show, how he had been persuaded to come out of retirement to do it, when Iggy suddenly appeared, impatiently waving his arms above his head and gesticulating wildly at us to start. Mat, although he could see that Bruce was just getting warmed up with his speech, counted the song in out of loyalty to Iggy, and Bruce's peroration was cut dead by the band kicking into the intro to 'No Fun' and Iggy literally barging onto the stage and almost knocking him over. In retrospect, I'm sure Iggy thought Bruce had said all he was going to say, but looking at the clip, it's really funny to see Bruce try desperately to be good-humoured about it while simultaneously getting out of the way quickly, before he got hurt.

We tore up a few songs at that party, even though we were only due to play for twenty minutes. It was the first time the aggression of the music had taken a real leap up, and it wouldn't be the last. Afterwards, Tony Sales asked me, 'Can I come see Jim, then?' I felt a bit awkward, as it's not often cool to take people backstage after the show, even old bandmates, and I didn't know if there had been any residual beef between Iggy and Tony. Nevertheless, I opened the door of the Winnebago, where Iggy was holding court with Josh Homme and his wife, Brody Dalle. I ushered Tony in and stuck my head around the door.

'Look what the fucking cat dragged in,' I announced cheerfully, whereupon Iggy's face lit up.

'Woah, Tony!' he said grinning, as he recognised his old bassist.

It was great to see them together again after so long. It's moments like that that still cause me to pinch myself. Did I really just reunite Iggy Pop and Tony Sales? They hadn't spoken in thirty years.

CHAPTER TWENTY-THREE

GUTTERDÄMMERUNG!

§

AH, BELGIUM. My memories of the place go back as far as my first foreign trip as a fourteen-year-old schoolboy on an exchange visit to an Italian family who lived in Brussels. On my first day there, I bought a copy of Deep Purple's *Machine Head*, which had just come out, and became obsessed for a while with the crisp virtuosity of their playing. Then, eighteen years later, there were those early gigs with Local Heroes, all squashed into the dodgy transit van with our gear. Fast-forward another three years and it was Thomas Dolby's *Flat Earth* sessions. And now, in 2017, *Gutterdämmerung!*

I had met the ebullient half-Swedish, Antwerp-based photographer Bjorn Tagemose in a restaurant in London, and we hit it off quite well. He explained to me that he'd spent six million euros of investors' money, and the last four years, creating something he described as his 'rolling midlife crisis': a gothic black-and-white movie called *Gutterdämmerung*. It was about a titanic struggle between sin and virtue and involved a lot of guns and bombs and scenes filmed in the actual trenches of the Somme. The script was written by Bjorn and Henry Rollins, and the resulting film is halfway between a B-movie horror story and a rock pantomime.

The film has a number of cameos by some major rock stars: Iggy Pop as the Archangel Vicious, Grace Jones as Death, and Lemmy as a general. Slash, Josh Homme, and Slayer's Tom Araya also make cameo appearances, and Eagles Of Death Metal singer Jesse Hughes plays a Christian fundamentalist hitman whose teenage porn star girlfriend, Tuesday Cross, represents fallen humanity.

Bjorn needed me to be the musical director to actualise the staging of the project, which required a live band synchronized to the movie and placed behind a giant gauze projection screen. I couldn't quite understand what it was all about at first, so I hopped on a train to Antwerp and visited him, to take it all in and try and grasp what he wanted me to do.

Imagine seeing a floor-to-ceiling cinema-sized screen that completely covers the stage in a theatre. On it is projected a pin-sharp, beautifully shot, black-and-white film—Bjorn's frankly mental story of good vs. evil.

In one scene, Iggy Pop theatrically hurls a guitar from his cloud in heaven down toward Earth. This represents 'temptation'. Iggy has a huge set of wings and horns sticking out of his forehead. The sound of rumbling thunder peals and an opera singer performs bits of Faust. Half-naked young women drape themselves at the foot of a medieval altar, while a twisted Mother Superior bludgeons one of her neophytes to death with a giant spiked candlestick.

Suddenly, the screen becomes translucent and virtually invisible, and you notice a full rock band set up behind the projection. The band strikes up Black Sabbath's 'War Pigs', while hooded monks shuffle into view swinging incense burners.

Henry Rollins, dressed as a priest, delivers a fire and brimstone sermon on the screen, to a cringing congregation. An LED array at the rear displays blood-red text and inverted crucifixes. At various points in the proceedings, characters die violent deaths and flash bombs go off. Mark Lanegan leans on a staff and opines about the animated skeletons writhing in a graveyard as we play Jefferson Airplane's 'White Rabbit'. Grace Jones trundles into view, dressed in a tattered black gown, holding a giant scythe, and standing astride a World War I tank.

Generalissimo Lemmy unleashes a firestorm over the battlefield with the order 'Kill them all!' as we tear into 'Ace Of Spades'.

With such camp nonsense, a multi-sensory experience is created to assault the eyes and ears and, hopefully, please both the most died-in-the-wool fan of heavy metal and the curious rock agnostic alike. The band accompanies the movie throughout with a live soundtrack containing a bit of everything from the history of hard rock: from Led Zeppelin to Slayer, The Deftones to Marilyn Manson, The Doors to Screamin' Jay Hawkins. This ambitious and perfectly bonkers production—part movie, part rock gig, and part panto—was to be my responsibility as bandmaster. I said a cautious yes and went home to practise Slayer's 'Raining Blood'.

This was new territory for me. Many of the New Wave Of Heavy Metal bands have legions of young fans, attracted by the manic energy and power of the music. What I didn't realise, until I put it under the microscope, was just how nerdy you have to be to want to play that stuff. Bands like Slayer, Slipknot, and Lamb Of God have guitar players who spend countless hours practising extremely fast micro-movements of their right hands to achieve the kind of pointlessly intricate buzzsaw riffs that characterise much of that music. In turn, there are legions of fifteen-year-old boys on YouTube who seem to spend hours and hours learning how to copy them. I can't imagine why fifteen-year-old boys have a particular penchant for pumping their right hands up and down so rapidly, but there you go.

Many wannabe Slayer enthusiasts play Slayer songs better than Slayer. For me, it was a make-or-break task to learn their frantic guitar style. Fortunately, just when I was about to throw in the towel, call Bjorn, and tell him it wasn't possible to play like that, I started to make some progress. It had taken weeks of failure and a very sore forearm before I made any headway with the technique. After a while, the economy of movement became easier. I was finally able to relax my muscles and train my hand and wrist to make the rapid accurate strikes necessary to master the parts. And I was actually having fun.

Despite learning how to play Kerry King riffs, my skills as a guitarist don't really extend to 'shredding'. I hired the wonderful Chris Jones from a Pantera tribute band to handle all the tricky stuff. This would leave me to hold down the riffs and provide the correct period sounds for the project's huge range of songs from different eras and styles. Iggy's drummer and bassist, Mat and Ben, joined me for it, and we added a young and very talented singer called Jesse Smith. Opera singer Cathy Van Roy would open the show on an unseen ladder, just behind the screen, shrouded in a black cape, her white face floating fifteen feet off the ground and appearing to inhabit a huge projection of a coffin on the screen in front.

We set up the full production as a dry run on a giant film soundstage near Antwerp. Henry Rollins joined us to perform his evil priest role live for the premiere. Bjorn had also persuaded Eagles Of Death Metal's Jesse Hughes and Dave Catching to appear with us in London.

After four days of intense technical rehearsal, we felt ready, and the band and crew boarded the Eurostar, bound for London. On this journey, after so much intense hard work, some tension-relieving alcohol was imbibed. We were looking forward to a couple of days of stress-free living in a hotel in Camden Town before the big opening. A gig at the O2 in Kentish Town had been organised as an initial 'preview event' for fans.

* * *

On our arrival in London in the late afternoon, I slumped fully clothed onto my hotel bed and fell into a wine-induced stupor. The next thing I know, the phone is ringing, and it's Bjorn in manic mode:

'Kevin, we are meeting Grace Jones in half an hour. Meet me in the lobby!'

I splashed water from the basin onto my puffy face, sprayed on some aftershave, and sprinted to the lift.

A full three hours later, we were still waiting in the bar of the swankiest hotel in Mayfair. Sipping tea, I said to Bjorn, 'Why are we still here?'

He was getting text messages from Ms Jones's assistant. She was still coming, they said, and it was worth waiting a little longer.

Sure enough, a ripple of excitement went through the lobby as staff rushed about and guests craned their necks to see the enigmatic diva sweep in from her limo. Pursued by a small number of minions toting a plastic bag of dripping fresh oysters and a bottle of Cristal champagne, she beckoned toward Bjorn and me, so we swept into the elevator and up to her suite.

The scene that met us, as her valet opened the door, was as if somebody had casually tossed a hand grenade into a liquor store that doubled as a laundrette. There were bottles and glasses everywhere, and clothes strewn all over the furniture.

Grace was warm and funny and immediately put us at ease, which I hadn't expected. She summoned a series of hotel chefs, who appeared at the door with knives with which to try to shuck the oysters in the plastic bag. Saltwater dripped onto the carpet, and none of the knifemen pleased her. To the accompanying sounds of U-Roy and Dennis Brown blasting from the stereo, Grace waved away the hapless kitchen staff. Dressed in only tracksuit bottoms and a bra, she shucked the oysters herself over the bathroom sink.

We drank the champagne and ate the lovely oysters while Bjorn pitched the idea of appearing at the *Gutterdämmerung* premiere in person.

'Just to say hi to the fans,' he said.

'Nonsense, darling, I'll come and sing!' she exclaimed.

I suggested that 'Nightclubbing' would be the obvious choice, as it was an Iggy Pop song that she had covered. I opened my laptop and showed her a clip of us performing the song with Iggy so that she could hear how we played it and practise her part. Grace seemed enthusiastic, so, arm in arm, we rehearsed the song there and then, amid much merriment and bonhomie.

In the cab on the way back to our hotel, I asked Bjorn if he thought she really would come to the gig.

'Honestly, I have no fucking idea, Kev.'

The day of the O2 date came, and we set up for *Gutterdämmerung*'s debut show. Jesse Hughes and Dave Catching arrived with the Eagles Of Death Metal tour bus, along with Jesse's girlfriend Tuesday and Joshua Tree guitarist Alan Johannes.

Jesse invited me to the Eagles' dressing room and, true to his reputation, had lines of various classified pharmaceuticals racked out on every surface, as well as open bottles of tequila.

'Hey Kevin' he said, holding out a short straw and a shot glass. 'Here you go, but be careful of that shit. If you would normally do a line two or three inches long, just do half an inch or you'll be up for three days, man.'

I declined his kind offer.

Just before showtime, there was still no word about Grace. If she was coming, we wouldn't know until the very last moment. We would therefore leave a 'detour' in the programme for her to sing or not, depending on whether she showed up at all, or whether she came and felt like doing something else.

About ten minutes into the performance, during some dialogue where we had to stand silently on the darkened stage behind the screen waiting for the next cue, the whispered news came from the wings.

Grace is here. 'Nightclubbing' is on!

We started the song, and the crowd went crazy as Grace sashayed onto the stage in a hooded, full-length, black leather vampire-cape thing, looking a million dollars. That woman knows how to make an entrance. Would she sing a single lyric or a note in tune or in time, though? The answer was an emphatic *nope*.

Grace had also visited Jesse Hughes's dressing room and had not only accepted a similar offer to the one he made me but completely ignored his warning about the potency of the goods. The diva had evidently hoovered up three rails of Jesse's 'gentleman's pick-me-up', and by the time she hit the stage, she was as crisp as a little beetle. The question was, 'Did it matter?' The answer was, 'Not even a bit.' We had been *Graced*, and that was good enough for the crowd, who absolutely adored watching her strut around the stage mumbling random lyrics in a random key.

The event had gone really well, and the band stayed up partying with the cast and crew late into the night. In the morning, there was a full double-page centrefold picture in the *Guardian* of Grace onstage, batwings akimbo.

Gutterdämmerung clocked up only eight performances in my three-year involvement with it. This was partly to do with the unusual nature of the production itself, but also partly because it is wholly the concept of Bjorn Tagemose, the maverick auteur who continues to take sole responsibility for its survival. With a cast and crew of twenty-seven, it's expensive to put on. I wish it well, and I hope that one day it will return to haunt and amuse us again.

* * *

The day after that first *Gutterdämmerung* show, November 13, 2015, was to turn dark—and I mean really dark. I returned home after the show, and in the evening Angelica and I attended a school quiz and wine night at Battle Abbey in East Sussex. As the event wrapped up at about 11pm, I turned on my phone, and it started to vibrate continuously.

The flood of messages took a minute to sink in. While we had sat there in the amiable surroundings of my son's school hall, doodling on the tablecloths, the Eagles Of Death Metal gig at the Bataclan in Paris had been attacked by Islamist gunmen. The assault on the theatre, and other shootings carried out simultaneously across the city, resulted in the deaths of one hundred and thirty people. I felt stunned.

Stories emerged gradually of the terror and mayhem that occurred that night at the Bataclan. Our *Gutterdämmerung* singer, Jesse Smith, had been wearing a floor-length leather coat at one point during the London show. EODM frontman Jesse Hughes had taken a fancy to it and 'borrowed' it as the band left for Paris on their tour bus in the early hours of the morning. At the Bataclan, that same coat was hanging on a hook on the back of the dressing room door, and it provided a roadie with an effective hiding place when one of the gunmen entered, looking for more victims. That stolen coat saved his life.

Shawn London, the sound engineer, was shot in the leg and thought he was about to die as he hid behind his console among dead bodies. Nick Alexander, who was selling merchandise in the foyer, was brutally gunned down and killed. Jesse Hughes may indeed be, in the words of a Queens Of The Stone Age member, 'a barely functioning collection of human cells', but when the shooting started, it only took him three milliseconds to react and run. Dave Catching and the rest of the band kept playing for eight bars before they cottoned on.

In subsequent tearful interviews, it looked as if Jesse's life was spiralling out of control. He made all kinds of spurious allegations about the involvement of theatre security guards in the attacks, which endeared him to absolutely nobody. While I sympathised with him, after he'd gone through something so dreadful, I couldn't understand why he singled out the mostly black staff members as accomplices. One thing was clear. The target of those gunmen could just as easily have been at our gig the night before in London—or anyone's gig, for that matter.

Since that day, I have scoped out 'where to run if they start shooting' at every venue I play. I never would have thought my life might be in danger from a concert crowd before, but since the Paris massacre, all performers are now potential targets. My guitar techs always make sure there is an escape route.

Only a year after the Bataclan outrage, we played with Iggy at Punk Rock Bowling in Las Vegas, in an open parking lot surrounded by tall buildings. A few months later and only a mile or two up the road, a shooter opened fire on a festival crowd across the street from a high window at the Mandalay Bay Hotel. Fifty-nine concertgoers died, and four hundred and nineteen more had gunshot wounds.

CHAPTER TWENTY-FOUR

THE NEXT DAY

JANUARY 10, 2016. It had become my habit to make tea while listening to the news early in the morning before the school run. The radio was barely audible as the kettle boiled, but something caught my attention. The unmistakable sound of a David Bowie hit, then another and then another, in quick snippets. BBC Radio 4 is normally ninety-nine percent spoken word.

I turned up the volume realising, instantly, that the only time you would hear this kind of song collage on a news program would be if the unthinkable had happened. Sure enough, he was gone. I spent the day in shock.

Since I'd started playing with Iggy again, I'd assumed that at some point I would see David again. I'd hoped he might turn up after a gig, crack a few jokes, and light up the room for us all.

Very soon the phone calls came. First it was friends and colleagues, then the local news radio station, then the BBC. Would I like to share my thoughts about working with David?

I felt increasingly bleak throughout the day. I retreated to my studio and began to play the songs and listen to the amazing *Blackstar* album, which had hit number one in the charts a few days earlier. I looked at the recent videos, particularly 'Where Are We Now?' and 'Lazarus', and I couldn't help but feel like crying.

I stumbled upon the 'Villa Of Ormen' Instagram page. As I listened and looked, I began to feel something other than just a sense of loss. It dawned on me how premeditated and calm Bowie must have been about his imminent demise. The deliberate secrecy around his health, the focused creation of new work, and the stark honesty of the songs on *Blackstar* showed he was still pushing boundaries and making no compromises right until his last breath. The stylishness of his exit from the world was as unique as his life had been, and it was something we should all celebrate. He died as he lived, re-inventing his world and, in doing so, re-inventing ours. *Where the fuck did Monday go?* He never wasted a day and was a cosmic joker to the end.

Having since toured with Mike Garson and other Bowie musicians, it's been a revelation to get inside the songs and gain new insights into Bowie's early work at a deeper level. I am struck by the continued love for it from audiences worldwide and the joy it still gives us to play those groundbreaking songs. Re-listening to *Ziggy Stardust*, *Aladdin Sane*, and *Diamond Dogs* from the perspective of the intervening forty-odd years makes me all the more astonished at what he did back then. In writing those songs he completely reframed the relationship between pop star and audience. He practically invented a new branch of popular culture based on his own ambitions as a performer and, in the process, tore up the Elvis/Beatles/Stones rulebook more than punk rock ever did.

Bowie was also a truly original, gifted writer of tunes. He had a way with a melody that was very rare indeed. Like a lot of things in life, you don't always realise the significance of them until way later. I look back on a lot of the places I went and the people I met as a result of working for David and feel both grateful and at the same time utterly amazed that any of it actually happened.

Months after he died, I was watching the memorial show at Brixton Academy. A succession of artists came up and sang his songs in front of a band of his own musicians. All of this took place only feet from where he was brought up, and where I had once briefly lived with Live

Aid saxophonist Clare Hirst. It was marvellous to see the incongruity of such disparate characters as rocker Earl Slick playing guitar next to jazz piano genius Mike Garson, brought together by the man's music. I wondered if there was any other artist who could have put such very different elements together and left such a dazzling body of work. If you could only listen to one pop artist from the whole history of music, David Bowie's name would be on a very short list indeed.

Only six months before Bowie died, I was in Keflavik, Iceland, for an Iggy gig. After the show, we found ourselves in the hotel bar until way later than normal, owing to the sun literally not going down. At about 3am, the sky goes a bit grey, but that's it. We had shared the festival bill with Public Enemy. After having a few drinks with Flava Flav (still wearing a clock around his neck) and hearing about his numerous offspring and grandchildren, I struck up a conversation with T-Bone Davis, who plays drums with Public Enemy on tour. His dad was Bowie's outstanding drummer Dennis Davis, who was with him from *Young Americans* through to *Scary Monsters*. At the time, Dennis was very ill in a clinic, and T-Bone told me that—despite the fact they had not worked together for three decades—David had helped for years with his father's medical expenses. Dennis died a few months after David.

CHAPTER TWENTY-FIVE

POST-POP
DEPRESSION

§

IN 2016, IGGY MADE AN ALBUM WITH JOSH HOMME, *Post Pop Depression*, which meant we had to take a three-month sabbatical from being his band and find other things to do. We were invited to the Albert Hall to watch Iggy play with Josh Homme's group, and I realised that night that I'd only ever seen Iggy perform from behind. 'Put the lights on in this shithole!' he shouted impishly, before taking a detour around the arena with his radio mic and climbing up things that weren't supposed to be climbed up. It was a fantastic gig and made me all the more appreciative of how lucky we were to be his regular band at this time in his life.

I think Josh must have looked at YouTube clips of the way we'd been performing with Iggy, as he went for a similar modus operandi with Iggy's back catalogue. Just as we had done, he kept to the same tempos as the records and stuck quite closely to the original arrangements of the older songs. The new stuff sounded great too, and songs like 'Sunday', 'Break Into Your Heart', and 'Gardenia' would become part of our repertoire once we resumed. Queens Of The Stone Age had their own tour planned, so Josh's involvement with Iggy came to an end after the gigs to promote the album. Soon enough, we were back in the saddle as the Iggy band, hitting the festival circuit once again.

Of course, David's death had affected Iggy. They had done so much great work together. We played 'Tonight' in the set and started covering 'Jean Genie' too.

Our first gig back was in Mexico at the Foro Sol stadium, which holds sixty thousand people. Metallica had asked Iggy to open their run, so we played to an audience of a hundred and eighty thousand people over three nights. We loved soundchecking in the piercing morning light of Mexico City, filling the huge empty space of the stadium with our raging sound bouncing off the bleachers, while Henry Rollins marched around the stage with his camera.

Rollins would often show up and hang with the band when we played with Iggy. I first met him on the *Gutterdämmerung* gig. His encyclopaedic knowledge of Iggy's career and his serious love of the music have kept him coming back to watch, make lists, and write. He is always writing. You might bump into him in a hotel breakfast room and he'll cheerfully say good morning, but if you ask to join him he is less amenable.

'Well, I won't stop you, but I warn you I'm not going to be good company this morning as I'm writing.'

Henry is not an antisocial person—far from it—he's just more focused on his work than ninety-nine per cent of humanity. And boy, can he work! I was only aware of him as the tattooed guy who fronted the seminal American punk band Black Flag. He seemed like a scary dude on some sort of mission to embody the spirit of macho aggressiveness. In truth, he is very engaging and civilised company, and he can talk a mile a minute—without hesitation, repetition, or deviation—about politics, religion, or skateboarding down the Eiger.

He will tell you excitedly how he once met Jimi Hendrix, Liz Taylor, and The Dalai Lama and spent the night camping in the Amazon rainforest with them. Just as you are starting to think he must be an eighteen-carat fantasist, he'll show you a photo from his laptop and you realise that not only is he telling you the truth but he's had hundreds of these types of experiences over the years.

These days he plies a successful trade as a stand-up raconteur, broadcaster, writer, publisher and traveller, He's like the Zelig of music.

He has been everywhere and met everyone. His one-man show is a great night out if you want an intelligent and refreshing view of the twists and turns of popular subculture and an idea of where it could go next.

* * *

In October 2016, we had gigs in Colombia, Peru, Chile, Ecuador, and Argentina. Playing five South American countries in ten days, it made sense to hire a private plane to get around. One might think private planes are all outrageous luxury, but some of them don't even have a toilet, while on others the toilet doubles as the galley, so you can find yourself having a shit with your knees pressed up against the hamper containing your lunch.

It's terrific, though, to bypass the usual public areas of airports. No queues, no shopping malls, no exhaustive security checks, just very attentive personal service from smiling cabin crew who seem to genuinely enjoy their jobs. Such a change from the brow-beaten crews on commercial airliners who wish you would just get sucked out of a hole in the side of the aeroplane or make snarky comments as they dole out the revolting brown liquid that passes for tea and coffee.

From there we followed Iggy through 2017, from Spain to northern Norway, and marvelled at his continuing energy. He seemed incapable of doing a bad gig. On his BBC 6 Music radio show, Iggy made it known that he was a fan of a small label called Burger Records, and he agreed to perform at their annual summer festival in Oakland, California.

We spent a few days in San Francisco getting ready, where we soon discovered that the homelessness problem had become out of control. Much of Downtown smelt of urine, and there were dozens of sleeping bags in every alleyway. Driving out to Oakland, the underpasses and seemingly any piece of waste ground played host to tent cities full of desperate people, many of them zonked on oxycontin or fentanyl. Two of our guys spent a couple of shifts in a food station, doling out free meals. Meanwhile, I was hopping between clinics and pharmacies trying to recover the hearing in my right ear due to an infection and paying $195 for some $3 eardrops.

The Burger Boogaloo was a stand-out show. It took place in a small park with no barriers on the stage, meaning it would be easily scalable by any number of determined stage invaders. It was clear they weren't used to hosting an act as big as Iggy Pop. It was like playing at someone's backyard party, and it was all the more exciting for that.

Pink Flamingos film director John Waters introduced Iggy with a very amusing self-penned homage, including stuff like, 'This man survived the 1970s, drug addiction, heterosexuality, Lou Reed, and David Bowie—in short, he's God!' This time, thankfully, Iggy let him finish before we struck up the thunder.

The band tore it up in front of the smallest crowd we had yet played to. People hurled themselves onto the stage throughout the set, and there were some hilarious tussles as our crew chased and wrestled with mad, whirling punters all over the stage, again and again. I'm sure it reminded Iggy of the old days with The Stooges. Terrific, good old rock'n'roll fun.

* * *

As 2018 dawned, I began putting together a one-man show, discovering that there is an audience that will come to hear me tell stories about my half-century in music and hear me play some of the songs I've been there for. I found I really enjoyed talking to small crowds in theatres or arts centres. It was a chance to develop as a raconteur and solo performer and a way to rekindle a love of live performance.

The monster gigs are great, but these intimate shows would prove far more nerve-wracking. And the preparation was way more intense than for a band gig. I found myself suffering from stage fright for the first time in years, but with a few shows under my belt, I began to relax into it. I was also becoming a dab hand (or rather dab foot) with a looper, enabling me to create full soundscapes and arrangements for one guitar. The audiences seemed to appreciate the stories, too, and it was great to be able to meet them and chat.

Around the same time, Mat Hector and I renewed our working relationship with Thomas Dolby when we accepted an invitation to go on an '80s Cruise' that would spend ten days sailing around the Caribbean out of Florida, to Nassau, with stopovers in Jamaica. Nine days on a boat, just to do two gigs with Thomas.

The idea appalled me at first when I looked online at photos and videos of these cruises and the strange and obsessive superfans who go on them, and I noticed to my alarm that the accommodation for musicians would be located on the lower decks. These tiny cabins have either a porthole that cannot be opened or, worse, no window at all. I emailed the promoters to explain that I suffer from claustrophobia and am prone to seasickness. Fortunately, when we arrived to board the ship, having been ushered through a gigantic warehouse in Fort Lauderdale with our fellow shipmates, long queues of people and luggage snaking around the building, I was taken aside and issued the key to a stateroom with a balcony on deck nine. The whole experience from that point on became not only tolerable but bloody marvellous. We were introduced to the owners of the cruise company, who proudly told us this was their seventy-second such outing. With two and a half thousand punters paying three thousand dollars a pop, just for the ticket without booze and internet, I worked it out to be seven and a half million dollars gross per trip.

After boarding, I purchased a Wi-Fi and drinks package that entitled me to water, coffee, and soft drinks. On day two, however, my magnetic keycard crapped out and refused to open my cabin door. When I went to the purser's desk to ask for a duplicate, the distracted clerk mistakenly printed the authorisation for 'prepaid alcoholic beverages' on my new card. The trip was getting better and better. From here on I would spend many hours sipping free G&Ts and sitting in the sunshine on my balcony, writing this book, and watching the seabirds skimming over the blue ocean. I could leave the balcony door open at night and enjoy the blackness out at sea, the distant sight of similar illuminated floating palaces, the slow swaying of the ship, the warm Caribbean breeze and the sound of the water.

I had always wanted to visit Jamaica, and when I got off the ship in Falmouth, I decided to walk beyond the area around the dock as far as I could go to try to meet someone local who wasn't there just to milk money out of the cruisers. After ten minutes of brisk walking, the bustling tourist zone was behind me and I found myself on a dusty lane at the back of the town, skirted by tumbledown buildings, moving toward the lush Jamaican countryside. I stopped to chat with a Rastaman sitting on a crate outside his house, knitting brightly coloured tams and smoking a large blunt. He had an old car tyre as a plant pot with a small palm tree and a large bush of ganja growing out of it. He introduced himself as Eglan.

As soon as I had established that I was not a tourist but a working musician from the ship and that I knew a thing or two about the history of Jamaican music—from nyabinghi through mento to rocksteady, ska, reggae, ragamuffin, and dancehall—I was accepted and treated to the kind of local hospitality that is not normally extended to the casual visitor. Eglan took me to a backstreet bar where I was made to feel welcome by the locals as we chatted about England.

At the second stop, Ocho Rios, things weren't quite so congenial. Instead of riding by taxi like everyone else, Mat and I elected to walk the half-mile into town from the dock. Before we'd even left the port area, we were offered cocaine twice, and on the way to town we were targeted by drug dealers a dozen times more. Half of those trying to hustle us were actually in uniform. There was no time to go further afield to escape the hassle zone, so we just grabbed a quick beer and return to the ship.

Back onboard, we visited the huge stateroom apartment at the stern that was the temporary home to sixty-eight-year-old Aussie heart-throb Rick Springfield. He looked alarmingly boyish for his age and we enjoyed boozing with him and his entourage. Rick was a veteran of these weird cruises and had started a kind of open-mic salon that he called Rick's Piano Bar. I joined one of these chaotic jams in front of a large crowd and brought the house down with my pretty random version of 'Purple Rain'. From then on, I would find myself accosted and complimented by cruisegoers at the breakfast buffet and in the bars in the evenings. I never imagined being a cruise-ship entertainer, but what the fuck!

We also saw The Tubes perform in the main theatre on the boat one evening, with Fee Waybill, still in the silver onesie and huge white wig with the twelve-inch platforms, a plastic water bottle shoved down the front of his crotch, singing 'White Punks On Dope'. I last saw them do this in London in 1975. The only difference now was that he was standing quite still as he sang and had to lean forward and put his hands on the bass player's shoulders to walk on and off in those enormous boots. Could you choose more wildly inappropriate footwear on a ship?

Our own gigs with Thomas Dolby were in a lounge bar at the front of the ship on an upper deck, attended by hordes of rabid fans wearing 'goonie' masks and all kinds of outrageous 80s-style wigs and costumes.

Leaving the boat and flying home from Miami, I experienced what is commonly called land sickness. Your body gets used to the subtle rolling movement of the ship, and it takes a number of days to adjust to life back on dry land. It's as if the world is tilting and rocking a bit when it clearly isn't. My first 80s music cruise, and hopefully not my last.

* * *

An enforced gap in the schedule while Iggy took a break from gigs left me time to finish work on my own songs and realise a dream. I finally released the solo album, *Run*, which I had started in 2010. It includes two songs I co-wrote with David Bowie and two that I wrote with Morrissey. The others are a personal testament from a musician turning sixty who still refuses to grow up.

If I've learned one thing in my time playing music and trying to avoid anything resembling real work, it's that you mustn't lose your nerve. All will be okay, and it doesn't matter a flying feck what anyone thinks as long as you keep going. And Iggy played the title track on BBC 6 Music!

Back on the road with Iggy in the summer of 2019, we play the Montreux Jazz Festival. He lost his footing while glad-handing people at the end of a set and fell headfirst onto a metal crash barrier, knocking out a front tooth. The band had already walked off the stage just before the encore, so we were somewhat concerned to see him arrive at his chair in the wings with blood dripping out of his mouth.

Iggy looked up at a concerned Henry McGroggan, loudly declaiming, 'I can't go back to the fucking dentist again.' I asked him if he wanted to call it a night. He fixed me with a gimlet eye while swigging beer to stop the bleeding, and without hesitation, spraying blood in my direction, he told me, 'Just get out there and fuckin' play!'

The last part of the gig kicked off with '1969' and continued for a full twenty-five minutes of Stooges songs at maximum thrash. The next day, Iggy would spend many hours strapped into the dentist's chair, having his grille rebuilt. That's called commitment to your art!

We finished our run of dates with a rollicking gig at Budapest Park, Hungary. Little did we know it, but this would be our final show together. All subsequent plans for 2020 were shelved as the COVID-19 outbreak engulfed the world. By the time Iggy was ready to go again, he would emerge with an album called *Free*, a collection of tone poems conceived with trumpeter Leron Thomas (aka Pan Amsterdam) and a new French band he'd put together. Their small series of theatre dates got postponed twice, then eventually went ahead eighteen months later, before finally morphing into a run of European festival shows.

I suppose it made sense to do those shows with Leron's line-up. What it meant, though, is that our five-year stint with Jim had come to a natural conclusion but in an unnatural way. What with the extra problems of using a British band after Brexit and delays due to COVID restrictions, it made no sense to continue. Though it was completely understandable and logical from a business standpoint, I can't pretend that it wasn't a perfunctory end to our time with Iggy Pop, and not quite the glorious finale I thought we deserved.

My relationship with Iggy would continue, though, via an interesting turn of events that had started with an email exchange earlier in the year. Out of the blue, Iggy expressed an interest in doing something entertaining for children. After the notorious TV teddy incident, I wasn't sure if this was a good idea, but I thought I might as well show him a project that Angelica and I had done together a few years previously.

Angelica had made a film set with characters in a box on the kitchen table as a craft idea to engage our son, Fox, when he was small. She called it *Squirrel Mountain* and shot it on a camcorder. She cast it with a mix of professional actors and friends who just fitted the bill. I wrote tunes to Angelica's lyrics and made recordings of the songs with a kazoo and ukulele, singing them in a silly falsetto. Thus, a funny, *WTAF have I just watched?* short film emerged, with woolly characters pushed around on sticks and hung from strings.

There was some initial interest from TV people we knew, but for now the film ended up lurking in a corner of the internet with a small but dedicated cult following. Then Iggy watched it and came back to us straight away to say how much he and his wife, Nina, had loved it.

'This is beyond,' he said, adding that he would like to play a character if we felt like doing more.

This felt like too good an opportunity to pass up, but at that point, due to the increasing needs of her elderly mother's care through her final years, Angelica couldn't find the time to work on it. Time passed, and we wondered if Jim would still be interested but, true to form, when Iggy says something, he means it. Not only that but he asked if we could write a character based on him.

Angelica came up with a new story that would see Iggy play a Squirrel Mountain superhero, 'hypnotising chickens' (a reference to the song 'Lust For Life') with a trail of frozen peas.

One of her oldest friends, the renowned sculptor Suzie Zamit, sculpted Iggy's head in miniature to attach to his little shirtless, fabric body. The five-inch-high figurine looked unmistakably like him.

I put a hard rocking track somewhat in the style of Iggy's *New Values* period to Angelica's wacky song 'Frozen Peas', which has him boasting of his superpowers along with his love of grilled cheese. Our actors added their performances to the new production, and *Iggy To The Rescue* was on the starting blocks.

After a gig in the Swedish city of Gothenburg, I stayed an extra day to visit Iggy's suite with my mobile studio and an expensive German microphone in a suitcase. He was a dream to work with. He made no changes to Angelica's script in any way and sang the 'Frozen Peas' song just as it was written, in a couple of excellent takes, right there in his hotel room. I had his performance in the bag and flew home to put the finishing touches to the soundtrack.

For more than a year, half the downstairs of our house was taken over by cameras, lights, cables, and a tabletop magical world, all made by hand. The filming was halted a few times when Angelica's mum died and COVID lockdowns came and went, before the project was finally completed and released in October 2020. The thirteen-minute film is now on Amazon Prime Video and YouTube. It is ostensibly a children's film but has plenty of thinly veiled adult references and wry jokes to make it a satisfying watch for older viewers too. It has won film-festival prizes around the world and appeals to little kids, stoners, and middle-aged Iggy Pop fans alike.

CHAPTER TWENTY-SIX

CH-CH-CH-CHANGES

§

BOWIE'S PIANO MAN, MIKE GARSON, WAS ARGUABLY RESPONSIBLE FOR INTRODUCING THE POP WORLD TO THE AVANT-GARDE. When we first heard *Aladdin Sane* in 1973, it was the piano that was the shocker. There was simply no frame of reference to compare it to anything we'd heard before. Mike's tumbling, atonal solo on the title track opens the door to a new world—a world where rules are made to be broken, but one in which, to break them, you really have to know them.*

I was truly excited, therefore, to be asked by Tom Wilcox to do an *Aladdin Sane* tour with Mike in 2017. The unconfident part of me imagined that such a musical genius as Garson might look at self-taught rock musicians as an entomologist might look at insects, but we emailed a bit and finally met in person in a festival field at the Los Angeles Coliseum, just before I took to the stage with Iggy for something called FYF (Fuck Yeah Festival).

Mr Garson was very charming and reassured me in his deep Brooklyn hit-man tones that he genuinely loved working with rock musicians. He struck me straight away as an easy-going and very cool guy. He absolutely loves Bowie's music, and nobody understands it better. We have since gone on to find a strong bond playing Bowie songs together.

* As Mike tells it, he was encouraged to be as abstract as he possibly could by Bowie on *Aladdin Sane*—another insight into David's prescience, bravado, and firm eye on the future.

I wasn't sure whether Mike's idea of having Gaby Moreno sing was a good one, however. Could she pull it off being a stand-in for Bowie on those iconic songs? I concentrated instead on getting inside Mick Ronson's head while learning his parts from the early songs, which showed just what a mature musician he was. After being the main influence on Bowie's music, to move aside on *Aladdin Sane* the way Ronno did showed real class. He played a lot of single-note riffs on the guitar so as to leave a natural space for Mike's piano to pull the music in whatever direction he wanted.

Despite not having toured in a 'splitter' van (gear in the back, people in the front) for decades, I was happy to put up with the discomfort for the opportunity to sit next to Mike Garson and talk music. As the longest-running live sidekick for David, he had seen much that I was keen to learn about. Originally, he'd been hired by Bowie as a live addition to the Spiders From Mars in 1973, but he lasted as a regular band member until 2014.

A professorial figure, Mike is also funny, generous of spirit and very modest. He told me he used to go to the library in Brooklyn as a youngster and take out huge stacks of classical, jazz, and pop sheet music. He'd go home and play it like most people would read novels, but for eight hours a day, and then he'd go back and get another stack the following week. He did this for years before he ever played for Bowie. On his audition for the Spiders, Mick Ronson apparently only had to hear him play for about twenty seconds before hiring him.

Despite his decades of being at Bowie's side, Mike still teaches private students at his home near LA. One guy turned up for a lesson with a digital keyboard under his arm and persuaded Mike to play something like his 'Aladdin Sane' piano break into it, just to demonstrate what it could do. Mike discovered that the guy had later gone to audition with a band, sat behind his keyboard, hit 'play', and mimed the part that Mike had recorded. He got hired for sounding 'a lot like Mike Garson'.

If anyone is the keeper of Bowie's musical legacy, Mike has a good claim. The other great thing for me was to work with a pianist who could be at home in the rock, jazz, and classical worlds. He's one of the very few musicians I've met who have no barrier between their imagination and what they can play. This is only achieved through total mastery of one's instrument—a thing that doesn't really matter in rock'n'roll.

Schedules and economics meant our tour was to be short and sweet—a quick trip around the north of England, Scotland, and London, six shows in total—but I relished all of it. Gaby Moreno was a surprise and a revelation. She won over the crowds easily with her voice and charismatic presence. The gigs also gave my sister, Janet, a chance to reprise her duet on 'Absolute Beginners'—the only time she has ever sung it live.

Mike also asked Steve Harley to come and sing at a few shows with us. We learned Cockney Rebel's epic song 'Sebastian', which was as mysterious and unintentionally amusing now as it was back then (it actually contains the lyric '*Generate me limply*').

Steve's a real trooper who overcame the challenge of polio as a child to become, with Cockney Rebel, a genuine phenomenon on England's 1970s glam-rock scene. I have never met anyone quite like him. He's like a rock star version of a disgruntled colonel from Tunbridge Wells who writes indignant letters to the *Daily Telegraph*. Put it like this: if there is nothing to moan about, Steve will find something to moan about. Sound technicians are always a target, as are venues, hotels, the state of the dressing rooms, food, the crapness of the music business, and so on. He also protested when I tried to teach him the right chords to 'Absolute Beginners', until the penny finally dropped. The fact that I was there when the song was created meant he had to give in, I suppose.

I don't wish to be too critical of Steve, though. He helped create the Mick Ronson Foundation in Hull and has raised money for young musicians to be awarded scholarships, which is more than I've ever done for upcoming talent. And, despite the moaning, I believe he really enjoyed the *Aladdin Sane* tour.

* * *

By chance, Bowie sideman Earl Slick was visiting my town for a one-man show he was doing in November 2019. I went along and we met in the bar before his gig. He invited me up to duet on a few songs with him, and it was like we'd known each other for years. I gave him my number and told him he was welcome to visit us anytime. I didn't expect that he would take me up on this quite so soon.

It turned out that Earl was staying a few miles down the coast with House of Love singer Guy Chadwick. Guy lives in a remote farmhouse and had put Slick in the guest chalet. When Slicky and his buddy Jesse left the local gig, they turned up late at Guy's, only to be met with some of the locals who had gathered at the cottage with violins and banjos. A great deal of strong alcohol had been consumed. Earl made his excuses and beetled off to the guest room, but he felt as if he has offended his host.

The next morning, my phone rang. It was Slick.

'Get me out of here, man!'

I duly drove over to pick him up. He spent a relaxing weekend as our guest as we talked music without any sign of a banjo or a violin.

Life is all circles. Late in 2019, Mike Garson called and invited me to join his show *A Bowie Celebration* (ABC) for a 2020 world tour as part of a band of Bowie alumni. This time, I would be replacing Earl Slick! The gigs were ecstatically received around the world. There's no sign of waning interest in David Bowie and his work, five years since he left us.

I was excited to play with Mike again, along with Bowie band stalwarts Carmine Rojas, Alan Childs, and Gerry Leonard. The set included the whole of *Diamond Dogs* and *Ziggy Stardust*.

Digging down into the music reminded me again of what an incredible writer Bowie was. It's harder than I thought to replicate his guitar parts on *Diamond Dogs* and learn the tricky changes in some of those songs. Imagine parting company with Mick Ronson and deciding to play all the guitars yourself on your next record. Bowie wasn't what you'd call a great guitarist, but his vision completely overrode his limitations.

The *A Bowie Celebration* shows weren't exactly a tribute—they felt more like a genuine 'celebration' of Bowie's oeuvre. A special bond conjured between performers and audience in mutual appreciation of a bona-fide pop genius. In playing those songs every night, I once again felt intimately connected to the days of listening to *Ziggy Stardust* and *Aladdin Sane* with my brother in the early 1970s. From obsessing over Ronno's guitar style back then, I would now get to give my own version of his screaming solo in 'Moonage Daydream'. Wielding my own Gibson Les Paul on some of the same stages across America where he played those songs when they were new, I remembered my vision in the cornfield all those years ago.

Our American tour at the beginning of 2020 was planned to last six weeks. Optimistically, as it turns out. We rehearsed in huge carpeted rooms in North Hollywood, where we were visited by some of LA's finest musicians, then it was all aboard the tour bus, ready to journey from San Diego across to Arizona and north to Canada. Then on through the rust belt cities and down the East Coast to Florida.

The start of the tour went well, apart from a couple of niggles. At the end of the show, I would race to the merch table, where my presence would cause people to hang out a bit longer than they would otherwise, and I would get the chance to sell them an album. They would also buy t-shirts and some of the official *Bowie Celebration*-branded stuff. After the first few shows, I was discouraged by Mike's tour manager from continuing this on the grounds that I was promoting my own merchandise above the band's. I complied, but I felt a bit hard done by. Little did I know that my problems were about to be put into perspective.

Just as we were really getting into our stride, disaster loomed. We hadn't reckoned on the total collapse of civilisation, but here it was. By the time the tour hit Seattle, all the gigs were being cancelled ahead of us and entire states were banning all public gatherings. What had started out as a bumper year got overtaken by Covid 19, and I was faced with the very real prospect of the end of live music for the foreseeable future. Apart from a few online sessions and podcast interviews, like everyone else whose working life all but vanished overnight I had to start thinking about living in a completely different and as yet unknown way. A more challenging future than ever before awaited. Always beginning again? Absolutely.

ABOVE The Young Ones: Martin Osborn, me, John Jacobs, and Mark Foster.

AFTERWORD

WHEN I FIRST STARTED WRITING THIS BOOK, I wanted to say something about my trajectory from bedroom guitar player to internationally renowned musician in a way that would describe this book neatly in a paragraph. The more I got into it, however, the more I realised that there was an issue that I wasn't addressing.

Central to my life has been the desire to make music. But I haven't dealt with the ambivalence I feel about my precise role.

When I first learned to play guitar in my teenage years, it was as a band member, purely for the love of the thing. I was happy to be the guitarist and nothing more. Pretty soon, though, I started writing songs. A new perspective opened up, and with it a new question:

Could I be an artist?

Much of my energy in my twenties was poured into this dream. I went from forming my own bands to getting record deals, then making albums of original material and trying to grow it into a mainstream success. I hit a brick wall, which, after I hit it pretty hard, bounced me off into a completely unexpected direction: that of sideman to some very big names.

I shelved my ambitions for artistic expression and never gave it a second thought. I willingly dropped my desire for fame and accepted being in the orbit of the stars with whom I worked. That is until much later, when the old urge to create returned.

My original opening to this book stated that I was entirely grateful and happy to have traded my plans to be an artist for the unarguably fantastic opportunities I have had as a guitar player. But truthfully there is a disappointment at the heart of it too. A feeling that I missed my calling.

In recent years, I have returned to singing and songwriting and started making records again. I harbour no illusions that they're going to make me famous, but they make me happy. They are my happy place.

I've also found some contentment in the role of storyteller and interpreter of the songs of my superstar employers. When we are young, we all have dreams that are entirely personal to us. Big dreams don't always work out, but sometimes we rise from the ashes and begin again.

* * *

I suppose we must accept that, like all things, our lives must pass. And most, if not all, the things we hold dear and true will fade away into forgotten irrelevance. But while we're here, we've got to try and find a little joy if not a little passion for something that may outlast us. Music has been life and breath to me. Despite all the cultural ups and downs of it, the harsh disappointments and the quiet triumphs are the measures of my tiny life on this earth.

Thank you for your kind attention to my story.

I'm an absolute beginner.

APPENDIX ONE

RULES FOR YOUNG MUSICIANS (AND SOME OLDER ONES)

Choosing the life of a musician is probably something that's harder than ever to do now. I was lucky enough to chase it at a time when it was possible to scratch a living and pursue seemingly unrealistic fantasies. If my kids had said to me, 'Dad, I want to do music as a living,' I would have found it hard not to warn them of the attendant difficulties they might face. Constant financial insecurity, self-doubt, criticism, repeated failures—these might all be 'character building' or pure folly in a world where our artistic value is diminishing and the encouragement from the music world is more about public profile than anything else.

I never wanted a job that would make me hate the world. Music has been my way of avoiding this fate and sticking two fingers up to conformity. It can still be a means to something that feels more human than just being a regular citizen caught in the sausage machine of life. Musicianship is something that—so far at least—'The Man' cannot take away from you.

Here are a few tips if you do choose to walk the tightrope and call yourself a musician.

- Turn up on time, reasonably SOBER and smelling good.
- COMMUNICATE. Start a WhatsApp group and use it.
- Learn the songs BEFORE you get to rehearsal.
- HELP others load and unload their gear.
- Make sure your gear works and bring ALL your own cables, plectrums, strings, batteries, etc.
- If you're the bandleader, LISTEN. Also, if you're not the bandleader, LISTEN.
- Sometimes the best way you can contribute to the music is by SHUTTING THE FUCK UP.
- DON'T upstage or play louder than the singer.
- When it's your solo, TURN IT UP.
- Don't overplay. NOBODY CARES about your amazing technique but you.
- ENJOY IT. It's only music.
- Keep some MONEY in your pocket for LUNCH. And enough for the cunt who's forgotten.
- Don't get fucked-up until AFTER the gig.
- Roadies and techs are PEOPLE. Love them and they will love you back.
- Don't be a twat to other bands. Give RESPECT.
- Dress sharp.

APPENDIX TWO
GUEST ETIQUETTE

It Has to be said that nothing gets the usually easy-going goat of a gigging musician more effectively than the dreaded 'guest list'. Everyone wants to come and see a gig as a guest. A free ticket is marvellous enough, but a free ticket with a backstage pass is golden. Unfortunately for us musicians, the whole process can become something of a challenge where, as the old saying goes, 'No good turn goes unpunished.'

I will endeavour to explain how to avoid the kind of potential anguish that can arise when guests assume that all musicians on the road are just having fun all the time. Or that we have the power to invite who we like, when and where we like, and that we'll always be available to socialise with them anytime.

The model guest will ask to be on the list for such and such a gig weeks in advance, turn up, and enjoy it. Then maybe (only maybe) you'll meet up, if the situation allows. If it's not possible to meet, they will just send a message of thanks afterwards and say how much they dug the show.

Many guests fall below these impeccable standards, and they can cross over into 'pain in the arse' territory. First, there's the 'can I meet Iggy?' brigade. No, you cannot meet Iggy. Then there are the ones who call you to ask for a pass on the actual day of the gig, having known about it for months. You'd be amazed how often this happens! I tell them, 'Sorry the list closed in 1953.'

The other thing we love is when a guest asks if they can bring four friends, then changes the friends' names two or three times in the run-up to the date.

Occasionally, I've had guests turn up to a festival the day before we are playing and expect free entry. Clue: your guest-list pass is to see us on the day we play and not a weekend pass for the whole festival!

Iggy's tour manager, the redoubtable Captain Eric Fischer, is as tolerant and kind a person as you could ever wish to meet. I have tried his patience more than once when the annoying phone calls kick off right from the runway, before we've even disembarked the flight. (Eric Fischer is hands-down the best tour manager I've ever met. He's always in the right place at the right time and often doling out pocket money! If you're ever in NYC, he runs a great burger place on a boat on Pier 66 called the Frying Pan.)

Another thing non-model guests will ask is, 'Can I watch from the stage?' Every gig has a different rule about this. Sometimes guests will be allowed onto the side of the stage and there will be a good view and maybe even a monitor speaker for them, as the sound can be pretty muddy from there. Other times they might be thirty feet behind the band and not be able to see or hear much at all. Sometimes there is a so-called 'closed stage' on which nobody except bands and crew are permitted. We seldom know this in advance. Guests will message you and say, 'Can I come backstage and say hi before the gig?' or 'We are at a bar in the Peace and Love Field next to the giant purple tent (about a mile away), come and meet us!'

Sometimes, people don't realise that we are actually at work and not necessarily free to roam about hunting for them. We are part of a well-organised team of fifteen people that operates in a coordinated way and runs on a tight schedule. Tour parties have to travel together, eat at the right time, and have enough headspace to prepare for the show, then check the (often unfamiliar) equipment with very little time. It would be lovely if every gig was like being on holiday and we could just wander about at festivals drinking and chatting with our mates all day and catching a few bands, but it really isn't like that!

APPENDIX THREE
A LITTLE ABOUT GEAR

Sometimes, people (mostly male, bald, and over forty) ask me about equipment. The usual questions revolve naturally around guitars. 'What type of strings do you use?' 'What gauge of plectrums do you prefer?' 'Are you a Fender or a Gibson fan?' 'What pedals are in your board?' 'Which amplifiers sound the best?'

This chapter is really only for those who find such stuff interesting. If you don't, you're welcome to skip this bit entirely, as I'm about to describe things that are utterly boring to the average well-adjusted person. But for those of us who are guitar nerds, fetishists and obsessives, I will crack on.

Firstly, it's worth saying that the qualities that make a great musician are never found in equipment. B.B. King would only have to bend a B-string to play a high E note and you would know it was him, whether he was playing his iconic black Gibson 'Lucille' or a cheap hundred-dollar guitar. In other words, ninety percent of what you sound like is found in YOU, not the gear. That said, there are obvious advantages to having access to very nice instruments and amps, so I will share with you some of my preferences and observations.

Guitars do have distinct 'personalities' and, just like with people, it takes time to form completely successful relationships with them. They vary in weight, width of neck, and tone. Forging a bond with a particular instrument cannot be rushed. Sometimes it works out and sometimes it doesn't. Finding out what a particular guitar does best, takes time—you can't hurry it. You wouldn't want to pick up an archtop to play punk rock, just as you mightn't play jazz on a Gibson SG. That doesn't mean you can't, but you'll be fighting an uphill battle.

This esoteric knowledge took me decades to acquire, and I'm still learning what tool is exactly right for the job. Some guitar brands are associated with very particular sonic characteristics. The two most famous American manufacturers, Fender and Gibson, have shaped the way guitarists think about music for the last sixty years.

Fender guitars have been my companions for much of my life, and the Fender Telecaster in particular has been my most trusted friend. For much of the 1980s, I used to play the more complex and sophisticated Stratocaster. But since I discovered the more basic Telecaster in the early 1990s, I have never been far away from one. Teles have a heavy slab body, too, so they make for a good weapon in an unruly stage invasion.

These two iconic designs share the defining Fender personality trait that one could broadly describe as 'woodiness'. Something about the way the necks are bolted (and not glued) onto the body of Fenders makes them chime and ring in a certain way. The Fender sound has less 'sustain' than the denser and more 'creamy' character of the Gibson (which has a glued-on neck), but it is very dynamic and responsive, often brighter and more easily recognizable.

Anybody who listens to Jimi Hendrix is hearing a player who understood the Fender sound better than most, particularly the Stratocaster. Every nuance of the way he touched the guitar is expressed so clearly through what I perceive as the inherent 'femininity' of the instrument. However much he modified the sound with experimental echoes and distortion boxes, the clarity of his relationship with that Fender still comes through.

Television's *Marquee Moon* album is also one of the most recognizably 'Fender-ish' records ever made in my opinion. Also, a lot of Captain Beefheart's guitarists showcase the Fender in a very distinctive way. Hitting a Fender guitar as hard as you can, without any distortion or effects of any kind, produces just about the purest essence of the sound there is. Listen to Beefheart's song 'Dirty Blue Gene' and you'll hear what I mean.

The polar opposite in the guitar world is the Gibson Les Paul. If you want to know what the equally iconic Les Paul sound is really about, listen to Paul Kossoff from Free, or some early Fleetwood Mac records with Peter Green. Anything by Thin Lizzy in the 1970s is very obviously the voice of the Gibson too, as is much of Mick Ronson's work with Bowie. Gibson's two best-known models, the Les Paul and the SG, have a sound that could be described as 'flutier' and 'rounder' than Fenders. The denser woods and glued-on necks of Gibsons give them more sustain.

You could say generally that Gibsons sound more musical when distortion is introduced, whereas Fenders break up in a grittier and less predictable way when overdriven. This is because, apart from the construction of the instruments, the electronic pickups in a Fender are 'single coil' and the ones in Gibsons, called 'Humbuckers', contain dual coils and more wire. Broadly speaking then, Fender guitars are better suited to cleaner and brighter sounds and Gibsons to heavier and darker sounds.

The reason I have only talked about the qualities of these two brands of guitars is that practically every other manufacturer is producing some version of these dominant designs. It's incredible to think that the electric guitar models invented in the 1950s have not really been improved upon in any meaningful way up to the present. They basically cracked it then, and no one's come up with anything better since.

I have a 1954 Fender Telecaster that has all the beautifully subtle overtones and character that comes with decades of being played and cared for. I recently stopped travelling with it as airlines, in their infinite wisdom, have now made it nigh on impossible to carry one onto an aircraft, even in a soft bag. I can't risk checking my valuable old Fender through the baggage handling system. I therefore bought a replacement—a newly made American Fender 50s replica model—in 2017 that is exactly the same in every detail of its design and construction as the one made in 1954. Though it doesn't have quite the subtle nuances in its character that the old one does, it's perfectly usable and sounds very similar to the untrained ear. If cared for properly, it will no doubt one day sound as good as my old '54, but long after I'm gone.

Guitar players often refer to a particular instrument as having 'mojo'. In a store with a wall full of Gibson Les Pauls, one or two of them may have the 'mojo' and the rest won't quite do it. What does this mean? It's a matter of very subjective opinion, but I will try to describe it.

Some guitars are just perceptibly more 'alive' than others. Something about the way they ring, the way they encourage you to play different things than you would normally. The way you feel, instantly, that you could play any style of music on one and it would work.

It's possibly a happy confluence of the quality of the wood and the right choice of hardware that can bring out the magic in a particular guitar. Very old and valuable vintage guitars are often better, just because they had the 'mojo' from the off and started life as someone's favourite, so they've been cared for ever since. They survived, therefore, where other more mediocre offerings may have been retired, or broken up for parts.

Newer guitars can definitely have special qualities straight from the factory gate, though. My advice to anyone buying a serious guitar is to have as many examples of the model you want in front of you as you can and spend a good ten or fifteen minutes playing each one. I guarantee that, if you find one with the 'mojo', you will discover it like that. If you can afford it, the big manufacturer's hand-built 'Custom Shop' models are worth the money as they have premium materials and the oversight of a master luthier.

If your budget doesn't stretch to an American classic, it's not the end of the world. You can be sure that some of the recent mass-produced Mexican, Korean, and Chinese instruments are better quality than they have ever been.

Having forged a relationship with a great electric guitar, the next thing that has an effect on your sound is the amplifier. Again, it seems to me that nothing has really topped the technology that was pioneered by Leo Fender and Jim Marshall in the 1950s and '60s. Old-fashioned vacuum tube (or valve) amplifiers are the only type that floats my boat. I've tried transistor amps and I've tried all the amazing and highly sophisticated software modelling devices that are everywhere now. I still haven't heard anything nearly as exciting as a 1950s American guitar plugged into a 1960s British valve amp and turned up loud. The sounds that made early rock'n'roll fans cream their jeans decades ago are, in essence, the same ones that are used by the likes of Radiohead, Arctic Monkeys, or a zillion other great guitar groups of today.

Many people are still producing modern versions of this tried and tested technology. There are lots of great boutique amp manufacturers around now making really fantastic stuff, even though it's based on seventy-year-old technology. Over the period I've played with Iggy, I have used a variety of old-fashioned valve-driven monsters. Blackstar, Marshall, Orange, Vox, and Hamstead amplifiers have all been my companions on big stages. All of them have their characters and flaws. I have stuck with the small boutique maker Hamstead for the longest, as you can't really ever make their amps sound bad, no matter how you try.

There is a whole new world of digital modelling amplifiers now that has quickly responded to a changing market. You can buy small boxes that plug directly into a recording device or a pair of headphones that will mimic any combination of analogue amp and speaker. Let's face it, there are fewer opportunities for guitar players to really let rip at high volumes, so bedroom devices are all the rage.

Having said that, even some very big live acts use digital modellers now. At our Mexican stadium dates with Metallica, I was amazed to see that all the guitar amps are rack-mounted Fractal Axe FX boxes situated offstage, and all the sound changes that James Hetfield or Kirk Hammett require are done by roadies backstage, leaving them free to pose away on their giant white stage set, without any unsightly equipment visible. Of course, standing at the side of the stage, all you can hear is the distant sound of the PA speakers out front and Lars Ulrich's drumkit being bashed and flailed at on an otherwise silent stage. No guitar amps roaring, just earpieces feeding the sounds back through the performers' ears. To me, that's not rock'n'roll.

When it comes to pedals, we are in an ideological and technical minefield of divided opinions, conflicting advice, bullshit, and very personal taste. Many purists are put off by the whole notion of so-called 'effects pedals' and consider any guitarist who uses them somehow inferior. This is clearly bollocks, but it stems from those who pay homage to the idea that a good guitar and a good amp should always be enough and further gimmicks are not needed (the notable exception being the occasionally permitted wah-wah).

Wilko Johnson once quipped, 'Pedals? I'm a guitar player, not a bleedin' cyclist!' Now that's true, and it's also true that the world's most iconic and influential guitar players from the past very often crafted their signature voices from just the guitar, an amp, and their fingers. But many of them only had need of a very limited palette. If you hear Wilko spanking a Telecaster with his bare hands, it is a unique and beautiful thing for sure, but that's all he did and all he ever needed. Keith Richards doesn't need a digital delay or a chorus pedal when he cranks out 'Brown Sugar', but that's always been the straightforward sound of the Rolling Stones, and it hasn't changed a lot. Perhaps it's worth remembering that it was Keef who first unleashed the fuzz pedal on the world in 'Satisfaction'. Jimi Hendrix brought phasing and modulation to an unsuspecting army of blues purists, too. So, the use of effects pedals does have an illustrious history.

If you're a professional sideman like me, your needs may be very different to those of a player who just uses one type of tone. There are times when I might have to play a set with an artist who has a very broad range of styles. Iggy's or Bowie's or Dolby's songs, for example, cover a lot of ground, sonically speaking.

Sometimes you need clean tones and often you need varying degrees of distorted ones. This can get very nuanced. Reverb, delay, and modulated sounds are often called for, too. In these situations, pedals can be very useful tools. There are times when you might have to get a roaring, overdriven guitar tone in a small room, or on a stage where it isn't possible to crank an amp up to trouser-flapping level. Certain flavours of overdrive pedals are a shortcut to making the sound you want, even if it's mostly to emulate an amplifier turned up very loud

and pushed into distortion. If you want to get really freaky with sounds, there are myriad options to do that. In the end, I like to get the basic relationship between the guitar and the amplifier right, and then be sparing with effects to make sure they are only there to serve the music and don't get too gimmicky.

I currently carry around a thirty-kilogram pedal board with about thirteen pedals on it, but most of them are different flavours of overdrive, distortion, and fuzz, with just two stereo reverb and delay machines that I don't use very much. The Holy Grail for most guitarists is how to get a great sound for rhythm during a song and then a killer 'lead' sound for your solos. The old-school method is to have the amplifier really loud, then turn the volume knob on the guitar down, but to crank it up when you need it. Most players now use booster pedals of one kind or another to achieve this, and it can work spectacularly well if you choose the right gear.

In my opinion, if you do go into the world of building a proper pedal board to cover all the ground you want, you will probably end up spending anywhere between £3,000 and £10,000. You may keep changing everything in it for about five years until you find the right combination of stuff that suits you. Then, if you're anything like me, you will use it less and less as you learn more about how to make the sounds you want efficiently just with your fingers and a little good taste. I play standard gauge .09 or .10 strings and historically would use .88mm Tortex picks, although I've recently been using heavier 1.5mm nylon picks and now prefer them. (You'd be amazed how much difference to your overall tonal approach comes down to a few fractions of a millimetre in the width of your pick.)

In the end, gear is only gear. The important thing is to be able to use it and not let it use you. A good guitar, a good amp, and really strong, agile fingers are the best way to get a great tone. The rest comes with time and a deeper knowledge of yourself.

APPENDIX FOUR
A LITTLE ABOUT MUSIC

There is a well-known Duke Ellington quote that goes, 'There are only two types of music, good and bad,' and I think he was archly correct.

Brian Eno's opinion is, 'The art of music has little to do with the craft of music.' What he means is, it doesn't matter how hard you've studied theory, or even whether or not you've studied it at all; the only thing that matters is what you try to *say*.

Would Miles Davis's trumpet style have reinvented jazz if he had been an overweight heating engineer from Walsall? Who knows? Miles himself said, 'The note is only ten percent. The attitude of the motherfucker who plays the note is ninety percent.'

The point is, there's always a story. The place, the time, and the person can be as important as the music itself. In other words, devoid of context, it doesn't mean as much. For example, there are some musicians of my acquaintance who swear that singing out of tune renders you a 'bad singer', but I think they completely miss the point. Trained singing technique, it seems to me, is virtually irrelevant when it comes to communicating the contents of your heart to a listener. When we hear Bob Dylan sing 'The Lonesome Death Of Hattie Carroll' or Mark E. Smith sing 'Totally Wired', John Lydon sing 'Poptones' or Nico sing 'All Tomorrow's Parties', despite the holes one could pick in the technical ability, we don't hear 'bad singing'. We hear consummate poets and storytellers using their voices to pierce the bubble of apathy that most of us live in, most of the time.

Good music finds its way into our subconscious and speaks to the essence of us. It might be disco, it might be Turkish folk music, or it might be heavy metal, but if it says something to you, then it's okay. Nothing makes me cry quicker than the sound of a classical choir singing Thomas Tallis or Arvo Pärt, or Aretha Franklin singing 'Ain't No Way'. These performers are displaying amazing technique, but that's not really the point. I can just as readily find myself transported by the primitive sound of Neil Young flailing at a single note on a distorted Les Paul, or by the horrendously out-of-tune flute solo in The Mamas & The Papas 'California Dreaming' (which is a full teeth-itching quarter-tone sharp) as I am by something that's the product of earnest study or technical prowess.

Music should sound like magic, and part of it is the sound of imperfection. Technical mastery is boring in and of itself. People like to hear tryers, to take part in the thrill of tearing up the rulebook. I understand that we don't all share this view. I played my mother the Miles Davis/Gil Evans classic *Sketches Of Spain* when I discovered it. I felt sure she would have her mind blown by the rich and sensuous harmony and the fluid freedom of Miles's playing, just like I had. But all she said was, 'The trumpet's a bit out of tune, dear.'

My first encounters with that very broad thing called 'pop music' were—unbeknown to me—occurring at what was probably something of a golden age, when artists were exploring how to break free from convention and really make something new. They weren't all striving desperately to forge a career, get famous, or make money. It wasn't even called the 'music industry' then. It was all self-taught, homemade, and a bit wonky.

In the intervening decades, we seem to have gradually retreated from the idea of invention, rebellion, and protest into a world where pop music is just another arm of corporate-led, conveyor-belt consumerism. It seems such a shame that the idealism and experimentation of the latter half of the twentieth century

have given way to perfectly pitch-corrected, over-produced vocals and mathematically time-corrected beats. Instead of its boldness nourishing us, pop's blandness seems to be dulling our appreciation, just as surely as processed food is giving us cancer and making us fat, while *Love Island* and *The X Factor* are rendering critical thinking redundant. It seems like aesthetic fascism to me, the silly idea that everything must be blemish-free, shiny, and polished to death. Free of mistakes, free of life.

The information contained in a pop hit from the digital era is flatter, simpler, less melodic, lyrically less interesting, more impoverished, and more homogenised than it was in decades gone by. I state this as if it were a fact, simply because it is. Pop's sole purpose now seems to be to anaesthetise the listener. Instead of tearing down the barricades, its overriding message now is, 'Keep calm, everything's fine.'

A combination of technical innovation and capitalist marketing has a tendency, inevitably, to render everything less vital and more easily consumable to a less discerning and more distracted audience. Yes, pop music's got a wider reach now, but it seems—to these old ears, anyway—shallower in intention and somewhat lacking in conviction. Where is the fire?

What young artists were doing in the 1960s and 70s, when I was growing up, was struggling to define their place in the world by trying to reinvent it. They were rejecting their parents' lifestyles and the 'trappings of the bourgeoisie' in favour of experimentation and a true exploration of freedom and dissent.

Far from rejecting conformity, a lot of pop nowadays embraces and promotes it. The way that records are made today is often with the same set of software-based sounds that are commercially available worldwide to everyone, so there's simply less dynamic variety in modern mainstream pop music. That's not just me becoming old and grumpy, it's a verifiable truth!

Pop today is used as an all-pervasive, ambient soundtrack to shopping and eating; you don't seem to be able to go anywhere without it being continuously piped into our public spaces. It used to be something we cherished, concentrated on, and cared about. It had resonance and inspired us to ask questions, to fight back. Now it's been relegated to mere 'content'. The post-war teenage tribal culture that bred rock'n'roll is largely a dead duck in a stagnant pond, and we are now adrift in a sea of homogeneity and aural diarrhoea.

There was even a moment in the 1990s, around the time you could buy a computer and make a record yourself at home, when the technical democratisation of early music-creation software poisoned 'alternative' music, too. The great John Peel, whose late-night Radio One show was so influential for so many years, had a strict rule. He would play the records that no one else would so that everyone would get a chance to hear their efforts on the radio at least once. He would never talk over the records, even over the end of a fade-out. But even the ultra-respectful Peel broke this rule once everyone with a laptop and half a brain could throw together something shoddy in their bedroom and burn a CD. He seemed almost to lose the will to live as he announced (over the record) that the tedious, repetitive electronic noodling limping from the radio for nine minutes plus was 'Armageddon Crumpets' by Drowned Hairbrush, featuring Frog Spigot from Nottingham. It appeared to sound the death knell for original guitar bands and people who wrote actual songs. It would be a long time before things got better.

There are, of course, many positives about the current era. By no means all 'modern pop music' adheres to my bleak theory of general crapification. We can be very broad in our listening habits now, thanks to the good old internet. For the artist still wanting to say something, the possibility of connecting with a niche audience, free of anything except their own homegrown 'marketing strategy', means there are some very interesting new talents finding fans very quickly out there, despite the dead hand of the good old music biz.

For those of my generation who wanted to discover new music, options were very limited back in the day. There was John Peel's nightly radio show on Radio 1 and *The Old Grey Whistle Test* on BBC TV, which seemed to be on at a different time every week and very late for school kids. I had to negotiate really hard with my parents to be able to stay up to watch Whispering Bob Harris. Drawing air through his enormous teeth, and showing off a new tank top and some enormous flared trousers, he would breathlessly introduce a bit of Neil Young or Frank Zappa to a waiting world.

Another good thing about the modern era is that many of the young alternative bands we see now are more technically accomplished than their age would suggest. Instant access to the whole history of every genre of music can give them a really wide perspective and a solid knowledge of where their influences are. There is a lot of original and fresh talent around, even if it's sometimes harder to find amid the deathless pop noise. For good or ill, in today's changed and fractured digital universe, pop stars aren't heroes and heroines anymore either. They are much more approachable and connected with their fans. It's a complex new world for veterans like me to navigate. As a child of the 1960s, I can't help feeling fortunate to have grown up in the era when it was all being invented for the first and only time—a time before big business figured out how to sell the kids' dreams back to them again and again.

APPENDIX FIVE
RANDOM CRITICAL ESSAYS

AMBIENT MUSIC

On my long walks on the south coast of East Sussex, I sometimes wear a decent pair of noise-cancelling headphones and delve into some musical areas that I previously haven't had a lot of time for. One of these forays has been into so-called 'ambient music', a phrase that may have been coined by Brian Eno to describe the kind of thing he has made from the 1970s to the present.

To those who remain blissfully unaware of the mechanics that go into producing such work, the experience of hearing ambient music must surely differ from that of someone who can instantly tell you how it was made (like me). I will say this. There is an awful lot of very similar, generic-sounding nonsense out there. Most of it involves software synthesizers of the sort that anyone can buy off the shelf. You call up a sound from the huge array of complex pre-sets available, plonk your finger on a key, and lo! a world of emergent harmonic loveliness floats from your speakers as if beamed from a distant ethereal plane. No discernible talent is required, other than the ability to switch on your computer and punch in your credit card details.

Then there's Eno. Brian's pieces nearly always have intent. They often start with actual chord changes or a melodic motif that didn't come straight out of a box. There are often real instruments involved. Leo Abrahams's guitar features, even though it's often been processed out of all recognition for effect. Sometimes there's even a distant hint of a lap-steel guitar or a harmonium or some other acoustic instrument. Pianos are often used, either a pre-fucked upright or, more likely, the rich and full tones of a Fender Rhodes, which fills up an awful lot of sonic space in a mix.

I suppose the idea is to experience this kind of work in a different way from listening to 'regular' music. It is certainly a very appropriate accompaniment to certain visual stimuli. If you hear almost any of Eno's early stuff while walking along the beach, for instance, the sight of the waves hitting the shore is a perfect match for his amorphous and coldly beautiful sounds.

EDM (ELECTRONIC DANCE MUSIC)

I'd like to talk about my relationship with the phenomenon known as EDM. Early electronic music from the 1970s was not so brutally automated. That's probably the reason why I liked it then and still do. It was often played by hand, on custom-made analogue instruments. The tuning was a bit unstable, and it was all a bit irregular and imperfect. You were hearing brand new sounds being created on records by Kraftwerk and Giorgio Moroder, for instance.

Sounds that had never been heard before. There is a living dynamic interplay going on and a lot of uncorrected mistakes and playing by hand. They are genuinely futuristic in intent but slightly wobbly in execution. For many of my generation, our introduction to electronica was Delia Derbyshire's amazing theme for *Dr Who*, which was made from bits and bobs of tape and magic from the BBC's Radiophonic Workshop. The fact that such a place even existed is amazing in itself, let alone that

it provided a nurturing environment for a young female composer to experiment freely with cutting-edge technology.

Nowadays, apart from a few original minds like Aphex Twin, so much electronic music is software-massaged into being mathematically perfect in every way. Computer sequencing has become so highly efficient that there is no room for flaws. Instruments stay bang in tune, and everything is in perfect time. Most of the sounds modern producers use have been expertly pre-made by very clever Japanese boffins in research facilities at the Roland Corporation, so all the composer has to do is dial them up from a software library. This doesn't, in my opinion, lend itself to much variety or originality. The electronic drums sound and all synth bass sounds are so similar on so many records that it renders it impossible to say who made it or why.

In a four-minute electronic dance song, you might literally only be hearing about twenty seconds of processed information, repeated again and again. Maybe some people can get real pleasure from this, but I am not one of them. I prefer Delia's genuinely off-the-wall explorations. After I had figured this out, I stopped feeling like I was missing out on something when I failed to join the rising tide of dance-music producers and started to realise that my failure as an 'electronic' musician was, in fact, my success as a human being. I have, of course, been off my tits in a club at 3am and had techno music blasted at me until I numbly submit. But at all other times, I'm proud to own a pair of ears that crave musical variety over robotic aural wallpaper (cue death threats).

DRUMMERS

Drummers are easily the most problematic area for me in a band setting. I don't mean drummers as people. I mean how and what they play. They are absolutely critical to whether a band works or it doesn't.

Some people think drummers are not really musicians at all but just hit things in a rhythmic way, hopefully in time with the music. But there's an old saying that goes, 'A band is only as good as its drummer.' And there is certainly a grain of truth in that. You could say with some certainty that an average band can sound great with a good drummer, and conversely that a good band can sound pretty dire with a poor one.

Let's start with the basics.

Timekeeping. Being able to play in time is, of course, a good quality in a drummer, but it's actually less important than you might think. There are loads of drummers with excellent timing who are a little, shall we say, boring. I always get quite agitated when I see polls of people's favourite drummers and Rush's Neil Peart is at the top. This goes to the very heart of how I hear music and differ in taste from a huge number of others. For me, the late Mr Peart— lovely gent though he surely was, and just as technically gifted—was the most unmusical and boring drummer I could possibly imagine. He was the antithesis of everything that there is to enjoy about a drummer's playing. No risks, everything in mathematical order, all sounding lovely but as dull as ditch water. His timing was flawless, but his taste was just so completely unadventurous. It's like listening to paint dry.

There are quite a few absolute legends for whom timekeeping was not at the forefront of their skillset. They had something else of value: personality. Think of The Who's Keith Moon, a flailing monster of a drummer who sure as hell wound up Pete Townshend with his random turns of speed and wild fills that you weren't entirely sure would land on the beat. He pushed and pulled like crazy, and the band had to try and follow, but his mad playing made those early Who records quite thrilling. Led Zeppelin's John Bonham's timing could also be quite erratic. What he did, though, was unbelievably exciting. He seemed to be able to drive that band like a steamroller stamping his mark on every song. It's a huge talent. He has a lot of fans because he could make the entry of the drumkit into any song immediately recognisable.

Drummers talk about having a 'pocket'—the space they occupy within the rhythm. For me, the groove is not mathematical, it's spiritual. Give me these self-taught wonderful, unpredictable, musical, and human players every time: Ringo Starr (The Beatles), Richie Hayward (Little Feat), John Bonham (Led Zeppelin), Carlton Barrett (The Wailers), who can literally bring me to tears; Charlie Watts (The Rolling Stones), Levon Helm (The Band), Clyde Stubblefield (James Brown), Howard Wyeth (Bob Dylan), and Hunt Sales (Iggy Pop). These are the musicians with whom I most identify in terms of what you must do to make music live and breathe. Their 'pocket' is infinitely connected to their experience of life and their character, and it is the most precious thing for a band guitar player like me to play with.

REGGAE AND CULTURAL APPROPRIATION

If cultural appropriation is a real thing in this age of so-called identity politics, I was as guilty of it as the next white kid. I'm unashamed to say that when I moved to Brixton in the late 70s, I immersed myself in listening to and learning to play reggae music. It wasn't that I was trying to steal anything—it was a proper thirst for knowledge. The first time I saw a real reggae band play, I was impressed beyond measure with the sound and the feeling generated between the players and the crowd. This was something I wanted to deconstruct and understand. The music was utterly repetitive but never boring. It was a particular fascination to me that the musicians could sound as fresh five minutes into a song as they did in the first minute. How did they do this?

In reggae, the drummers play the 'one drop' beat, where the hi-hat drives the rhythm, and the snare (often played 'side stick') and bass drum drop together on the third beat of the bar (as opposed to the two and the four, as in nearly all rock music). The guitarists usually play a bouncing chop on the two and four of the bar together with piano or organ chords that bubble, and then there are the massive, sinuous bass lines, which seem to be the most important melodic element, rumbling underneath and dictating the mood. The singer is then free to fly his or her top line over this solid danceable foundation.

I studied, I practised, and then it started to come. I learned to play 'the drop' with the right feeling and the right weight. It dawned on me slowly but surely that this was a form of meditation—a truly spiritual expression. It was magic from minimalism; beauty and transcendence from the simplest of rules. An egoless technique in the service of something greater than oneself. Add to that, the horn sections with their uniquely wonky tuning and the singers quoting black history, bits of the Old Testament, and social comment, the stoned-out productions using buckets of tape echo and spring reverbs.

I was a proper Brixtonian white kid in total thrall to the spell cast by Jamaican music. It is, of course, culturally born of blackness and black experience, and therefore always beyond my direct reach in that regard as a white boy, but the musical skills I learned in the study of reggae have stood me in good stead in almost every other area of my work. It's counterintuitive to think that the execution of something as simple as a reggae 'chop' could be so critical, but a guitarist with super-sharp timing and the ability to play repetitively, with absolute commitment and flow and a perfect lightness of touch, is solid gold in so many ways. This led to an appreciation of how to play funk and how even hard rock is improved by bringing along your 'reggae head'. So many white musicians play in an uptight and nervy way, always slightly ahead of the beat (Brian Eno's guitarist friend Leo Abrahams refers to it as 'The Honky Discount'). Later, when I learned to produce and record, I discovered how often a (usually white) musician's performance can be massively improved by retarding the timing even by twenty milliseconds or so.

I wanted to conquer that incipient tendency to rush and reach for something a bit deeper in my playing. Nowadays, when people tell me they enjoy my guitar style, it's precisely because I learned, quite early on, to challenge the natural inclination to busyness that dogs so many self-taught rock musicians. Of course, there have been many great musicians who have brought frenetic energy and rawness to the world, but I wanted to have the ability to play in any band, anywhere, and sound like I belonged there. I wanted to learn to not waste energy but put it in the right spot. Reggae was my touchstone, my teacher—a deep resource to mine for golden principles about taste, and understatement.

There's one other thing to say about reggae music. It was a beautiful enough thing to see a band or play the records, but you haven't heard it properly until you have stood on a street corner at Notting Hill Carnival, or in a Harlesden dancehall, and experienced the full power of a Rasta Sound System. I saw some of the best: Coxsone Dodd, Jah Shaka, Moa Anbessa, Solution Sound, Jah Observer, and many more. Huge custom-built wooden speaker cabinets adorned with stencils and chicken wire, shaking the foundations, the bass penetrating your whole skeleton and the treble cutting like a knife is a life-enhancing vibe. True, I am a white boy, but roots music has held me in its sway for a long time.

ACKNOWLEDGEMENTS

Thank you to all whose support helped me write this book.

My wife Angelica Campion, without whose encouragement and prudent counsel I could not have finished this book.

Thanks for the valuable time and attention of Paul McAlpine, Darren Coffield, Tom Wilcox, Nadja Rogers, and Kathryn Flett.

KEVIN ARMSTRONG, MAY 2023

Unless otherwise noted, the photographs in this book are from the author's archives. All efforts have been made to contact copyright holders, but if you feel there has been a mistaken attribution, please contact the publishers.

ALSO AVAILABLE FROM JAWBONE PRESS

What's Exactly The Matter With Me? Memoirs Of A Life In Music P.F. Sloan and S.E. Feinberg

Who Killed Mister Moonlight? Bauhaus, Black Magick, And Benediction David J. Haskins

Lee, Myself & I: Inside The Very Special World Of Lee Hazlewood Wyndham Wallace

Seeing The Real You At Last: Life And Love On The Road With Bob Dylan Britta Lee Shain

Long Promised Road: Carl Wilson, Soul Of The Beach Boys Kent Crowley

Eyes Wide Open: True Tales Of A Wishbone Ash Warrior Andy Powell with Colin Harper

Eternal Troubadour: The Improbable Life Of Tiny Tim Justin Martell with Alanna Wray McDonald

Throwing Frisbees At The Sun: A Book About Beck Rob Jovanovic

Confessions Of A Heretic: The Sacred & The Profane, Behemoth & Beyond Adam Nergal Darski with Mark Eglinton

The Monkees, Head, And The 60s Peter Mills

Complicated Game: Inside The Songs Of XTC Andy Partridge and Todd Bernhardt

Perfect Day: An Intimate Portrait Of Life With Lou Reed Bettye Kronstad

Adventures Of A Waterboy Mike Scott

Becoming Elektra: The Incredible True Story Of Jac Holzman's Visionary Record Label Mick Houghton

I Scare Myself: A Memoir Dan Hicks

Shredders! The Oral History Of Speed Guitar (And More) Greg Prato

Fearless: The Making Of Post-Rock Jeanette Leech

Tragedy: The Ballad Of The Bee Gees Jeff Apter

Shadows Across The Moon: Outlaws, Freaks, Shamans And The Making Of Ibiza Clubland Helen Donlon

Staying Alive: The Disco Inferno Of The Bee Gees Simon Spence

The Yacht Rock Book: The Oral History Of The Soft, Smooth Sounds Of The 70s And 80s Greg Prato

Earthbound: David Bowie and The Man Who Fell To Earth Susan Compo

What's Big And Purple And Lives In The Ocean? The Moby Grape Story Cam Cobb

Swans: Sacrifice And Transcendence: The Oral History Nick Soulsby

Small Victories: The True Story Of Faith No More Adrian Harte

AC/DC 1973–1980: The Bon Scott Years Jeff Apter

King's X: The Oral History Greg Prato

Keep Music Evil: The Brian Jonestown Massacre Story Jesse Valencia

Lunch With The Wild Frontiers: A History Of Britpop And Excess In 13½ Chapters Phill Savidge

More Life With Deth David Ellefson with Thom Hazaert

Wilcopedia: A Comprehensive Guide To The Music Of America's Best Band Daniel Cook Johnson

Take It Off: KISS Truly Unmasked Greg Prato

I Am Morbid: Ten Lessons Learned From Extreme Metal, Outlaw Country, And The Power Of Self-Determination David Vincent with Joel McIver

Lydia Lunch: The War Is Never Over: A Companion To The Film By Beth B. Nick Soulsby

Zeppelin Over Dayton: Guided By Voices Album By Album Jeff Gomez

What Makes The Monkey Dance: The Life And Music Of Chuck Prophet And Green On Red Stevie Simkin

So Much For The 30 Year Plan: Therapy? The Authorised Biography Simon Young

She Bop: The Definitive History Of Women In Popular Music Lucy O'Brien

Relax Baby Be Cool: The Artistry And Audacity Of Serge Gainsbourg Jeremy Allen

Seeing Sideways: A Memoir Of Music And Motherhood Kristin Hersh

Two Steps Forward, One Step Back: My Life In The Music Business Miles A. Copeland III

It Ain't Retro: Daptone Records & The 21st-Century Soul Revolution Jessica Lipsky

Renegade Snares: The Resistance & Resilience Of Drum & Bass Ben Murphy and Carl Loben

Southern Man: Music And Mayhem In The American South Alan Walden with S.E. Feinberg

Frank & Co: Conversations With Frank Zappa 1977–1993 Co de Kloet

All I Ever Wanted: A Rock 'n' Roll Memoir Kathy Valentine

Here They Come With Their Make-Up On: Suede, Coming Up ... And More Adventures Beyond The Wild Frontiers Jane Savidge

My Bloody Roots: From Sepultua To Soulfly And Beyond: The Autobiography Max Cavalera with Joel McIver

This Band Has No Past: How Cheap Trick Became Cheap Trick Brian J. Kramp

Gary Moore: The Official Biography Harry Shapiro

Holy Ghost: The Life & Death Of Free Jazz Pioneer Albert Ayler Richard Koloda

Conform To Deform: The Weird & Wonderful World Of Some Bizzare Wesley Doyle

Happy Forever: My Musical Adventures With The Turtles, Frank Zappa, T. Rex, Flo & Eddie, And More Mark Volman with John Cody

Johnny Thunders: In Cold Blood— The Official Biography, Revised & Updated Edition Nina Antonia